Principles of International
Physical Distribution

Principles of Export Guidebooks

Series Editor: Michael Z. Brooke

Principles of
International
Physical Distribution

Jim Sherlock

Copyright © Jim Sherlock 1994

The right of Jim Sherlock to be identified as author of this work has been asserted in accordance with the Copyright, Designs and Patents Act 1988.

First published 1994

Blackwell Publishers
108 Cowley Road
Oxford OX4 1JF
UK

238 Main Street
Cambridge, Massachusetts 02142
USA

British Library Cataloguing in Publication Data

A CIP catalogue record for this book is available from the British Library.

Library of Congress Cataloging-in-Publication Data

A CIP catalog record for this book is available from the Library of Congress.

ISBN 0-631-19169-0

Typeset in 11½pt on 13½pt Garamond Light by Aitch Em Wordservice, Aylesbury, Buckinghamshire, Great Britain.

Printed in Great Britain by Hartnolls Limited, Bodmin, Cornwall.

This book is printed on acid-free paper.

Contents

List of Figures

Foreword

I am writing to welcome this informative book on international physical distribution written by Jim Sherlock, the Chairman of The Institute's Education Committee. His text provides the detail, not often brought together in one place, that exporters have to acquire to be confident in their profession.

There will be a warm welcome for this distinguished book.

The Earl of Limerick, President,
The Institute of Export

Series Editor's Introduction

In launching the fourth book in this series of guidebooks to the profession of exporting, the series editor – along with others associated with the project – is grateful to Jim Sherlock, the Chairman of The Institute of Export's Education Committee for writing it.

Like the book on trade and payments, which covers some of the same ground, *International Physical Distribution* is necessarily more technical and detailed than some in the series. The author's contribution to the development of you, the reader, rests on his experience as a teacher and consultant and I present this book with great pride to the exporting public.

All the books in this series are preoccupied with bringing products to foreign markets (what else is export about?) and this book – which reviews the whole subject of international transportation – takes us into the mysterious realms of Incoterms and export documentation which are lucidly explained.

May I welcome you, the reader, and hope to meet you again in the other books in the series which cover all aspects of export which you need to know – law (for the non-lawyer), trade and payments, international marketing, market research and export management, in addition to the first book in the series which is a review of the whole subject. The main focus of Jim's book is on the market itself – how to service it. He makes the point that export marketing is of little value if the products are not delivered or the payment collected.

Michael Z. Brooke

 # About The Institute of Export Examinations

The Institute is grateful for the initiative of Michael Z. Brooke, the series editor, and Blackwell Publishers in publishing this unique series of books specially written for the Professional Examinations.

The authors for the series have been carefully selected and have specialized knowledge of their subjects, all being established lecturers or examiners for the Professional Examinations.

The books have been written in a style that is of benefit not only to students of The Institute but also to commercial organizations seeking further information about specific aspects of international trade.

Professionalism in export is vital for every company if they are to compete successfully in world markets and this new series of books provides a sound basis of knowledge for all those seeking a professional qualification in export through The Institute of Export's Professional Examinations.

The book covers the following parts of The Institute's syllabus.

International Physical Distribution

Objectives of the syllabus

1 To explain how to organize an export office.

2 To explain the considerations affecting payment for goods and services.
3 To explain the documentation and other procedures that the office handles.
4 To set out the basic requirements for securing marine and credit insurance.

The export office

The role of the export office with emphasis on its administrative structure and the options available, including their advantages and disadvantages; its liaison with sources of supply of goods and supporting services; order processing routines, records, checklists and sources of commercial data. Emphasis to be given to processing the export order in a professional manner with regard to simplified documents and electronic data processing techniques.

Incoterms 90

An understanding of Incoterms 90 with emphasis on the responsibilities of the buyer and seller; insurance and transportation obligations to link in with 'Principles of Law Relating to Overseas Trade' and 'International Trade and Payments' and the transfer of title to the goods from seller to buyer.

Marking and packing

An appraisal of the various forms of marking and types of packing pre-commodity/consignment relative to transport mode(s), regulatory bodies, stowage, costing, documentation and mandatory procedures.

Freight rates and transport modes: characteristics

The physical and cost characteristics of all transport modes, their rate structures and combinations, total distribution costs, quality of service and commodity suitability.

Statutory export/import procedures

Basic appraisal of the Customs obligations imposed on sellers (or their agents) to deliver the goods in a cost effective manner. To include the changes brought about by the Customs 88 Project:

– The Harmonized Commodity Description and Coding System (HS).
– The Integrated Customs Tariff (TARIC).
– The Single Administrative Document (SAD).
– Customs Handling of Import and Export Freight (CHIEF).

In addition, among the procedures that should be understood are: licensing (export and import); prohibitions and restrictions (export and import); VAT (export and import); and ATA carnets.

Export documentation

Complete understanding and role of all the documentation associated with Incoterms 90, including Bills of Lading/Charter Parties/Sea Waybills/Short form documents; Air Waybills; CMR/CIM consignment notes; insurance documents; invoices of all types; certificates of origin; exchange controls and other formalities, including dangerous goods – to link in with 'Principles of Law Relating to Overseas Trade' and 'International Trade and Payments' relative to Documentary Letters of Credit, bank documents and passing of title of goods.

Export order processing

An understanding of techniques of effectively handling export enquiries, issuing quotations and processing the order through to receipt of payment. Effective control of and liaison with other parties, preparation of checklists.

Sources of information

Understanding the role of Liner Conferences, Shippers' Councils, Credit Insurers, Chambers of Commerce, IMO, IATA, BOTB, ICC, SITPRO, PIRA, RHA, COI, ECGD and THE.

Cargo insurance

An understanding of the purpose of cargo insurance and its fundamental principles. The basic policy and standard clauses, including the extent of 'cover'. Arranging insurance, the responsibilities of each party, claims procedures, determining who has an 'insurable interest' in the cargo and commercial adjustments related to claims.

Postal and small packet services

An understanding of overseas postal and courier services; charges and documentation.

Shipping office

The role of shipping personnel and their duties. The involvement of a freight forwarder and other parties servicing international transactions.

International trade and shipping terms/abbreviations

A basic understanding of the terms used in the process of handling export business in all its areas, including transportation, insurance, customs, documentation, etc.

Costing and accountancy

Evaluation of the costing methods available to determine the most acceptable distribution arrangements for a particular consignment, using the Transport Distribution Analysis technique. Understanding transactions in foreign accountancy procedures, credit control and payment for services in the context of processing the export sales contract.

Information technology

An appraisal of current developments which influence the processing of export business, embracing transportation, documentation, computer technology, legislation, etc.

R.T. Ebers FIEx,
Director of Education & Training,
The Institute of Export

Acknowledgements

The author acknowledges his debt to the following and thanks the people concerned.

Understanding the Freight Business (Derek Downs)
Export Trade Connections (Neil Guy)
Exportlink Ltd (Tony Symes)
Herbert Watson Freight Services Ltd
Davies Turner Ltd
Manchester Chamber of Commerce & Industry
The Arab British Chamber of Commerce
The Freight Transport Association
Eagle Star
Export Practice & Documentation (Alex Walker)
Import/Export Documentation (Alan Branch)
Schmittof's Export Trade

Dedicated to the memory of
Bert Ibbetson, FIEx

1

Physical Distribution in Perspective

The main purpose of this book is to examine in some detail the complex and technical problems associated with international physical distribution. It will address the problems all exporters face in getting goods from where they are made to where they are used and the relationships between correct procedures and getting paid. So why should we start by looking at marketing?

One reason is that the broadest overview possible of a company's activities is from the marketing point of view. This enables us to look at all the business activities within international trading companies and attempt to put those activities into some sort of perspective. In particular, as this book is specifically about physical distribution, it helps us place those procedures into a wider perception of business activities.

Hopefully it also shows that the physical distribution function of any business is just as important as, for example, the sales function. This comparison is deliberately chosen because in many companies there is an unfortunate tendency to regard certain functions as being peripheral to, and certainly less important than, others. It is a shortsighted exporter who believes that the sales department is more important than the shipping department. Each function must play its part in order for the business to perform successfully and this is even more obvious in the complex area of international trade. The specific relationships within export departments are examined in chapter 2.

It also allows us to briefly look at the planning activities, in particular the marketing plan, which underpin the more specific, day-to-day, procedural functions with which this book is primarily concerned. ¡All successful businesses take control at a broad strategic level, by planned decision making and then attempt to operate efficiently on a day-to-day basis in an attempt to service the business obtained by good planning. Therefore a broad understanding of the elements of that planning is essential as the foundation of a more specific understanding of the technicalities of international physical distribution.

Finally, the marketing overview allows a comparison of domestic and international trade, and the differences between the two. A company which thinks that its home sales department can easily deal with overseas markets is a company that will find out the hard way that they certainly cannot, at least not without a wholesale transformation of procedures and a programme of specialized staff training and development. This is more of a problem now than it has ever been, particularly where the Single European Market is concerned, because of the misguided idea that Europe is now simply an extension of our home market. Not only is this patently ridiculous in terms of sales and marketing but even from the more basic perception of physical distribution many differences remain. From January 1993 it has been technically incorrect to refer to shipments from the United Kingdom to other Community members as 'exports', but they remain 'overseas' sales and distinct practical differences exist between them and true home sales. A study of the rest of this book will illustrate the truth of this comment.

So where better to start than with a definition of marketing?

Defining Marketing

> Getting the right goods to the right people in the right places at the right time and the right price. (Anon.)

This is probably one of the best known definitions of marketing and just one of the hundreds which have been produced over the years. Another which is just as useful in this context is:

Deciding what the customer wants; arranging to make it; distributing and selling it at the maximum profit. (Durham University)

The important points in both of these definitions are, firstly, that marketing is about finding out what people want first, not making it and then attempting to sell it; the marketing process begins with research not production; and, secondly, that the process of distribution, the need to get goods to 'the right place at the right time', is an essential element of good marketing and not a separate, and less important, function.

Definitions of words can help but the more practical question concerns the **how** of marketing rather than the **what**. That is, if a company were to accept the need to be responsive to market demand, to be 'customer orientated', as a means of becoming more successful in competitive markets, then how would it go about doing it? Firstly the difference between selling and marketing is important.

Figures 1.1 and 1.2 illustrate the basic difference in the processes, the major point being that selling starts with production, followed by the need to sell enough to make a profit, whilst marketing starts with market research in order to identify current market needs and profits from a satisfied customer.

Figure 1.1: The selling process

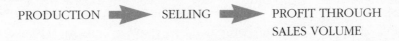

PRODUCTION ➡ SELLING ➡ PROFIT THROUGH SALES VOLUME

Figure 1.2: The marketing process (I)

MARKETING RESEARCH ➡ INTEGRATED MARKETING PLAN ➡ PROFIT THROUGH CONSUMER SATISFACTION

The other important distinction is the fact that selling is totally a one way process whilst marketing is based on a continuous feedback from the customer and adaptation by the company to changes in consumer demand.

Figure 1.3 is perhaps more instructive as an overview of the marketing process and helps us introduce physical distribution as a vital element of that process.

Figure 1.3: The marketing process (II)

THE MARKETING PROCESS (II)

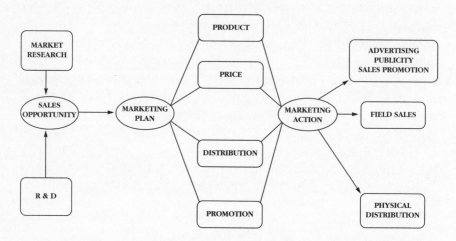

The beginning of this process is research carried out as a continuous activity in the market place, often underpinned by the internal research and development which improves a company's capability to produce. Once research has identified **where** demand exists, and the company is capable of producing goods, or services, to meet that demand, then decisions need to be made as to **how** that demand might be serviced successfully. The so called '4 Ps' approach is a simplistic, but nevertheless useful, interpretation of the basic decision making areas of the marketing plan.

All important strategic decisions which successful companies make can be categorized into the four elements of **Product**, **Price**, **Promotion**, and **Place** (or **Distribution** ... the '3 Ps and a D' doesn't really have the same ring to it). No amount of planning is beneficial without implementation and figure 1.3 illustrates the more obvious and visible activities of a company.

Planning is not a process that can be seen but it does result in the high profile activities of selling, promotion and physical distribution which are clearly visible as the practical results of the planning. As stated earlier the function of physical distribution is just as important as others and the diagram deliberately places it alongside selling and promotion. Later in this chapter we will look a little more closely at the elements of the plan with specific reference to overseas markets, but first the point should be made that the process is the same whether we consider home or overseas trade. It is not the marketing process which changes from home to export markets, or even from one export market to another, but the application of that process which will differ from one market to another.

The concept of market orientation, by definition, means that companies will attempt to discover the differences exhibited from one market to another and adapt to them in order to maximize profitable business. The differences encountered between the UK home market and overseas markets form a formidable list, and it is an ignorance of these differences which very often explains the failures of UK companies overseas.

Domestic Versus Export Markets

All trading organizations exist in a market environment which is always dynamic, that is, subject to change, and often volatile. In many cases these market movements are very unpredictable and adapting to them is a difficult task for even the most flexible of companies. The market environment is made up of a whole range of **uncontrollables**, and the elements of the marketing plan, the **controllables**, represent the company's attempt to operate with maximum success in the face of the uncontrollable elements of the market.

A comprehensive list of the factors which may differ between the United Kingdom and overseas markets and, in fact between one overseas market and another, would occupy a disproportionate section of this book, but a brief list of the most obvious points would include:

Type of economy — Mixed private and public, state planned, capitalist, for example.

Level of economic development — Subsistence, developing or developed.

Technological development — What is obsolete in one market may be state of the art in another.

Cultural or religious — In many markets these two factors may be one and the same thing. They can lead to many problems in product design, packaging and promotion in particular.

Political and legal — Again often inseparable and leading to a wide variety of regulations and legislation. May also affect the stability, or otherwise, of the commercial environment.

Commercial practices — What is perceived as sharp, or even illegal, practice is not the same in all markets.

Competition — The number, size and quality will vary.

Taste — Very few products are sold in exactly the same form all over the world.

Language — Totally innocent words in one language can be quite offensive in another.

Climate — There are obviously extreme differences from one part of the world to another.

While it could be argued that many of these distinctions could also apply to the regions of a domestic market, like the United Kingdom, for example, there is little doubt that the extent of the differentials is invariably far greater when operating in overseas markets.

This is by no means a full list but does serve to illustrate the point that the international trader is attempting to operate in a potentially infinite number of differing commercial environments, each market segment requiring individual approaches, which means that what is successful in one market is by no means sure to work in others. It is the company's ability to make the right decisions in those areas within its control, in order to accommodate the differences in the range of markets with which it deals, which makes the difference between success and failure! One of the first things the exporter has to accept is the need to **differentiate** from one market to another if profitable sales are to be maximized.

It is the decisions made in the areas actually under the control of the exporter which illustrate this differentiation in practice, that is, within the areas identified as the four Ps earlier in this chapter. All of these decisions should be based on a firm foundation of accurate and topical market information.' The possibilities within these areas and some examples of these differences can be illustrated by a brief examination of the main components of the marketing process. ⸲

Marketing Research

Quality research underpins all successful export marketing and, if carried out professionally, will always be cost-effective in that any research costs will be recouped by the benefits derived from the proper identification of market potential, the maximum exploitation of that potential and the avoidance of mistakes. The relevance of the latter point will perhaps be better illustrated by the examples of some of the expensive mistakes companies have made in overseas markets, which are mentioned later in this chapter, all of which could have been avoided by simple research.

What is the purpose of marketing research? The simple answer is that it helps decide **where** the company will operate, in terms of a logical market selection strategy, and then **how** those markets will be exploited for maximum returns.

Market Selection

It is clearly important for exporters to develop a market selection strategy which means that they choose the markets rather than the markets choosing them. But first we should ask the important question as to whether we should in fact be exporting in the first place. It might seem a little illogical in a text book based on international trade but there are situations in which many companies would do better if they did not export. One of the reasons for this is that many companies are actually exporting for the wrong reasons.

Bad Reasons for Exporting

Disposing of excess production

Not only does this devalue the potential of overseas markets but also evidences no permanent commitment to export, in that if and when the home market takes up the excess then the export markets are ignored. It is no surprise that such an attitude does nothing to develop overseas sales. A company with a permanent excess of production capacity should also be considering the efficiency of their capital investment. A permanent excess points to an underlying structural problem.

Marginal cost pricing

Sometimes linked with the above and based on the, often incorrect, assumption that sales in export markets have to be made at low prices. This process of pricing goods based on a recovery of direct costs only, and making no contribution to indirect costs, is one which can be legitimate as a short term policy in markets quite separate from those paying the full price. In this respect export markets are prime targets but too many companies simply adopt marginal pricing as a permanent policy, without considering the great potential for profitable sales overseas if they were only to approach the markets more professionally.

Prestige

Some companies operate under the misguided opinion that there is somehow great merit in dealing with a very large number of overseas markets. They appear to think that such a global image is evidence of their success. The truth is that in many cases they are trading badly in a large number of markets because the span of control is so wide. Such companies would often do much better if they were to be more selective about the markets with which they deal rather than adding new markets just because they are there.

Good Reasons for Exporting

Increased profits

Either by an increase in volume sales based on the expansion of the size of a company's market network or, and it is often possible, by obtaining better profit margins in export markets compared with home market levels.

Spread of risk

A selective and controlled market expansion policy will decrease the company's dependence on, for example, its home market. Given the instability of most markets it is clearly preferable for a company to avoid having 'too many eggs in one basket' as it were.

Extension of the product life cycle

As is examined later in this chapter there is often a situation in which the decline of the home market for a product, perhaps because of technical obsolescence, is not reflected in other markets. Because they are at a different stage of their economic development, they can often offer an expanding, as opposed to a declining market.

Even out seasonal fluctuations

Products which have a seasonal demand can benefit from the fact that such a cycle is not the same in every part of the world. In simple terms it is always summer somewhere for the deck chair manufacturer.

National interest

It is the interests of the UK economy, and therefore of all UK companies, that we should maximize our export business. In fact there are a variety of services available to the exporter, many of which are free, which are specifically designed to encourage this.

For most companies this reason for exporting would not exactly be on the top of the list.

So the first decision a company should make is the conscious one to enter overseas markets. This should be based on a long term commitment to export and a logical and informed market selection strategy.

Market Selection Criteria

These can be simplified into three major requirements which all companies should look for in new markets. In order of importance they are **potential**, **accessibility** and **similarity**.

Potential

The most obvious attraction of new markets is the potential they offer for increased business. This can be measured in a number of ways, the most obvious of which would be pure sales value, but also volume, or profit or even market share, could be of as much interest dependent on a company's particular requirements. For example a company with large production capacity would perhaps be more interested in the volume of units sold than the profit margin on each item. A company looking for control in a market may value a large market share even if that means lower profit margins.

It should also be borne in mind that current market size is not necessarily guaranteed to remain and trends in the market must also be considered.

Accessibility

Not only must new markets offer current, and future, potential, but also that potential must be accessible to the exporter.

This is of very great importance in international trade where barriers to trade exist which may make certain markets inaccessible to certain suppliers. From the purely physical distribution point of view there is hardly a place on earth that an exporter could not physically deliver goods. An elephant could be dropped on to the top of Mount Everest, if one wanted to. The problem is the cost of such physical distribution, which is clearly not the same for every supplier in an overseas market.

The UK exporter has to compete with domestic suppliers in the overseas market, and with competitors who are geographically closer, whilst facing greater physical distribution costs. It is no surprise that Canada's biggest single foreign supplier is the United States of America, or that the Irish Republic's number one supplier is the UK. Even if this problem can be overcome the exporter is still faced with a bewildering array of barriers to trade in the form of regulations which effect goods imported into a country. Many of these rules and regulations are based on legislation in the country of destination, and are often operated by the Customs & Excise authorities of those countries. They can be broken down into two broad categories:

1 Tariff barriers
 (a) Customs Duties.

(b) Taxes.
(c) Excise.
(d) Levies.
(e) Licensing.
(f) Quotas.

2 Non-tariff barriers
(a) Technical standards.
(b) Health and safety standards.

Many of the above can simply debar entry into the market, as they are generally designed to do. It should also be noted that suppliers can also find that export controls in their own market can impose significant barriers.

These aspects of accessibility of overseas markets and export controls will clearly figure, in much more detail, later in this book.

Similarity

Finally the exporter would wish that, given the above requirements are met, any new markets are as similar to current markets as is possible. There is no great merit in expansion into markets which exhibit totally different characteristics to current ones. The less changes that are necessary to the current marketing plan the easier will be the market development.

The fact that some 65 per cent of UK exports are to western Europe, and another 15 per cent or so to the USA, does indicate that whether exporters actually consciously apply the above criteria or not, they do operate in practice.

It should be noted that it is a little simplistic to describe an overseas market purely in geographic terms. To identify a market simply by political boundaries, as in France or Germany, very rarely represents the actual nature of the market. What the exporter must endeavour to do is define the **segment** of the market which contains its potential purchasers. This may be in terms of an **end user profile** describing the typical consumer or an identification of the industrial **sector** containing organizational buyers. Whatever the product the exporter must have a very clear concept of the segment of the market which will be **targeted** in the marketing plan.

Methods of Market Research

The two basic reasons for marketing research, that is market selection and market planning, do actually correlate with the two distinct methods of collecting information. Thus the process of market selection can often be achieved through the use of desk research. Sometimes referred to as armchair research, this involves the company in collecting information without actually venturing into the overseas market. Such information will invariably be **secondary** information, in that we are secondary users and the information is available to other companies. The sources of such information are very wide ranging in a developed market such as the UK.

Sources of Secondary Information

Department of Trade and Industry

In conjunction with the Foreign & Commonwealth Office the DTI offers an integrated package of services through it Overseas Trade Services division (OTS). A brief breakdown of these services would include:

1 Area Advisory Groups of the British Overseas Trade Board (BOTB) can give specialist advice.
2 Export Data Service: Export Market Information Centre (EMIC) and Export Information Service (EIS).
3 Export Market Research Scheme (50 per cent of cost).
4 Export Representative Service.
5 Overseas Companies Status Reports.
6 Market Information Enquiry Country desks in London.
7 A range of publications including *Hints to Exporters* and *Sector Reports*.

A Guide to Export Services can be obtained, free of charge, from your local DTI regional office.

Customs & Excise

Import and export statistics, tariff levels, regulations and so on.

Trade Associations

Specific product and market information. Can also help with promotion via sponsorship of exhibitions and missions.

Chambers of Commerce

Wide range of assistance, particularly documentation and regulations. There are a number of bi-lateral chambers, for example UK-Belgium Chamber.

International banks

Wide ranging economic and financial information. Free regular reports on market groups. Status reports on individual buyers.

Technical Help to Exporters

Part of the British Standards Institution. Advice on, and copies of, overseas technical standards.

Market research organizations

Commercial bodies specializing in business information, for example Dun & Bradstreet International. Also a wide range of consultants who can be expensive and more appropriate to field work.

Bibliographic

Published information covering almost every aspect of world markets. Most large libraries have a commercial section; the best in the UK is EMIC (see above). Also an increasing use of computerized databases, for example Spearhead for EC legislation.

The general problem for UK exporters is not a lack of secondary information but exactly the opposite. It is necessary to be as specific as possible about the objective of the research in order to pinpoint the relevant data.

Figure 1.4 illustrates the relationship between the market selection criteria mentioned above and the appropriate types of secondary information.

Figure 1.4: Market selection criteria and appropriate types of information

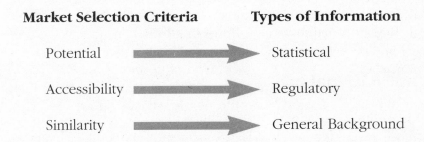

Market Selection Criteria	Types of Information
Potential	Statistical
Accessibility	Regulatory
Similarity	General Background

All the above types of information can be collected by Desk Research but it has to be accepted that as the questions become more specific, particularly in relation to the marketing plan, then the need for more specialized **field work** becomes more obvious. The use of specialized methods of research such as interviews, questionnaires, observation and test marketing in the overseas market is often required to produce **primary** information to answer specific questions such as product design, market prices, channels of distribution and optimum methods of promotion.

The apparent contradiction is that the market research scheme begins with secondary information, as this is general and usually free or low cost, and is followed by the more specialized and expensive collection of primary information, which contributes to the formulation of the marketing plan.

The Marketing Plan

Sometimes referred to as the marketing mix because it represents a mixture of decisions made in specific areas but which must blend together. 'The correct mix is the recipe for success'! The exporter has to make decisions designed to exploit, to the full, the potential identified in overseas markets. As we have seen it is possible to rationalize these areas into the four broad categories of Product, Price, Promotion and Place.

Product

All exporters must accept the fact that most successful products are modified for sale in overseas markets; very few products are sold in exactly the same form in all markets and the reason for, and nature of, modifications will differ from one market to another.

Illustrative of this point is the fact that most products which are thought to be the same throughout the world are, in many cases, not the same at all. The taste of Coca-Cola actually varies from one group of markets to another; it is, for example, sweeter in the Middle East than in western Europe. It is also claimed that Nescafé coffee is sold in at least forty different flavours worldwide.

The reasons for such product modifications are numerous but include:

1 Technical standards, for example voltage, calibration, food packaging.
2 Size, weight or volume, for example food packs, clothing sizes.
3 Taste, for example design, colour.
4 Method of use, for example a bicycle might be a means of transport or a piece of leisure equipment.

5 Materials, for example Corned Beef and bone china do not sell in Hindu countries.

These are just a small selection of examples of product modifications, and reasons for them, from the many that exist in international trade. There are some products which are sold without modification throughout the world, for example Scotch whisky, and some, but only some, French perfumes, but even then certain brands will be more or less popular from one market to another. Also some products, usually of a technical nature, which are used in the same way in all parts of the world, may not be modified, but even then other aspects of the marketing plan will almost certainly differ.

To be technically correct we should in fact refer to **product/ market** strategies, as each product package should relate to a specific market segment. This process is known as **product positioning** and links in with the segmentation process mentioned as part of market selection.

Figure 1.5: Product life cycle

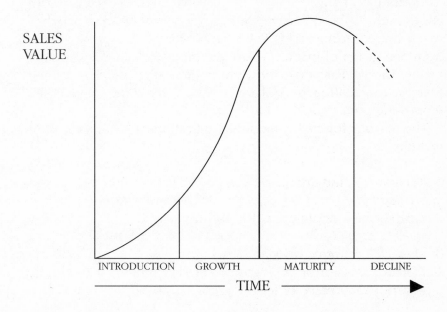

17

Exporters must also realise that buyers are often buying not just the physical entity of the product, but a whole package of things which go with it. This is known as the **total product concept** and includes elements such as reliability, reputation, image and prestige as well as the more tangible elements such as the packaging itself, credit terms, guarantees and warranties and pre and after-sales service.

Finally, exporters have to accept that even if current demand is being satisfied it is unlikely that the situation will never change. All products go through a life cycle which begins with an introduction to the market, followed by a period of growth and then a maturity when the best returns are made, but this is inevitably followed by decline. All products will decline eventually – the problem is to determine the time scale (see figure 1.5).

There is a clear need for a long term product development and replacement policy to attempt to ensure a constant product portfolio of mature and profitable products.

The value of market research is not only in ensuring that the product is suited to market requirements, but also that costly mistakes are avoided. The company that produced a range of ladies' fashion garments for Scandinavian countries naturally produced a 'winter' range because it is often cold in that part of Europe. Unfortunately, they realised too late that the UK concept of a winter and summer range of clothes was of no relevance to Scandinavian countries, where the distinction between 'indoor' and 'outdoor' is far more important. The market is actually for lightweight, indoor, clothes; functionality is more important than fashion for outdoor wear.

The list of expensive mistakes is almost endless. A bone china dinner service specially designed for Italian taste, did not sell at all due to the absence of a pickle bowl. White false teeth produced for the Far East did not match the betel nut stained teeth of the potential recipients, who objected to a mouth which resembled a piano keyboard.

Packaging may be more important than the product as the company selling powdered milk into west Africa found out. Their traditional metal container was replaced by a more cost effective cardboard box. Sales fell drastically because it is difficult to carry water, and even more difficult to cook, with a cardboard box. The company totally misunderstood the method of use of their product. As did the exporter of depilatory creams who discovered, too late, that the majority of their west African market was male, and not female, who used the cream as an alternative to shaving.

Even when the product is right for the market, the name it is given can render it unsaleable. Some years ago the Chevrolet Nova caused quite a stir in Latin American markets; 'no va' is Spanish for 'won't go', and Toyota's competitor to the Mini would not have sold so well if they had persisted with the name Toyolet. It may therefore be necessary to sell the same product with a range of different names.

Basic marketing research could, and in some cases did, avoid the long term cost of such mistakes.

Price

Price, as an element of the marketing mix, may be designed to do more than just maximize profits. It may attempt to create a market share, generate early cash recovery, establish compatibility across a range of products (price lining), or generate a specific rate of return.

In chapters 3 and 6 the technical process of price calculation, from an Ex Works to a Delivered price, are examined in some detail. The marketing plan is concerned with where the Ex Works price came from in the first place.

Basically the exporter has two choices in arriving at a selling price. The most common, because it is the easiest, is the least effective and that is **Cost Plus** pricing. The direct, and hopefully indirect, costs are calculated and a percentage profit margin is added. This produces the **minimum price** the company is prepared to accept, the same price for every customer and every market. The final Delivered price may differ, because the physical distribution costs are different, but the bottom line Ex Works price remains the same.

All companies should have a very clear idea of their minimum price, but to operate on that basis only, ignores the potential for more profitable sales should the buyer be prepared to pay more. Sensible companies need to know the **price the market will bear** to complete the picture. Such information gathered from market research and, it has to be said, trial and error, will lead to an understanding of the **maximum price** the company can achieve. It will also naturally lead to a system of **differentiated** pricing in that the price obtainable from one market, and even one customer, will differ from place to place.

The truth is often even more complex, as most products exhibit some sort of price-elasticity. There is rarely a price the market will not bear, but different prices will generate different sales volume. The typical situation is that the lowest price will generate the highest volume sales, and vice-versa. What exporters need to establish are the price-volume relationships which exist for their products in overseas markets. (See figure 1.6.)

Figure 1.6: Price-volume relationship

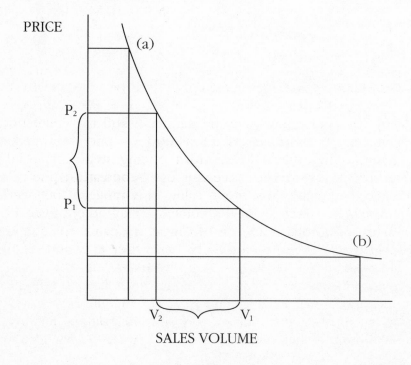

(a) The highest price will generate the lowest sales volume.
(b) The lowest price generates the highest sales volume.

In practice the extremes of this curve are very unreliable and the exporter will attempt to define the range P_1 to P_2 and its relationship with V_1 and V_2.

Between the two options of Cost Plus and Market Price exist hybrid versions in which the percentage add-on may be varied from market to market, and in which the price level in the market is established by the market leader, or by world commodity prices, in which case research is less of a problem. (See Figure 1.7.)

Figure 1.7: Pricing strategies

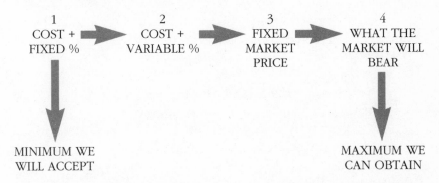

Many companies, knowing the minimum and maximum price parameters in their markets, are able to use price as a marketing tool. They may choose **skim** pricing strategies to take high profit, low volume, sales, or use **penetration** pricing to take high volume, low profit, sales, or a range of options in between. In extreme cases a company may accept even loss making sales in the interest of long term gains. All of these strategies will be supported by the other elements of the marketing plan.

To operate successfully the exporter must have a very clear understanding of all business costs, the margins necessary to achieve profit targets and the price/volume relationships available in each of their markets.

Promotion

All goods need promotion in order to sell. The type and extent depends on the products themselves, distribution channels, markets and end-users. The **promotional mix** forms an important element of the marketing mix, and describes the combination of promotional activities which are available to the exporter. This can be broken down into four components:

Advertising

Any paid form of non-personal presentation or promotion of ideas, goods or services by an identified sponsor. Involves the use of specialized media – press, television, radio, cinema, outdoor.

Publicity

Non-personal and unpaid publication or broadcast. Involves the above media and, usually, requires newsworthy items of general interest. In the UK the Central Office of Information and the BBC External Services can be very helpful.

Personal selling

Oral presentation in conversation with one or more prospective purchasers for the purpose of making sales.

Sales promotions

Those marketing activities, other than advertising, publicity and personal calling, that stimulate consumer purchasing.

The above are often referred to as **marketing communications** in that they represent the methods by which the seller communicates, and makes contact with, the buyer. It is obvious that the need to differentiate from one market segment to another is vital to the success of any promotional activities.

When we looked at market research earlier in this chapter the DTI featured as a major provider of information. It should also be mentioned that they offer financial assistance towards participation in overseas missions and exhibitions. Such activities invariably must be organized by a non-profit making body which is typically a Trade Association or a Chamber of Commerce.

The need for quality research is evidenced by the many examples of mistakes in communications, the cost of which could have been avoided by marketing research.

Many mistakes originate from simple errors in the translation of advertising copy from one language to another. The Parker leak-proof fountain pen which prevented the embarrassment of ink stained shirts found a totally new market when embarrassment was translated, in Spanish, as 'emberazer' which actually means 'pregnancy'. Parker had apparently produced a new form of contraceptive.

Almost apocryphal is the case of the company, already mentioned in this chapter, who manufactured depilatory creams. They planned an expensive magazine promotion in the Middle East which involved the use of an advertisement which had been successful in a number of other areas. This involved two colour photographs depicting a pair of shapely legs before and after the application of the cream. The process was fluently described in the advertising copy below the illustrations. This company was not caught out by a problem with the Arabic translation because they had learnt that the only safe way to translate from one language to another is to have one translator handle the English to Arabic, and another to then translate the Arabic back into English. Any problems in interpretation are usually revealed. The problem in this case was not the quality of the Arabic, but that the company had not considered the fact that Arabic reads from right to left, and they had not reversed the photographs. They seemed to be promoting something that made hair grow.

As a final example, even the largest of companies can get caught in the language trap. CocaCola's famous global message that 'Coke gives life' was variously translated as 'Coke raises the dead' and 'Coke brings your ancestors back from the grave'.

Place (distribution)

The exporter faces two major decisions in regard to the distribution of the goods. One is the problem of International Physical Distribution, which is actually what the rest of this book is about. The other is the common use of a variety of different forms of intermediaries between the seller and the final end-user.

Because of the gap, both geographical and cultural, between the UK exporter and the overseas buyer, there is often a need for some form of intermediary to bridge the gap. This gives rise to what can appear to be a complex web of organizations involved in the servicing of the end-users.

Indirect Exports

Perhaps the easiest way for a UK company to get its goods into an overseas market is to deal with UK-based intermediaries. These will perform a variety of business activities but the most common forms are:

Export Merchants

Buy on their own account and resell overseas at a profit. In many cases this is how a company's goods first arrive in foreign markets.

Confirming Houses

Act as agents for overseas buyers and pass on orders to the UK suppliers. They often finance the transaction and earn commission from the buyer.

Buying or Indent Houses

Again act as agents of overseas buyers but may have more control of the purchasing process. In some cases they will have complete freedom to fill the indent (list of requirements) at the most competitive rates available.

In all the above cases the UK exporter deals with the export house as a home sales customer. The only distinction is that the terms are invariably Free on Board (FOB) but even then it is the export house which arranges the shipment; the seller will deliver to the port or depot against their instructions. What we are more concerned about here is the process of direct exporting.

The basic choices available to the direct exporter are listed in figure 1.8.

Figure 1.8: Channels of distribution

DIRECT
+
COMMISSION AGENT
(BROKER)
+
DISTRIBUTOR
(STOCKIST)
(WHOLESALER)
(DEALER)
+
RETAILER
+
LOCAL COMPANY
(SALES)
(STOCK)
(ASSEMBLY)
(MANUFACTURE)
+
LICENSE
FRANCHISE

Direct Sales

We should not ignore the possibility that the exporter may be able to deal direct with the end-user without the need for any form of intermediary. This is often the case where the product is an industrial durable, such as large capital items of plant and machinery, and there is direct contact between producer and consumer. In some cases this would include custom built equipment. The exporter is able to arrange a small number of large consignments for direct delivery to the buyer.

Commission agent

The term 'agent' has a wide ranging legal interpretation, but in this context it refers to the very common form of export intermediary, the Commission Agent. Because UK exporters generally lack a detailed knowledge of the range of export markets within which they operate, they will feel the need for advice and support from knowledgeable parties. Also the geographical gap means that a representative based in the market is very valuable in terms of customer service and full exploitation of the market.

The commission agent will represent a number of principals in a specific territory. They will usually specialize in certain product areas and therefore handle a compatible range of goods, manufactured by their principals. They are involved in a variety of activities to do with the selling process, which can include promotional activities, pre and after-sales service, debt collection and problem solving, as well as the more obvious personal selling function. However they do not normally handle the goods and the exporter still has to physically deliver the goods to the end-user, and collect payment.

In return for their efforts the agent will receive a commission on sales in their territory. Typically this is between 5 and 10 per cent of those sales which is paid following receipt of payment from the buyer (or should be). Two brief points need to be made about the calculation of commission payments:

1 The percentage of commission paid will be applied to an

agreed value and that value should not include any ancillary or third party costs, such as freight or insurance premiums for example. The commission should be calculated ideally on the ex-works price of the goods which, after all, is where the seller is making a profit. It is inequitable for an agent to expect to make a commission on the physical distribution costs.

2 There is an important distinction between mark-up and margin which many exporters ignore, to their cost. Take the example of an invoice for £100 to a customer in a territory where the commission agent earns 10 per cent commission. A simple calculation you might think:

	£
Basic invoice value (ex-works	100.00
Plus 10% commission	10.00
Ex-works invoice to the buyer	110.00

The shipment is made and the buyer pays on time (use your imagination) and at the end of the month the exporter pays the agents their commission. They receive 10 per cent of the sales value, that is, £11.00 – £10.00 have been added but £11.00 paid; £1 of the seller's profit is lost to the agent. Now this may seem to be splitting hairs but if you were to add a few zeros to the numbers, and multiply by a few hundred consignments, then the exporter is giving away significant amounts of what they thought were their profits.

The misunderstanding centres around the distinction between the **mark-up**, which is an add-on to the basic cost, and a **margin** which is a percentage of the subsequent gross price. How do we get it right? Well to be exact:

To pay 5% commission add   5.26% mark-up
To pay 7.5% commission add 8.11% mark-up
To pay 10% commission add 11.11% mark-up

There are some round numbers but only when considering much higher figures which are not normally paid as commissions. But for the sake of symmetry:

25% mark-up gives a   20% margin
33.33% mark-up gives a 25% margin
50% mark-up gives a   33.33% margin

and if we wanted a 50 per cent margin we would need a 100 per cent mark-up.

Distributor

Often referred to as stockists or dealers, distributors purchase goods from the exporter, sometimes on an exclusive basis (sole distributors), and resell in the territory. The cost to the seller is the discount which must be given the distributor to allow them a mark-up in order to make their profit on the resale. These discounts vary enormously but typically they would be higher than average commission levels, ranging from 20 per cent to over 50 per cent. The higher rates do reflect the greater responsibilities of distributors who not only physically handle and sell the goods but also hold stock, arrange domestic deliveries, install and service, and collect payment from the end user, as well as everything that a commission agent will do.

Whilst there are no rules, it is often the case that the stockist of industrial goods will be described as a distributor, whilst the stockist of consumer goods is referred to as a wholesaler.

The advantages of such arrangements to the exporter are that a small number of large consignments can be made, rather than a large number of small ones, which is much more economic; and the end-user is able to get off-the-shelf deliveries. Generally speaking the volume of sales in a market would have to justify the holding of stock, but certain products demand off-the-shelf delivery and the exporter has little choice.

Some exporters arrange for **consignment stocks** in a market. This describes the situation in which the distributor does not pay for the goods until they are resold, that is, the stock-holding is financed by the supplier. The more common situation is that the distributor agrees terms with the supplier and pays at the due time whether the goods are sold or not.

For consumer products the stockist or wholesaler may on-sell to, or the exporter supply direct to, retailers, who will them-selves on-sell to the end-users. It is logical that large retailers and chains should choose to deal direct with manufacturers and the exporter does still benefit from an economic consign-ment size.

Local company

If sales levels in a market justify it, then the exporter may choose to make a direct investment in the market by setting up a local company, that is, local to the overseas market. These may be wholly owned subsidiaries of the UK company, or part of a joint venture with another exporter or, more likely, a local national. In some markets nationals of that country must retain a controlling interest in the companies so formed.

The local company may be a simple sales office, in which case it does no more than a commission agent would, or may be a stockist, or import components and act as an assembler or even act as a full scale manufacturer. In the latter case there would obviously have to be sufficient long-term sales revenues to justify the investment, and stability, both economic and political, would be essential.

License

Concerned with the sale, not of goods, but of 'know-how'. This may simply be a transfer of production knowledge, in exchange for a fee, which enables an overseas company to manufacture certain goods themselves rather than import them. It may involve more complex legal arrangements which involve the transfer of what is known as **intellectual property** in the form of licensing agreements over long periods of time. The intellec-tual property may be a patent (design or process) trade name, trade mark or copyright, and a disclosure fee and regular royal-ties will be paid. Many countries are more interested in the acquisition of the ability to produce themselves than they are in the import of finished goods.

The licensing of retail outlets for consumer goods is generally referred to as a **franchise** operation.

Selection of Distribution Channels

Thus the UK exporter has a wide choice of solutions to the problem of making goods available to the overseas buyer, and there are many factors which will affect that choice.

1 Product: industrial or consumer. Specialized products need storage, installation, training, maintenance and so on. Purchasing quantities . . . direct to large buyers, distributors for small ones. Quality levels . . . distinction between exclusive and 'off-the-peg'.
2 Market: size; consumer habits; availability; and special arrangements.
3 Source of manufacture.
4 Strategic organization . . . who decides?
5 Company resources . . . financial and managerial.
6 Timing . . . long-term plans may preclude short-term choices.

In addition to the factors above it may also be that the company is attempting to fit channel decisions into a broader marketing strategy. In particular the choices made in terms of Product Positioning may logically link with channel strategies such as:

1 Selective: specialized product needs, for example foodstuffs, electrical, construction.
2 Exclusive: non-specialized product through selected intermediaries, for example high fashion as opposed to off-the-peg.
3 Intensive: mass market products through any intermediary.

Also the company's concept of its reputation and image in a market will make it more, or less, concerned with the standing of its representatives in the market.

The selection of the correct marketing mix for a particular market is obviously not a simple thing for the average exporter.

It requires quality research, an understanding of the options and a little experience would not go amiss. But any planning is better than none and every company, including small ones, will benefit from any research and planning it is able to do, because the more a seller is able to identify and react to market demand the more successful they will be.

At the beginning of this chapter we introduced the concept of **market orientation** and emphasized its importance in dynamic and competitive markets. This concept is important in home markets but becomes essential when the exporter is faced with the almost infinite variety of situations encountered in overseas markets. The more volatile the market, then the more important it becomes for the seller to adapt and accommodate. The UK exporter that ventures into foreign markets thinking they are simply extensions of the home market will invariably face a rude awakening.

International Physical Distribution

The title of this book and the basis of the following chapters. What we have hopefully established is the principle that physical distribution, call it 'shipping' if you like, is an essential and integral part of the marketing process. Our definition of marketing included the words 'right place, right time', and no matter how effective a company is in terms of strategic decision making, it ignores the physical distribution problem at its peril.

Choosing just the right target markets, producing products which exactly meet demand, at a price the market will pay, and selling and promoting them so well that the buyers are 'beating' a path to our door', is all totally pointless if the goods never arrive, or arrive too late, or arrive in the wrong place, or arrive damaged, or, worst of all, are delivered but not paid for because the documentation is faulty.

Each element of the marketing plan must play its part in the success of the company in overseas markets, and none are more important than the others. Remember it is the 'right mix which is the recipe for success'.

What the rest of this book addresses are the complex and

technical aspects of international physical distribution. It is a highly specialized function which impacts directly on the purpose of virtually all business activities – that is the need to get paid. The importance of documentary procedures in particular cannot be underestimated in terms of collecting payments overseas, and the level of accuracy necessary to protect the interests of the exporter means that apparently minor errors can have major consequences.

A study of the subsequent chapters in this book will go a long way towards establishing the level of expertise necessary to avoid problems, rather than just solve them, and minimize the possibility of non-payment. It may also help in passing an Institute of Export examination.

2

The Export Office

We began chapter 1 with a broad examination of the marketing process and attempted to relate this to the unique problems associated with its implementation in overseas markets. (Note that other books in the series cover both the marketing issues in general and market selection in particular – see the list in the introduction). What we now need to do, in order to move forward into the specific operational areas of the export trade, is to home in on the aspect of the organization which performs these operations, that is, the Export Office. The day-to-day servicing of overseas markets requires a very wide range of complex functions to be efficiently performed in order to achieve the objective of profit, and in fact, the rest of this book is a detailed examination of those procedures.

But first one final overview of the activities of business organizations from a marketing perspective. Another of the many definitions of marketing is:

> 'The income producing side of the business.'
> (McNair, Brown, Leighton and Englent)

This may not, at first, sight appear to be a particularly valuable statement in terms of an understanding of marketing, but it actually shows an important and in-depth perception of the true nature of business functions. Well, it did take four people to write it.

It is possible to identify only four functions which go on in any commercial organization. These are:

1 Production/Purchasing.
2 Personnel.
3 Finance.
4 Marketing.

Every business activity can be placed into one of the above four categories. Production and purchasing are linked in that the merchant will buy goods and sell in the same state, the manufacturing company must purchase raw materials or components and process them in order to produce something to sell, but they are part of the same process of producing goods for sale.

Personnel, or, if you prefer, Human Resource Management, concerns itself with the provision of adequate labour at all levels of the organization. This will involve not just hiring and firing, but all the extremely important aspect of staff training and development.

Finance will operate at every level, from the bookkeeping aspects of financial accounts, through the cost controls and standard costing of the Cost and Works Accountants, to the budgetary control and planning strategies of the Management Accountant.

Finally, marketing will cover a wide range of activities including market research, pricing strategies, channel management, promotion and selling. Obviously there are many specific functions which are not mentioned above but all business activities could be fitted into those four categories. So what does this have to do with our definition of marketing? Simply that if you were to examine these activities from the point of view of revenue, that is whether they actually produce money coming into the business as opposed to sending money out of it, then marketing is the only function which is 'income producing' – all the others either spend money, or count it. See figure 2.1.

Before any accountants or production managers start writing in, let us hastily accept that, of course, all business activities, including marketing, involve operating costs. Every activity can be identified as a cost-centre. Also, it is not suggested that

Figure 2.1: The 'income producing' side of the business

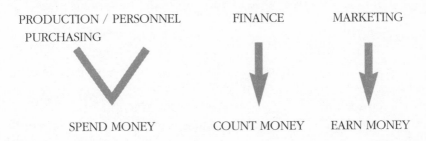

PRODUCTION / PERSONNEL   FINANCE   MARKETING
PURCHASING

SPEND MONEY   COUNT MONEY   EARN MONEY

the production of products or the control of finance are less important to the company than, for example, selling and promotion. Every function must play its part in achieving the company's objectives.

This is simply an acceptance that marketing, and certainly specific aspects of it, is the, so-called, 'revenue buying' function of the business. Hence the fact that a marketing definition which describes it as 'the income producing side of the business', not only has the great advantage of brevity, but also displays quite a broad understanding of all business activities.

What we are more specifically concerned with, from now on, are those aspects of the marketing function which are concerned with overseas markets. If we assume that a company which is serious about marketing will organize its structure to enable a specialization in export markets, then it is logical to expect that an Export Office will be set up. This is not as obvious as it may seem as some companies appear to think export can be 'tacked-on' to, for example, the home sales department. Or that it is a part-time activity which can be handled on a couple of half days per week. This is a particular problem in companies where home sales represent a large proportion of total sales, and exports are seen as 'the jam on the bread'. In such cases it is no surprise that these companies remain 'part-time' exporters. We will obviously proceed from the premise that exporting will operate as a distinct and specialized function within the organization and it is therefore logical to start by examining what goes on in an export office, who does it and how is it organized.

The Export Office

Functions

It is possible to break the functions of an export department into just two areas: sales, that is, order getting, and shipping, that is, order filling. Add to these specific functions the need for overall **control** and the whole department can revolve around those three.

It is perhaps easier to identify what particular things are done within each of these areas if we were to identify the duties of the individuals responsible for their operation. See figure 2.2.

Figure 2.2: Duties of Export, Sales and Shipping Managers

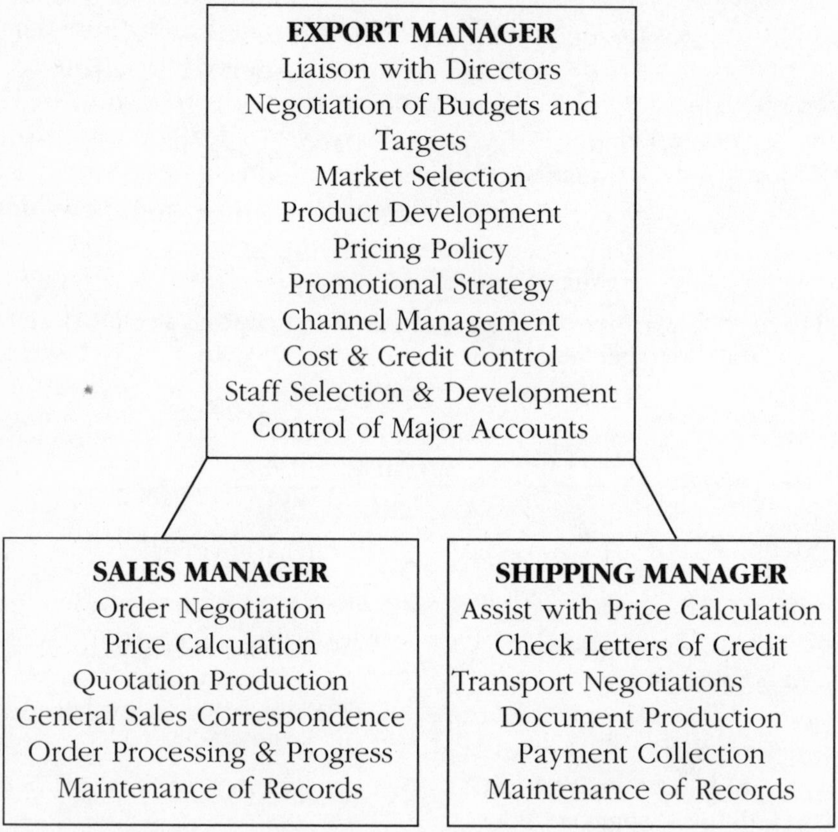

EXPORT MANAGER
Liaison with Directors
Negotiation of Budgets and Targets
Market Selection
Product Development
Pricing Policy
Promotional Strategy
Channel Management
Cost & Credit Control
Staff Selection & Development
Control of Major Accounts

SALES MANAGER
Order Negotiation
Price Calculation
Quotation Production
General Sales Correspondence
Order Processing & Progress
Maintenance of Records

SHIPPING MANAGER
Assist with Price Calculation
Check Letters of Credit
Transport Negotiations
Document Production
Payment Collection
Maintenance of Records

In figure 2.2 we have assumed a simple structure of a Sales and a Shipping Manager directly responsible to an Export Manager. It is, of course always possible that there could be an Export Director, or the Export Manager could report to a Marketing Director. Also, it is not unusual that an Export Sales Manager should run the sales office and an Export Marketing Manager handle the field sales operations. There are no rules which can apply to every company because all will be different in terms of size, product range, type and number of markets, channels of distribution and even their stage of development.

In particular, the size of the export office will have a great effect on its organization. Some companies' export departments will consist of one man or woman, perhaps with secretarial support, in which case any division of labour is somewhat irrelevant. On the other hand is the company with major export business and which employs many hundreds of people within its export department. In such a case it is essential that the functions are defined down to very specialized levels of responsibility.

It is in these latter cases, where larger companies are concerned, that organization structures become very important. A typical, hierarchical, structure of a medium to large export department would probably look like figure 2.3.

Figure 2.3: Hierarchical structure of an export department

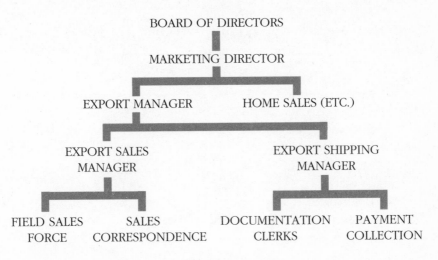

BOARD OF DIRECTORS

MARKETING DIRECTOR

EXPORT MANAGER   HOME SALES (ETC.)

EXPORT SALES   EXPORT SHIPPING
MANAGER   MANAGER

FIELD SALES   SALES   DOCUMENTATION   PAYMENT
FORCE   CORRESPONDENCE   CLERKS   COLLECTION

The larger the company then the greater the degree of specialization. This would be apparent on the bottom row of the organization chart.

Figure 2.3 is an example of the most common form of organization chart, that is a horizontal chart, and is useful when looking at the organization of the Export Office as a distinct unit.

The criteria used as a basis for a horizontal organization chart can vary from company to company, one of the most common being on the basis of markets as demonstrated in figure 2.4 However it is also just as possible that divisions are made on the basis of products (figure 2.5) or type of end-user (figure 2.6).

Figure 2.4: Horizontal organization chart (Market)

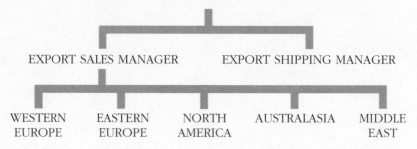

Figure 2.5: Horizontal organization chart (Product)

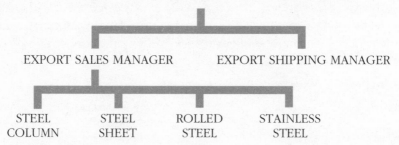

Figure 2.6: Horizontal organization chart (Industry)

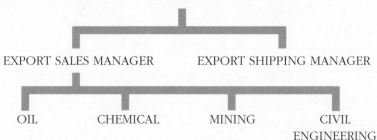

It is not uncommon in large companies that, for example, each market section will itself be broken down into product or end-user based subsections.

All of these organization charts are based on a breakdown of the sales function, based on a variety of criteria, and show shipping as a distinct and separate activity. In such cases the shipping department could also be organized along the same lines. That is to say shipments to certain markets or to certain end-users, or of certain products may be arranged by specialist sections. It could also be the case that other criteria might be applied and prominent among these would be method of transport. It is not uncommon for shipping sections to specialize, for example, in surface and air freight as separate disciplines.

On the other hand it may be that each country section will perform all those functions related to servicing the markets, including the shipping and payment collection tasks. In these cases the operational elements of the export order process will be organized in a vertical structure which is concerned with the elements of the process from enquiry to final payment and allows specialization in procedures as well as products or markets.

Before we look at this vertical process we should clarify the use of organization charts.

Organization Charts

The larger the company becomes the more important it is to adopt a rational organization of its activities, and for that organizational structure to be known to all personnel involved in it.

What this defines is:

1 specific duties/job descriptions;
2 responsibilities, up and down the structure;
3 internal lines of communication;
4 external lines of communication;
5 lines of command; and
6 internal sources of advice and information.

In a small company it is quite possible for everybody to know everybody else, and in fact be in regular daily contact, but in larger organizations even the names and extension numbers of individuals is vital information.

The hierarchical model of the organization chart, which we have used earlier in this chapter, is the most common, containing a varying degree of information regarding the specific functions of each section, but there are other ways in which an organization structure can be graphically displayed.

Some of these are illustrated in figures 2.7, 2.8, and 2.9.

Figure 2.7: The Pyramid

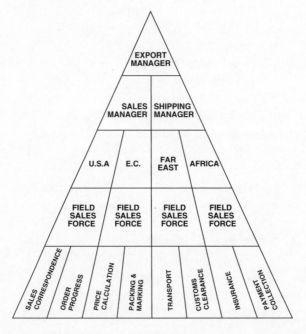

Figure 2.8: The Atom

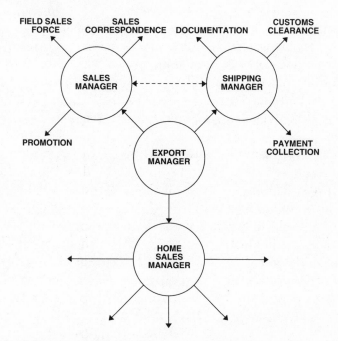

Figure 2.9: The Onion

The most common horizontal organization in exporting companies is based on a market breakdown. This recognizes the importance of market knowledge to the success of the export effort and allows those involved to establish personal contacts in those markets. The same argument applies should the company feel that product or end-user knowledge is more important. However, we have already established that within each of these sections there is a need for procedural expertise regarding the order processing elements.

Some companies duplicate each element of the process within each section, others decide to specialize in terms of function rather than market, for example, and establish sections which handle different elements of the order process. For example, one section will produce all the quotations irrespective of the market. In its ultimate form the vertical organization will not even distinguish between home and overseas sales. The advantage of this form of organization is that personnel can become highly specialized in term of procedural requirements and, from the point of view of 'order filling' needs, this is often very efficient. It can be seen as a production line based on a chronological series of processes from:

ENQUIRY ➤ ORDER ➤ SHIPMENT ➤ PAYMENT

A company which was large enough could attempt to get 'the best of both worlds' by organizing departments horizontally, based on markets, and then organizing vertically within each of those departments. The regular movement of people across sections and departments can not only offer them some variety, but also allows the accumulation of expertise across markets and functions.

As this book is concerned with the practical day-to-day procedural elements of the export order process, then it will be useful, at this early stage, to decide what we mean by this process. The following list (figure 2.10) and the brief explanations are, in fact, a representation of much of the content of subsequent chapters of this book.

Figure 2.10: The export order process

Enquiry

Quotation

Order

Letter of Credit checked

Order acknowledgement

Order process and progress

Packing and marking

Space booking

Documents prepared
Transport
Customs
Insurance
Payment

Goods dispatched

Payment received

Virtually every element of this process is examined in detail in the following chapters, but for now it may be useful to at least clarify the logic of this layout.

It is rather obvious that the beginning of the process is the enquiry from a potential overseas buyer. This may have been instigated from many sources such as personal contact, advertising or recommendation or it could simply be a regular buyer coming back for more. The enquiry will take almost as many forms as there are overseas buyers; it could even be a verbal request, but is often a simple piece of correspondence detailing their requirements or it could be a more formalized tender document.

The quotation in response may be just as informal as the verbal contact, or an extremely formalized completion of tender documents. Generally it is a written quotation on the exporter's standard form. The format of the export quotation and the information it contains is covered in chapter 3.

The next stage, we hope, is receipt of the order from the buyer. We must ensure that the order conforms with our quotation and is still acceptable and that, if a Letter of Credit was requested, that it is available and in an acceptable form. As can be seen in chapter 12, the time to check a Letter of Credit is when it is first received not when the goods are packed in the warehouse ready for dispatch.

The internal documentation necessary to process and progress the order is not directly a subject of this book, but we will, in chapter 13, examine the process of producing a range of external and internal documents using one-run systems. It is logical that both internal and external documents are rationalized into such a process.

An element of the process which is often underestimated in terms of its importance is the packing and marking of export consignments. This represents a cost element which cannot be ignored and good practice is essential in order to get the goods to the destination at the right time in good condition; this good practice is covered in chapter 4.

The booking of transport space is invariably an informal process, often requiring no more than a telephone call from the exporter or their agent. This does not, however, mean that the Contract of Carriage so raised is an informal one and exporters should be aware of the implications of these transport arrangements. The nature of Contracts of Carriage, and the related documentation, are examined in chapters 5 and 7.

Many of the problems with international physical distribution are associated with documentation. The international trader is faced with what appears to be a mountain of 'bits of paper', and it is sometimes difficult to see any sense or logic to it. Such logic does exist but it requires a step back from the mountain to rationalize it. The breakdown of export documentation shown in the order process of transport, customs, insurance and payments is an attempt to break the mountain down into four smaller hills. It is somewhat simplistic but every document used in international trade can be placed into one of these four categories. This is examined in more detail when we start to look at export documentation in chapter 7.

Documents to do with the international transport of goods are covered in chapter 7, Customs & Excise procedures and documentation in chapters 8, 9 and 10 (there is a lot to it), cargo and credit insurance features in chapter 11, and last, but by no means least, payment methods are addressed in chapter 12.

The problem of producing correct documentation must be solved by exporters because in many cases, whether payment is received or not will directly depend on the quality of documentation produced. Even the banks specifically state that they deal 'in documents only'. Whilst it may seem ridiculous, the quality, or even the very existence, of the goods can be totally irrelevant to the transaction and final payment.

As a final illustration of the importance of correct documentation it is an often quoted statistical fact that something like 60 percent of document sets presented to banks against Letters of Credit are rejected, on first presentation, because of documentary discrepancies; it seems that a lot of exporters do get it wrong.

External Organizations

The process we have examined in this chapter is clearly an internal one which must be organized and co-ordinated by the company. Just as clearly it involves contact with, and use of, a wide variety of third parties outside of the company. Many of these are used by choice in that they offer service, help and advice to the exporter. Others are imposed on the exporter by the procedural elements and are unavoidable.

The obvious third parties would include: international carriers – shipping lines, airlines, and road and rail hauliers; freight forwarders; banks (international sections); Customs & Excise; insurance brokers and companies; and Chambers of Commerce.

However, there are also a large number of more specialist organizations, all of which do their best to increase the number of abbreviations and acronyms with which exporters are bedeviled. These include:

DTI	Department of Trade & Industry
COI	Central Office of Information
ICC	International Chamber of Commerce
FIATA	Federation Internationale des Associations de Transitaires et Assimiles
IMO	International Maritime Organisation
ICAO	International Civil Aviation Organisation
IATA	International Air Transport Association
SITPRO	Simpler Trade Procedures
THE	Technical Help to Exporters (Part of the British Standards Institution)
GCBS	General Council of British Shipping
PIRA	Research Association for the Paper and Board Printing and Packaging industries.
BIFA	British International Freight Association
ABCC	Association of British Chambers of Commerce or Arab-British Chamber of Commerce

Whilst a list of abbreviations is not particularly enlightening every one of the above mentioned organizations is examined in the relevant parts of this book in terms of their specific functions. Indeed some we have already detailed in the first chapter. Please consult the index.

We should also not forget the very large number of professional bodies, particularly the Institute of Export, and the various Trade Associations, who are able to offer expert help to their members.

And finally a mention of the most important third party for every company, the **customer**. The only way an exporting company can be sure of long term success in overseas markets is by creating satisfied customers. This not only entails the production and sale of want-satisfying goods, but also the efficient movement of those goods to the end-user. Many exporters are quite capable of producing and selling quality products, but their effort is often wasted because of an amateurish approach to the problems of international physical distribution. A study of the subsequent content of this book will go a long way towards solving these problems.

3

The Export Quotation

As described in chapter 2, the logical beginning of the export process is the enquiry from an overseas buyer and the quotation in response from the exporter, and it is here where things start to go wrong. Many of the problems which exporters face could be avoided by an improved understanding of the nature of export quotations, the correct procedures for their production and the contractual consequences of the information they contain.

A variety of quotation formats exist in practice and will be examined in this chapter, but it may be useful to first identify the range of information contained in most export quotations. This would include:

1 Goods description – size, quantity and so on.
2 Prices.
3 Delivery period (lead time).
4 Terms and method of payment.
5 Validity.

All of which are perhaps not as straightforward as might appear.

1 As the description of the goods is directly relevant to the range of tariff and non-tariff barriers that they might attract at destination then exporters should carefully consider the wording even at this early stage of the process. If choices

exist it could be advantageous to be selective as to product descriptions. (More on this in chapter 10.)

2 Perhaps the most important element of the quotation and one which many exporters actually get wrong. Firstly the price makes no sense without a specific Trade Term, such as the very common FOB and CIF, and the importance and meaning of these terms is not always understood, and secondly the actual process of calculating an accurate export price is one which is beyond many exporters. Both of these factors are examined in some detail in this and following chapters.

3 One of the most common mistakes made at this stage is the habit of exporters to suddenly become super optimists as far as delivery times are concerned. Whilst it is tempting to quote short lead times in order to make the quotation more attractive to the customer, the long term consequences of the subsequent late deliveries do really make it pointless. It is far better to promise 12 weeks and deliver in 10, than to quote 10 but deliver in 12. From a purely practical point of view the deadlines imposed by carrier's schedules and Letters of Credit mean that the consequences of late delivery can be far more severe than simply an unhappy customer.

4 The exporter's estimate of the risks involved with certain customers and certain markets leads directly to, hopefully, sensible choices regarding the method of payment and the credit terms granted. A brief point here; the credit risk in international trade is now perceived as being worse than it has ever been, and this does not just refer to developing countries. About a third of the nations in the world are bankrupt in strict business terms, and as businesses would have been liquidated long ago. Credit risk management is essential to all exporters and starts at the beginning of the process, not at the end when attempting to collect money. (See chapter 12)

5 It should be noted that the quotation made by a UK exporter may be seen in English law as an *invitation to treat*. That is, the order from the buyer is actually an **offer** to buy which is **accepted** by the acknowledgement or acceptance of the seller. The strict legal situation is not quite as simple as this,

but it does mean that an order can be refused by the seller, should they so wish. This may not be the best way to promote good customer relations but may be necessary should the situation have changed or if the order is received after a long delay. The best way to clarify the situation for both parties is to specify a validity period on the quotation and thus avoid any possibility of misunderstanding or conflict.

Forms of Export Quotation

Verbal

This speaks for itself in that in many cases price and delivery information may be given during personal meetings or over the telephone. It is very important that such quotations are confirmed in writing as soon as possible so as to avoid any possible misunderstanding. Don't forget, a verbal contract isn't worth the paper it's written on.

Standard letter

The most common form of quotation which requires no specific format as long as it contains the relevant information mentioned above. Many companies use preprinted letterheads, and these may merely cover price lists, and not state any quantities or specific requirements.

Tender documents

Particularly when dealing with overseas governments, or state buying agencies, the enquiry is received in the form of a tender document. These are also often related to large projects, but not exclusively to large companies, as smaller exporters may tender for parts of a larger tender. There are a number of problems associated with tenders, which include:

1 There is no standard format and the exporter is required to complete the tender document. This involves some quite time consuming investigation of the tender itself in order to complete it correctly and to ensure that the stated terms are acceptable.

2 The requirement for Bonds or Guarantees. This is common in the Middle East but appears to be spreading to other countries and involves the provision of a Tender Bond by the seller along with the completed tender document. This will need to be issued by a bank and promises an amount of money (often five per cent of the tender value) in compensation should the tenderer withdrew the tender before expiry or refuse the order when placed. This compensates the buyer for the expenses involved with the complex process involved in examining all tenders. It may also be seen as a sign of good intent by the tenderer. A typical example of a Tender Bond is shown in figure 3.1.

When the order is placed and accepted it will then be necessary for the seller to produce a Performance Bond which again guarantees an amount of monetary compensation should the seller not perform according to the contract conditions. (See figure 3.2.) The problems associated with these Bonds relate to the fact that the banks make a charge for their issue, and regard any monies guaranteed as being unavailable to the exporter. That is to say that the seller's facility at the bank will be reduced. When one considers that Performance Bonds can be valid for six years or more, then this can be quite restrictive.

Also, most overseas governments insist on unconditional, sometimes referred to as **on demand**, guarantees. This means that the buyer simply has to call on the bond and the bank will pay, there being no requirement for any proof of the seller's breach. The only possible solution to this, assuming that conditional guarantees are not acceptable, is to arrange, through a credit insurance company, for Unwarranted Calls cover. The other solution is, of course, not to give them, but this almost certainly means that the tender would not be considered.

Figure 3.1: Example of a Tender Bond

GUARANTEE NUMBER:

We understand that   (APPLICANT'S NAME) ('the Applicant')
                             (APPLICANT'S ADDRESS)

are tendering for the (DESCRIPTION OF GOODS) under your invitation to Tender (TENDER/CONTRACT NUMBER etc.) and that a Bank Guarantee is required for (AGREED PERCENTAGE OF CONTRACT) ......% of the amount of their tender.

We, (NAME OF APPLICANT'S BANK) hereby guarantee the payment to you on demand of up to (AMOUNT IN FIGURES) say, (AMOUNT IN WORDS) in the event of your awarding the relative contract to the Applicant and of its failing to sign the Contract in the terms of its tender, or in the event of the Applicant withdrawing its tender before expiry of this guarantee without your consent.

This guarantee shall come into force on (COMMENCEMENT DATE) being the closing date for tenders, and will expire at close of banking hours at this office on (EXPIRY DATE) ('Expiry').

Our liability is limited to the sum of (AMOUNT IN FIGURES) and your claim hereunder must be received in writing at this office before Expiry accompanied by your signed statement that the Applicant has been awarded the relative contract and has failed to sign the contract awarded in the terms of its tender or has withdrawn its tender before Expiry without your consent, and such claim and statement shall be accepted as conclusive evidence that the amount claimed is due to you under this guarantee.

Claims and statements as aforesaid must bear the confirmation of your Bankers that the signatories thereon are authorised so to sign.

Upon Expiry this guarantee shall become null and void, whether returned to us for cancellation or not and any claim or statement received after expiry shall be ineffective.

This guarantee is personal to yourselves and is not transferable or assignable.

This guarantee shall be governed by and construed in accordance with the Laws of England.

Figure 3.2: Example of a Performance Bond

GUARANTEE NUMBER:

We understand that you have entered into a Contract (TENDER/ CONTRACT NUMBER etc.) ('the Contract') with (APPLICANT'S NAME & ADDRESS) ('the Applicant') for the (DESCRIPTION OF GOODS) and that under such Contract the Applicant must provide a Bank Performance Guarantee for an amount of (AMOUNT IN FIGURES) being (AGREED PERCENTAGE OF CONTACT) ......% of the value of the contract.

We (NAME and ADDRESS OF APPLICANT'S BANK) HEREBY GUARANTEE payment to you on demand of up to (AMOUNT IN FIGURES) say, (AMOUNT IN WORDS) in the event of the Applicant failing to fulfil the said Contract, provided that your claim hereunder is received in writing at this office accompanied by your signed statement that the Applicant has failed to fulfil the Contract. Such claim and statement shall be accepted as conclusive evidence that the amount claimed is due to you under this guarantee.

Claims and statements as aforesaid must bear the confirmation of your Bankers that the signatories thereon are authorised so to sign.

This guarantee shall expire at close of banking hours at this office on (EXPIRY DATE) ('Expiry') and any claim and statement hereunder must be received at this office before Expiry and after Expiry this guarantee shall become null and void whether returned to us for cancellation or not and any claim or statement received after Expiry shall be ineffective.

This guarantee is personal to yourselves and is not transferable or assignable.

This guarantee shall be governed by and construed in accordance with the Laws of England.

Buyer documents

These are similar to Tender documents but usually less complex and are often related to business with Buying and Confirming Houses in the UK working on behalf of overseas buyers. The enquiry will be made using a set of documents part of which must be completed by the exporter. This is rarely difficult and helps to tie up the documents from the enquiry stage as the eventual order will be part of the same document set. A typical example of this procedure would be dealings with Crown Agents who represent ex-Commonwealth governments.

Pro-forma invoice

This document acts as a quotation as it is intended to exactly demonstrate what the final invoice will look like should the order be placed. That is, it is an advance copy of the final invoice. In this case it is obvious that the quantity and type of goods required will have to be clearly specified. As can be seen in figure 3.3, it is laid out in invoice format, and invariably contains a breakdown of the, so called, ancillary charges, such as freight charges and insurance premiums, commonly being prepared as a CIF quotation.

This type of quotation is extremely common when dealing with developing countries and is specifically related to the requirement for an Import Licence, not, as is often thought, to raise a Letter of Credit.

Licensing controls are examined in more detail in the Customs & Excise sections of this book, so for now it is enough to say that most developing countries use **specific** Import Licensing control regimes, which require the potential importer to obtain a licence for each consignment. The information on the pro-forma is essential to the buyer's licensing authorities and the licence will be issued for the exact amount. In some cases the importer will be granted an annual licence, for certain goods and a limited value, but the value of each consignment will be deducted from the floating balance of the licence.

This does mean that the exporter will have to be very sure of

The Export Quotation

Figure 3.3: Pro-forma invoice

(c) SITPRO 1992

PROFORMA INVOICE

Seller (name, address, VAT reg. no.)			Proforma Invoice number		Sheet no.
Jim Sherlock PLC Shady Lane Bolton Lancs			1234		1
			Proforma Invoice date 24.06.1994	Seller's reference	
			Buyer's reference 5678	Other reference	

Consignee	VAT no.	Buyer (if not consignee)	VAT no.
Sweeping Sing Fat High Street Singapore			

		Country of origin of goods U.K.	Country of destination Singapore
		Terms of delivery and payment C.I.F. Singapore Irrevocable and Confirmed Letter of Credit	

Vessel/flight no. and date First available	Port/airport of loading Liverpool	
Port/airport of discharge Singapore	Place of delivery	

Shipping marks; container number	No. and kind of packages; description of goods	Commodity code	Total gross wt (kg)	Total cube (m3)
S F 1234 SINGAPORE	5 cartons each 200 x 200 x 75 cms	390114	5,000	7.5
		Total net weight (kg) 4,700		

Item/packages	Gross/net/cube	Description	Quantity	Unit price (sheet)	Amount
		High Gloss Card 123	500 sheets	£10.00	£5,000.00
		High Gloss Card 456	500 sheets	£ 5.00	£2,500.00
		Total F.O.B. Liverpool			£7,500.00
		Estimated freight and insurance charges			£ 900.00
		Total C.I.F. Singapore			£8,400.00
			Value		

Name of signatory J Sherlock
Place and date of issue 24.06.94   Bolton
Signature

PR01

Export Trade Connections, SITPRO approved licensee No 10

54

the accuracy of the price quotation as any cost increases before delivery cannot be passed on. The ethics of quoting inflated freight and insurance charges, in order to cover for any possible increases, are discussed at the end of this chapter.

Whilst on the subject of the pro-forma invoice, and in relation to the comments made earlier regarding credit risk, we should also mention its other major function which is to obtain **pro-forma payment**. This actually means advance payment, sometimes referred to as Cash With Order, and is clearly the safest method of payment for any seller.

Some years ago advance payment was very unusual, and only occurred where the buyer had little, or no, choice as to supplier. So, for example, a company like Unipart could insist on cash with order in risk markets, and Marlboro operated on the same basis in West Africa. Most suppliers are not in such a strong position but nevertheless the incidence of advance payment has clearly increased. The reason for this is that many UK exporters perceive the risk of non-payment, or delay in payment, as being so great in many markets that the only basis on which they will do business is cash in advance. The buyer has no alternative and in many cases is not unhappy to deal on such a basis. This is not uncommon when dealing with African, Near and Far Eastern and sometimes Latin American markets. When the eventual shipment is made the exporter must still produce a final invoice which should be identified as being for 'Customs Valuation Purposes Only', and should, of course, be for the full amount paid.

International Delivery Terms

The major elements of the export quotation have been briefly discussed earlier in the chapter, but it is obvious that the price(s) quoted are central to its purpose. It can also be seen that for an exporter to simply say to an overseas customer that a particular product is, for example, £5.00 per Kilo does not really say much, in that the goods could cost them £5.00 in a warehouse in Manchester or £5.00 in their warehouse in Tokyo, and there is obviously a big difference between the two.

For the export price to make any sense then there must be some expression as to what is included, and not included, in that price, as in £5.00 per Kilo FOB. It is here where the use of delivery or trade terms is necessary, as has been the case for centuries.

It is natural that international traders have established, over long periods of time, a range of standard expressions to cover most types of contract, but the most important development was in 1936 when the International Chamber of Commerce produced the first version of *Incoterms.* This publication has been amended and updated on five separate occasions since then and the current version is *Incoterms 1990* (ICC Publication No 460), available from your local Chamber of Commerce. Further updates will be produced from time to time.

What Incoterms does is to provide definitive definitions of 13 trade terms in common use, in the form of a very detailed breakdown of the seller's and buyer's duties, and whilst exporters can invent any term they choose, it is clearly better to use terms for which standard definitions are available. It has to be said that it is also unlikely that terms could be produced which are superior to the ICC Committee's work, or that an Incoterm is not available to suit any requirement.

As the trade term specified on the quotation is such a vital factor in the conditions of the contract of sale between seller and buyer, and as it has such a direct relevance to the price calculation, it is extremely important that all exporters have a firm grasp of the meaning of the various Incoterms.

Incoterms 1990

Group E	EXW	Ex Works
Departure		
Group F	FCA	Free carrier
Main Carriage	FAS	Free Alongside Ship
Unpaid	FOB	Free On Board
Group C	CFR	Cost and Freight
Main Carriage	CIF	Cost, Insurance and Freight
Paid	CPT	Carriage Paid To
	CIP	Carriage and Insurance Paid To

Group D	DAF	Delivered At Frontier
Arrival	DES	Delivered Ex Ship
	DEQ	Delivered Ex Quay
	DDU	Delivered Duty Unpaid
	DDP	Delivered Duty Paid

The 13 listed terms all identify a very specific point, on the journey from the seller to the buyer, for the passing of **costs**, **delivery** and **risk**.

Costs

As we have already seen the export price quoted makes very little sense without some reference to what is included in the price and what isn't. Each trade term acts as a statement as to what costs will be met by the seller, and are therefore already included in the quoted price, and what costs will have to be paid by the buyer, in addition to the purchase price. Thus an ex Works price means that the buyer will have to pay all the costs of the physical distribution of the goods, but a DDP price means that the seller has included all those costs in the quoted price.

Delivery

This defines the individual responsibilities for the arrangements for delivery of the goods. In this context it is not enough for an exporter to quote, as in the previous example, £5.00 per Kilo, because it is also necessary to define a particular geographic location. Thus the UK exporter needs to be specific, as in £5.00 per Kilo FOB UK Port, or even more specific, as in £5.00 per Kilo FOB Liverpool. The point of delivery, once identified, confers obligations on both parties for the transport arrangements and production of the relevant documentation.

Risk

One of the most contentious issues in international trade is the relative responsibilities of the parties involved when the goods are damaged or lost during transit. It is important to establish first of all where the risk of loss or damage to the goods passes from the seller to the buyer, which is defined by the trade term, and secondly to attempt to establish exactly where the loss or damage occurred during the transit. This latter problem is addressed by the documentation governing the transport of the goods and is covered in chapter 7. In simple terms if loss or damage occurs before the point specified by the trade term then it is the seller's problem (they have not in fact delivered in accordance with the contract) but if loss or damage occurs after that point then the seller has fulfilled a contractual obligation and it is the buyer's problem.

Trade Terms

So where are these points in the journey identified by the various trade terms? Figure 3.4 shows the points in the journey identified by the Incoterms.

Ex Works (EXW)

Goods simply need to be placed at the disposal of the buyer at a named place of delivery. This is most commonly the seller's premises, but it should be noted that the seller has no responsibility for loading the goods or ensuring that they leave the factory or warehouse grounds.

Figure 3.4: Incoterms

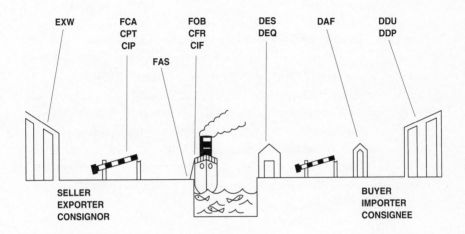

Free Carrier (FCA)

The seller must deliver the goods into the custody of the carrier, named by the buyer, at the specified terminal. This often refers to an inland depot in the UK, which may or may not be a Customs Clearance Depot, or, in the cases where the goods are a full load direct from the exporter's premises, then the point at which the goods are loaded on the vehicle provided by the buyer, or the full load is handed over to the carrier.

This term is appropriate to all modes of transport, that is:

SEA   (Container Base or a Full Container Load taken over by the sea carrier)

AIR   (Airport)

ROAD (Carrier's depot or full load loaded on buyer's vehicle)

RAIL   (Goods or loaded waggon handed over to rail carrier)

Free Alongside Ship (FAS)

The seller must deliver the goods alongside the named vessel at the named port of shipment. This is quite unusual in the UK.

Free On Board (FOB)

The seller must deliver the goods on board the vessel named by the buyer and, more specifically bear the risk of loss or damage until the goods cross the ship's rail at the port of shipment. Whilst it is common for the seller to actually book the shipping space, it should be noted that it is, technically, the buyer's responsibility. The expression 'FOB with services' describes the situation in which the seller arranges the space booking.

Cost and Freight (CFR)

The seller must arrange, and pay for, the carriage of the goods to the named port of destination.

Cost, Insurance and Freight (CIF)

The seller must arrange, and pay for, the carriage and cargo insurance of the goods to the named port of destination.

However, in both of the above cases, the risk of loss or damage to the goods passes at ship's rail **port of shipment**, in exactly the same way as with an FOB contract. Whilst this might appear to be a contradiction. it is perfectly possible for an overseas buyer to make a claim on insurance taken out by the exporter, in that there is a transfer of **insurable interest** at the ship's rail port of shipment. Thus the terms CFR and CIF are definitions of who pays for what, rather than who is responsible for what.

Carriage Paid To (CPT)

The seller arranges, and pays for, the carriage to the agreed point, which will invariably be a depot at destination.

Carriage and Insurance Paid To (CIP)

The seller arranges, and pays for, the carriage and cargo insurance to the agreed point.

In both of the above cases the risk of loss or damage to the goods passes at the same point as in an FCR contract, that is when the first takes over the goods, which will be at the UK depot or where the full load is taken over.

Just as with FOB, CFR and CIF contracts in which the risk passes at ship's rail port of shipment, the same logic applies to FCA, CPT and CIP where the risk passes when the first carrier takes over the goods.

Delivered Ex Ship (DES)

The seller arranges, and pays for, the carriage to the named port of destination and must place the goods at the disposal of the buyer on board the vessel.

Delivered Ex Quay (DEQ)

The seller arranges, and pays for, carriage to the quay at destination and must place the goods at the disposal of the buyer, Cleared Duty Paid.

Delivered At Frontier (DAF)

The seller arranges, and pays for, the carriage to the named point of delivery at the frontier. There is no obligation to arrange cargo insurance and risk passes at the frontier.

Delivered Duty Unpaid (DDU)

The seller arranges, and pays for, carriage to the named place of destination. There is no obligation for insurance and the import clearance charges are the responsibility of the buyer.

Delivered Duty Paid (DDP)

The seller must make all arrangements, and pay the costs, for delivery to the specified destination. There is no obligation to arrange insurance. In the cases of DDU and DDP the specified destination is often the buyer's premises.

An examination of these terms will reveal immediately that an Ex Works contract is much easier for the exporter than would be a DDP contract. However the seller must consider what the buyer might prefer in terms of a package deal, rather than simply take the easy way out by quoting Ex Works. Also the exporter should appreciate that for a number of these terms the obligations for transport and insurance, often to an overseas destination, differ from the point at which the risk of loss or damage passes from the seller to the buyer. Figure 3.4 shows the points at which risk passes from the seller to the buyer, although the seller's obligations in terms of costs would be different.

The final point to make about the selection of appropriate trade terms is relevant to the introduction of the, relatively, new terms of FCA, CPT and CIP. Their introduction reflects the in-creased use of electronic messages rather than paper and the changing nature of international movements, in that the tradi-tional port to port transit of goods, where the ship's rail was an important point in the journey, has given way to the depot to depot movement of unitised (mostly containerized) loads.

What this leads to is the, almost, heretical statement that FOB, CFR and CIF are actually obsolete for the majority of exports and imports. The fact that they are still the most commonly used terms is somewhat unfortunate. Figure 3.5 shows a com-parison of these terms.

Figure 3.5: Comparison of trade terms

	PORT >> PORT	DEPOT >> DEPOT
	FOB	FCA
	CFR	CPT
	CIF	CIP
RISK PASSES {	SHIP'S RAIL PORT OF SHIPMENT	CUSTODY OF THE FIRST CARRIER

The point is that the only really identifiable points on a modern international transit are the Departure and Destination depots, rather than the point where the container or road trailer crosses the ship's rail, and terms which identify the depot rather than the port are far preferable. In fact it could be argued that there are only four terms of any real relevance:

EX WORKS	➤	SELLER'S PREMISES
FCA	➤	UK DEPOT
CIP	➤	DESTINATION DEPOT
DDP	➤	BUYER'S PREMISES

This is particularly true for trade within the Single European Market. As there are arguably minimal differences between domestic, home trade, movements and those within the Single Market, it is logical that, just as FOB Manchester or CIF Glasgow make little sense in the UK, then FOB and CIF make no more sense in Europe. The only logical terms in domestic trade are either delivered or not, that is Ex Works or Delivered, and it is also logical that they should apply to the Single Market. Add the UK depot (FCA) and the destination depot (CIP) and that is all you need.

Export price calculation

The calculation of accurate export selling prices is clearly dependent on the relevant trade term but does, at the risk of stating the obvious, depend on the starting point of an accurate Ex Works price. The trade terms directly affect the component, and cumulative, elements of the price which are added on to an Ex Works base. On the assumption that most companies are able to calculate an accurate Ex Works price, based on a production costing plus a profit margin, then the components of the final quoted price would be:

Export Price Calculation

EXW	Production costs + profit
	+
	export packing
	+
FCA	inland carriage and insurance
FAS	to named
FOB	port or depot
	+
CFR	international freight
CPT	to named destination
	+
CIF	
CIP	Cargo Insurance premium
	+
DES	discharge costs
DEQ	
	+
DAF	on-carriage
DDU	
	+
DDP	customs clearance

The methods of calculation of these component elements, in particular the freight charge and the insurance premium, are covered in later chapters and a fully worked example is included at the end of chapter 6.

A final point regarding the ethics of pricing, particularly where the exporter is attempting to compensate for any possible increases in ancillary costs by a deliberate over-estimation of the cost elements.

I once worked for a company which produced pro-forma invoices sometimes six months in advance of an eventual shipment. The problem of predicting freight and insurance charges so far in advance was aggravated by the fact that the quantity of goods produced was subject to a tolerance of about 10 per cent, and the estimated packing specification was a work of fiction from the warehouse foreman. Given this background, it seemed logical to me to overestimate just about everything in the calculation, almost a 'take away the number you first thought of' method, to ensure that the company did not lose money when we eventually shipped, invariably against a Letter of Credit.

I was admonished on more than one occasion by the Export Manager who pointed out, absolutely correctly, that carriers make a profit on freight, and insurance companies make a profit on insurance, not exporters. An exporter's profit is in the Ex Works price of the goods and it is unethical to attempt to make a profit on ancillary or third party costs. The more pragmatic point is that a buyer is perfectly correct to be annoyed if such cost are exaggerated and can easily find out by producing a Letter of Credit which demands, for example, a Bill of Lading showing the freight calculation.

UK exporters are having to accept the inevitability of calculating and offering delivered prices to more and more customers and therefore have to develop the expertise necessary to produce accurate prices, and not take the easy way out by making Ex Works quotations which end up in the buyer's waste paper bin.

Questions for Discussion

1 Why is it important that delivery terms are stated precisely in an export contract? What can happen if they are not, and how can exporters and buyers avoid any possible disputes?

2 You have been asked to quote a 'Delivered Duty Paid' price for an export order. The buyer requires a detailed breakdown of all costs from Ex-Works onwards. Using a product and destination of your choice as an example, list the appropriate items and indicate how costs would probably be calculated.

4

Inland Transport

Proceeding on an optimistic note we can now assume that our perfectly calculated and presented quotation has been accepted immediately and we have a buyer desperately awaiting the goods. Stretching credulity to the limits, let us also assume that the goods have been produced exactly on schedule and are sitting in the warehouse in pristine condition.

This represents the beginning of the international physical distribution process and there are a number of technical areas that immediately become apparent in terms of the packing and marking of export goods and the delivery into the hands of the receiving authorities or international carriers who will handle the transit overseas.

Packing and Marking

The vital importance of correct packing and marking of export consignments is often not appreciated by many companies, even though they take great pains with other elements of the export process. This is particularly short sighted when one realises that in virtually all export sales it is the seller who will be responsible for adequate export packing and correct marking. It is only in the unusual case of an Ex Works contract in which the seller is **not** aware of the transport arrangements, for example mode and destination, that export packing would not be mandatory, and Ex Works Unpacked is very unusual.

Also the notion that because goods are containerized they need less packing is one which can lead to enormous problems. Whilst containers can reduce certain dangers they can also produce problems all of their own, in particular sweating, water damage and cargo shifting are problems specific to containerized cargo.

The fact is that there is very little point in a firm producing a competitive product, achieving good order levels and producing perfect documentation, if the goods get to the customer smashed to pieces, or with half of them missing, or they arrive in perfect condition in the wrong place. Negligence at this stage will not only negate all the good work which may have gone before, but can be extremely expensive in terms of direct financial loss, time taken in corrective action and loss of customer goodwill.

Many companies attempt to avoid problems by having specialist packing and marking departments, very often related to, or part of, the warehousing or transport sections. However, this is no solution if such a department packs for home and export deliveries and makes no distinction between the two. This is, unfortunately, not an unusual situation. It may also be the case that specialist external packers are used, which generally means that the goods are adequately packed and marked but this will often increase the cost and impose time delays.

What must be accepted is that packing and marking for export is a highly specialized function, and what is considered adequate for domestic dispatches is invariably inadequate for overseas dispatches.

There are a number of reasons why export consignments face greater risks of theft, pilferage and damage than do domestic consignments.

Distance

On a purely statistical basis there is more likelihood of loss or damage, the longer the transit. Overseas consignments can travel over 15,000 miles to some destinations; the average UK domestic journey is a stroll by comparison. The risk is related not only to the greater distance, but also the longer time of transit. Quite apart from the increased chance of theft or damage, the longer the journey then the more chance there is of the goods being lost or diverted en route.

Increased handling

Most loss and damage occurs to goods during handling. The number of times the goods are actually handled, loaded and unloaded on an export consignment is invariably greater than that for a domestic dispatch. A conventional, non-containerized, movement of goods could be handled anything up to 12 times on the one journey. One of the advantages of the use of containers is the fact that handling is reduced to a minimum with subsequent reductions in loss and damage.

Quality of handling

Not only do goods tend to be handled more often when exported but also the quality of handling may leave something to be desired. This is a particular problem in developing countries where there may be a lack of modern and specialized handling equipment, the consequences of which are exacerbated by a lack of properly trained, and motivated, labour. Whilst many ports and depots overseas are fast improving, and the development of containerisation has demanded centralized and mechanically equipped locations, there are still certain destinations which require the exporter to pack in units no heavier than 50 Kilos because the unloading will be carried out by hand. The lack of literate labour can also be a problem in terms of the marking of the goods, often involving colour codes as opposed to words.

Environmental conditions

Overseas consignments are often subject to far more arduous

conditions than are domestic transits. Because of the range of geographic and climatic conditions encountered on an international journey the goods may encounter a wide variety of different conditions. As an extreme example of this, it is a real packing problem to prepare foodstuffs for an air freight journey during which the pressure could drop by 4 lbs per square inch and the temperature range from −40°F to +130°F.

As a final point, the exporter should be aware that goods need to be prepared for the whole of the journey, not just the easiest part. Even containerized goods are broken down and on-carried towards the end of their journey in conditions which may be much inferior to those prevailing at the beginning. It is a sensible exporter who prepares goods for the worst possible element of the transit, not the best possible.

So what do we expect from our packing? It must:

1 Protect;
2 Contain; and
3 Identify.

The packing protects against damage and pilferage, contains the goods so that they can be handled, even when protection may be less relevant, and bears the marks which enable the goods to be identified. Whilst there is little problem in identifying what export packing is required to do, the actual choice as to how goods will be packed is far more difficult. An increasing problem is the huge choice of methods which exporters now have.

Packing Methods

Cartons

The most widely used type of outer packing now used, and available in a range of materials, in particular, double or triple walled cardboard or fibreboard. This combines adequate protection, in most cases, with low cost and lightness.

Cases or crates

Traditionally made of wood, but less common now because of the ever-increasing cost of timber. The case is a solid box, whilst the crate is composed of a skeleton, or slatted, structure. Apart from the material cost and the added weight (which increases the freight cost) it may also be necessary, for certain markets, for the wood to be treated with pesticide and be certified as such.

Bales

Used regularly in certain trades where goods can be compressed and then wrapped, often with hessian, and banded. Sometimes referred to as a 'truss', particularly when not banded.

Drums

Produced in a very wide range of materials apart from the traditional steel variety. Suitable for many liquid and powder goods.

Sacks

Again available in a range of materials, from paper to plastic, and often used when containment is more important than protection.

In addition to the above there is also a range of highly specialized forms of export packing suitable for specific goods, such as carboys, glass containers for corrosive liquids, steel cases for highly pilferable items, shrink wrap for goods damaged by moisture, and so on.

For advice on the range of packing materials available the exporter can, of course, consult the manufacturers, but must accept that they may be biased. A good forwarder, or carrier, can also be very helpful. An element of the British Standards

Institution known as Technical Help to Exporters, and the Paper and Board Printing and Packaging Industries Research Association (PIRA) can also offer specialized advice.

Given a fair knowledge of the choices available to the exporter what factors actually impact on the method eventually chosen?

Factors Affecting Choice of Packing

Nature of goods

The special requirements of the goods must be considered. They may be bulky, fragile or valuable, or may require special packing, handling and stowage, perhaps to avoid sweating or tainting. The very special requirements of Dangerous Goods are examined later in this chapter.

Destination

This relates to the distance to be travelled, the quality of handling and the range of climatic conditions experienced by the goods. Also there may be specific regulations, in the country of destination, regarding the type of packing. Typically this would be an insistence on the treating of organic packing with insecticides, or even a total ban. This would not only affect wooden cases or crates, but also wood wool and straw.

Mode of transport

The need for protection, and the particular packing regulations, will differ from one mode of transport to another. As a broad example, it is often the case that packing for air freight needs to be less robust than for sea freight, on the grounds that the transit is shorter and handling more sophisticated.

Customer's requirements

In some cases the type of packing the exporter would normally use is replaced by a type requested by the customer. Assuming the buyer is prepared to pay any extra costs which this may involve, then the exporter would normally comply. Care should be taken if the buyer requests inferior packing in an attempt to save money, if only to ensure that the seller has no contractual obligations for damage in transit.

Cost

Last but by no means least. If cost was not a factor in the selection of packing methods then the great majority of goods would be packed in solid wooden cases. Because this is a very expensive method cheaper, but adequate, alternatives must be found, such as cartons. We should also remember that the freight charge is based on the Gross weight of the shipment, that is it includes the weight of the packing, known as the 'tare' weight. Heavy packing is therefore not only a cost factor in its own right, but also increases the freight charge.

The use of second-hand packing as a means of reducing cost may be possible but the exporter should take great care to ensure that the packing is still adequate, and that any previous marks are completely removed. There is a potential risk that the carriers may issue claused receipts if they consider packing to be inadequate (see chapter 5).

Marking for export

Once the goods are packed the exporter must then ensure that they are marked sufficiently well to ensure that they get to the intended final destination. In this context the only rules as such which apply are those concerning the marking of dangerous goods and these are addressed later in this chapter. As far as non-hazardous goods are concerned then only recommendations are available from Simpler Trade Procedures (SITPRO) and the

International Cargo Handling Co-ordination Association (ICHCA).

For air, road and rail movements it is not uncommon that the goods simply carry the full address of the consignee, in which case they would be labelled as opposed to marked. The parties involved should seriously consider whether the naming of the consignee poses any security problems in terms of the possible identification of the nature of the goods.

Where sea freight shipments are concerned it is far more common for the goods to carry what are basically coded shipping marks. These have the great merit of being simple and do not clutter the packing with large amounts of, possibly irrelevant, information. SITPRO suggest that the marks should be 'sufficient and necessary for goods in transit'.

A typical mark is shown in Figure 4.1.

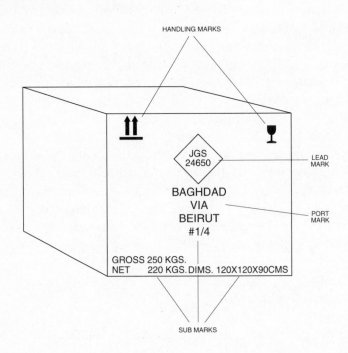

Figure 4.1: Typical shipping mark

LEAD MARK   Identifies the consignee and, maybe, the consignment or order reference number.

PORT MARKS It is important that the mark not only contains the final destination but also that the port of discharge is clearly displayed.

SUB MARKS These, for example, include Gross and Net Weights in Kilograms, dimensions in Centimetres, and running numbers which identify the unit number, for example 4 of 8, or 4/8 would identify case number 4 of a total of 8 cases.

HANDLING MARKS A range of standardized pictorial handling marks have been established through the International Standards Organisation (ISO) and give clear instructions regarding the handling of goods which are recognized throughout the world. They include:

Figure 4.2: Handling marks

Sling here   Fragile   Use no hooks

This way up   Keep away from heat   Keep dry

Center of gravity

Exporters should also consider:

Legibility
Lead marks and Port marks should be at least 7.5 cms high and Sub marks at least 3.5 cms high. Care should also be taken that any banding does not mask the marks.

Indelibility
Obviously the mark needs to be permanent in all conditions. One which washes off in the rain is not particularly effective.

Position
It is important that the marks are always visible and this therefore requires at least two, and sometimes three, marks on different sides of the goods.

Once the goods are packed and marked for export the next logical stage is to deliver them from the exporter's premises into the receiving authority's, or the carrier's, possession at the port or depot agreed in the contract. Two specific documents are related to this procedure.

Export Cargo Shipping Instruction (ECSI)

Where a forwarding agent is being used to arrange the shipment, and probably, the documentation, it is necessary to give them clear instructions. The standard document which does this is the ECSI which is used in two basic forms, one for surface freight (see figure 4.3) and one for air freight which is often referred to as the Shipper's Letter of Instruction (SLI). If the forwarder has also arranged for the goods to be collected from the exporter's premises it is normal for the documents, including the ECSI, to be released to the driver. In the case of direct delivery to the port or depot then the ECSI must be available to the forwarder before arrival of the goods.

Figure 4.3: Export Cargo Shipping Instruction

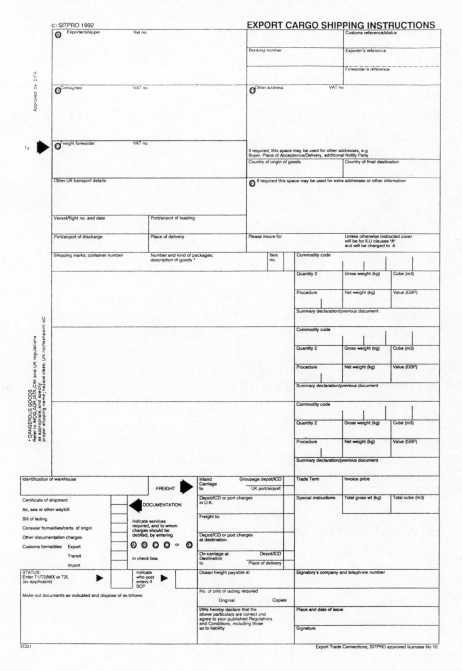

Standard Shipping Note

Designed to cover the delivery of the goods into the depot or port. This document is an excellent example of the work of SITPRO in reducing the number of export documents. It was introduced in 1975 as a replacement for the large number of different Port or Dock Notes which served the same purpose for each separate port authority. It is composed of six colour coded copies:

Copy 1 & 2 Retained by Receiving Authority
       3 To International Carrier
       4 Returned to Shipper/Agent
       5 To Inland Haulier
       6 Retained by Shipper/Agent

The standard document therefore gets the goods into the depot or port and provides receipts for all involved parties. It will be followed by the receipts from the international carriers in the form of a Bill of Lading or Waybill (see chapter 7). It is also acceptable to the Customs & Excise as an 'approved commercial document' if the goods are to be post-entered (see chapter 8).

All of the above information regarding the packing, marking and delivery of the goods is applicable to the movement of non-hazardous cargoes. The exporter must accept that if hazardous goods are involved then the procedures and restrictions are more complex and certainly more rigorously applied.

Dangerous Goods

It is extremely important that all exporters should be aware of the requirements for the movement of dangerous cargoes even if they do not normally deal with them. There are many examples of exporters who generally deal in non-hazardous goods but from time to time may be involved in declarable goods and do not have the procedures to cope. The company which dispatched a number of batteries, full of battery acid, as a favour to a customer, without declaring them were very lucky that it was only the driver's trousers which ended up with holes in them.

The importance of correct procedures cannot be stressed too much, simply because the consequences on non-compliance can be drastic. From the purely financial point of view it is very important that goods are packed, marked and declared accurately to the carriers. If incidents occur the carrier will naturally attempt to avoid liability and missing or inaccurate declarations will invariably impose severe penalties on the exporter. Apart from this, purely commercial, consideration there is a very clear moral obligation on exporters to make absolutely certain that those involved with handling dangerous goods are aware of what the goods are; many accidents occur because carriers are ignorant of the exact nature of the goods they are handling. Not only does this generate incidents but also exacerbates the consequences of any accidents. It is the involvement of people in such close proximity to goods that imposes such a strong moral obligations on exporters to 'get it right'.

The following section is intended only as a brief overview of dangerous goods procedures and reference should be made to the publications mentioned in the text for operational detail.

International regulations

The United Nations Committee of Experts on the Transport of Dangerous Goods produce revised 'recommendations' every two years in a publication known as the 'Orange Book'. This is then incorporated, with adaptations. in the published regulations of each of the authorities involved with the major modes of international transport. These are:

SEA   International Maritime Organisation (IMO)
        International Maritime Dangerous Goods Code (IMDG Code)

ROAD   Economic Commission for Europe (ECE)
        Accord Dangereux Routier (ADR)

RAIL   Central Office for International Rail Transport (OCTI)
        Reglement International Dangereux (RID)

AIR   International Civil Aviation Organisation (ICAO) Techni-
        cal Instructions

The UK takes account of all these provisions in producing detailed regulations, in the form of Statutory Instruments, for each transport mode. Before we look at these an overview of the basic principles for all international modes of transport will be useful.

Fundamental requirements for all dangerous goods procedures are:

1 Identification of goods;
2 Packing requirements;
3 Marking requirements; and
4 Documentary declarations.

Identification of goods

One of the first requirements is that the correct technical name of the product or substance must be used and not brand or proprietary names. Thus 2,000 litres of 'Gramoxone' would be unacceptable because that is a brand name; these goods should be described as 2,000 litres of Paraquet Dichloride in Solution.

Word descriptions of goods are, however, not specific enough for the detailed identification necessary and more precise classification systems are needed. The broadest classification is the United Nations Commodity Classification system which covers all goods, including dangerous ones. The UN 4 digit code must be included in the written declarations.

In addition the International Maritime Organisation, which is an arm of the UN, classifies goods into nine hazard classes. This is the basis of the IMDG and other modal classifications (with amendments for air freight) and also leads to a standardized hazard warning labelling system. The classes are:

CLASS

1 Explosives

2 Gases
   2.1 Flammable (Note, same meaning as Inflammable)
   2.2 Non-Flammable
   2.3 Poisonous

3 Flammable Liquids
   3.1 Flash point below 18°C
   3.2 Flash point 18° to 23°C
   3.3 Flash point 23° to 61°C

4 4.1 Flammable Solids
   4.2 Liable to Spontaneous Combustion
   4.3 Emit Flammable Gas in Contact with Water

5 5.1 Oxidising Substances
   5.2 Organic Peroxides

6 6.1 Poisonous Substances
   6.2 Infectious Substances

7 Radioactive Materials

8 Corrosives

9 Miscellaneous Substances (not covered by other classes)

Packing requirements

There is a simple UN classification of packing groups which is based on the broad level of hazard. They are:

Packing Group I High Hazard
             II Medium Hazard
            III Low Hazard

For international road and rail freight the group numbers become (a), (b) and (c).
   Each transport mode also specifies more detailed packing

types for each class, which relates to internal as well as external packing and, in some cases, to the size of packing units. Most packing also needs to be 'performance tested' and approved by authorized testing stations, which, in the UK, are operated by the Paper and Board, Printing and Packaging Research Association (PIRA).

Marking requirements

These do differ from one mode to another but there is general acceptance of the standard hazard warning diamonds and the UN number. Figure 4.4 illustrates the standard warning diamond for each hazard class.

Figure 4.4: Hazard warning diamonds

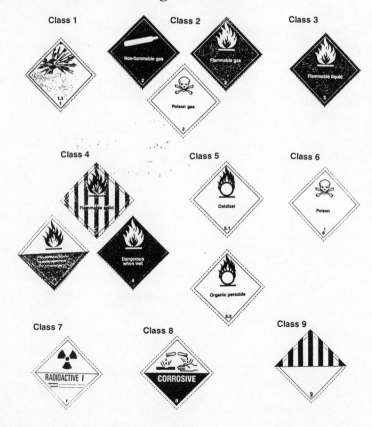

Figure 4.5: Dangerous Goods Note

DG

DANGEROUS GOODS DECLARATION, SHIPPING NOTE
& CONTAINER/VEHICLE PACKING CERTIFICATE
© SITPRO 1982

DANGEROUS GOODS NOTE

Special information is required for (a) dangerous goods in limited quantities (b) radioactive substances (class 7) (c) tank containers and road tankers (d) in certain circumstances a weathering certificate is required

SHADED AREAS NEED NOT BE SHIPPER COMPLETED FOR SHORT SEA RO/RO/RAIL

Exporter	1	Customs reference/status	2
		Booking number	3	Exporter's reference 00484	4

Manchester. M11 4AP
ENGLAND

| | | Port charges payable by: exporter / freight forwarder | 5 | Forwarder's reference | 6 |

Consignee / 7A other (name & address)

Klybeck
Switzerland

| Freight forwarder | 7 | International carrier | 8 |

For use of receiving authority only

| Other UK transport details (e g ICD, terminal, vehicle bkg. ref., receiving dates) | 9 |

Consecutive no. or DG reference allocated by international carrier (if any) 10A

| Vessel | Port of loading | 10 |

| Port of discharge | Destination | 11 |

TO THE RECEIVING AUTHORITY
Please receive for shipment the goods described below subject to your published regulations and conditions (including those as to liability)

SYSTEMFORMS LTD. 01 505 6125
SITPRO APPROVED LICENSE No. 29 (288)

| Shipping marks · Number and kind of packages, description of goods ·
SPECIFY HAZARD CLASS, UN·ADR, RID, IMDG CODE (AS APPROPRIATE) FLASHPOINT °C | 12 | Receiving authority use | Gross wt (kg) Net wt (kg) | 13 | Cube (m³) of goods | 14 |

20 INTERMEDIATE DYESTUFFS
KLYBECK   KEGS   2 CHLOR 4,6 DINITROANILINE DRY MILLED
48307-26

TRANSPORT CLASS : HARMFUL
UN NO. 2811
IMO CLASS 6.1
IMDG 6206
PKG GR III
ARD CLASS 6.1,17*C
RID CLASS 6.1,17C
ICAO CLASS 6.1
FLASHPOINT 154 DEG.C.
EMS 6.1-06

GROSS WT.
2802 kg

NETT WT.
2622 kg

PROPER SHIPPING NAME · PROPRIETARY NAMES ALONE ARE NOT SUFFICIENT

MUST BE COMPLETED FOR FULL CONTAINER/VEHICLE LOADS

CONTAINER/VEHICLE PACKING CERTIFICATE	15	DANGEROUS GOODS DECLARATION	Total gross weight of goods	Total cube of goods
It is declared that the packing of the container has been carried out in accordance with the provisions shown overleaf		I hereby declare that the contents of this consignment are fully and accurately described above by the correct transport/proper shipping name(s) and that the shipment is packaged in such a manner as to withstand the ordinary risks of handling and transport by sea, having regard to the requirements of the goods, to be carried and that the goods are classified, packaged, marked and labelled in accordance with the requirements of the Merchant Shipping (Dangerous Goods) Rules 1981 as currently amended (further declaration appropriate for goods are classified, packaged and marked to comply with the requirements of the Carriage by Agreement concerning the International Carriage of Dangerous Goods by Road (ADR) and of Annex 1 (RID) to the International Convention concerning the Carriage of Goods by Rail (CIM) or type of arrangement made between the contracting parties to these Agreements		
Name of company		The shipper must complete and sign box 17		
Signature of person responsible for packing container	Date 23.2.90			
Prefix and container/vehicle number	16	Seal number(s)	16A	Container/vehicle size & type	16B	Tare wt (kg) as marked on CSC plate	16C	Total of boxes 13 and 16C	16D

DOCK/TERMINAL RECEIPT		Name and telephone no. of shipper preparing this note	17
Received the above number of packages, containers, trailers or appliances in apparent good order and condition unless stated hereon		NAME STATUS OF DECLARANT	
RECEIVING AUTHORITY REMARKS		SHIPPING OFFICER	
Haulier's Name		DATE 23.2.90	
Vehicle reg. no.		Signature of declarant	
DRIVER'S SIGNATURE	SIGNATURE AND DATE		

Documentary declarations

It is essential that any exporter shipping hazardous goods makes a written declaration certifying that the goods are properly classified, packed, marked and suitable for carriage. The document used for surface freight movements is the Dangerous Goods Note (DGN) as shown in Figure 4.5. The DG note not only identifies the exact nature of the goods but also replaces the Standard Shipping Note, which is not appropriate to dangerous goods, and acts as a written application for shipping space rather than the usual informal verbal booking.

For air freight consignments the declaration is not the DG Note but the International Air Transport Association's (IATA) Shipper's Declaration as shown in Figure 4.6.

The above are requirements which broadly apply to all modes of transport but each individual means of international transport has adapted and extended these procedures.

Dangerous goods by sea

The International Maritime Dangerous Goods (IMDG) Code has been ratified in the UK by the Merchant Shipping (Dangerous Goods and Marine Pollutants) Regulations 1990.

It is important to note that the operational manual familiar to many and known as the '*Blue Book*' (*Report of the DTI's Standing Advisory Committee on Carriage of Dangerous Goods in Ships*) has now been replaced by the 1990 edition of the IMDG Code, which will be regularly updated. In addition to the four volume Code there is a supplement which contains Emergency Procedures, Medical First Aid Guide, Reporting Procedures and Guidelines for Packing Cargo in Freight Containers.

This means that the information needed from the exporter also includes the EmS number (Emergency Schedule) and MFAG number (Medical First Aid Guide).

Finally, exporters should never attempt to identify goods with the IMDG page number. The IMO publications exist in various languages and therefore page numbers may differ and amendments may alter the page running order.

Figure 4.6: International Air Transport Association's Shipper's Declaration

SHIPPERS DECLARATION FOR DANGEROUS GOODS

Shipper	Air Waybill No.
	Page of Pages
	Shipper's Reference Number
	(Optional)

Consignee	
	IATA

Two completed and signed copies of this Declaration must be handed to the operator

WARNING

TRANSPORT DETAILS

This shipment is within the limitations prescribed for *(delete non applicable)*	Airport of Departure
PASSENGER CARGO AND CARGO AIRCRAFT AIRCRAFT ONLY	

Airport of Destination

Failure to comply in all respects with the applicable Dangerous Goods Regulations may be in breach of the applicable law, subject to legal penalties. This Declaration must not, in any circumstances, be completed and/or signed by a consolidator, a forwarder or an IATA cargo agent.

Shipment type *(delete non-applicable*

| NON-RADIOACTIVE | RADIOACTIVE |

NATURE AND QUANTITY OF DANGEROUS GOODS *(see sub-Section 8.1 of IATA Dangerous Goods Regulations)*

Dangerous Goods identification						
Proper Shipping Name	Class or Divi- sion	UN or ID No.	Subsi- diary Risk	Quantity and type of packing	Packing inst.	Authorization

Additional Handling Information

I hereby declare that the contents of this consignment are fully and accurately described above by proper shipping name and are classified, packed, marked and labelled, and are in all respects in the proper condition for transport by air according to the applicable international and National Government Regulations.

Name/Title of Signatory

Place and Date

Signature
(see warning above)

Dangerous goods by road

The Accord Dangereux Routier (ADR) is ratified in the UK as the '*European Agreement concerning the International Carriage of Dangerous Goods by Road*' (*Green Book*) which is available from HMSO. This provides provisions which govern the goods and the vehicle. Annexe 1 covers goods classification, packing and marking; Annexe 2 covers vehicle type, loading, stowing, safety equipment and driver training.

The nine IMDG classes broadly apply but ADR does make a distinction between 'restrictive' goods which cannot be moved without special arrangements with the transport authorities of the countries of transit and 'non-restrictive' goods which can be moved as long as they meet ADR provisions. Within the classifications ADR groups goods under item numbers which are expressed as 1°, 2°, 3° and so on, for example Benzine is '3,3° (b) ADR'.

The standard hazard warning diamonds are acceptable under ADR but, in addition, the vehicle must be placarded with rectangular orange plates (sometimes referred to as Kemler plates) which not only identify the hazard but also carry a telephone number for specialist advice. A final and very important requirement under ADR is the need for **Transport Emergency Cards** (Tremcards) to accompany the goods. (See figure 4.7.) They carry written information as to the substance and appropriate emergency action, including first aid, which is of great value to the police and fire services in the event of an accident. The Tremcard system has been developed by the European Council of Chemical Manufacturers' Federations (CEFIC), and is acceptable throughout Europe with the proviso that the Tremcards are carried in the languages of the countries of transit. Should dangerous goods be carried by road for a destination outside Europe, which would include road delivery to a port for subsequent sea freight outside Europe, then the ADR does not apply. Similar requirements are imposed by the Road Traffic (Carriage of Dangerous Substances in Packages etc.) Regulations (PGR) 1992, which includes the need for Tremcards, placards and driver training.

Figure 4.7: Transport Emergency Card

	CEFIC TEC (R) - 219
TRANSPORT EMERGENCY CARD (Road)	January 1976 Rev. 1
	UN No. 2672

Cargo

AMMONIA DISSOLVED IN WATER (not more than 35%)
(Aqueous Ammonia ; Ammonia Liquor ; Ammonium Hydroxide Solution)
Colourless solution with perceptible odour

Nature of Hazard
Volatile
Corrosive

Contact with liquid causes skinburns and severe damage to eyes
The vapour causes strong irritation to eyes and air passages
Heating will cause pressure rise with risk of bursting

Protective Devices
Suitable respiratory protective device
Goggles giving complete protection to eyes
Plastic or rubber gloves, apron and boots
Eyewash bottle with clean water

EMERGENCY ACTION — Notify police and fire brigade immediately

- Stop the engine
- No naked lights. No smoking
- Mark roads and warn other road users
- Keep public away from danger area
- Keep upwind

Spillage
- Drench with water
- If substance has entered a water course or sewer or been spilt on soil or vegetation, advise police

Fire
- Keep containers cool by spraying with water if exposed to fire

First aid
- If the substance has got into the eyes, immediately wash out with plenty of water for at least 15 minutes
- Remove contaminated clothing immediately and wash affected skin with plenty of water
- Seek medical treatment when anyone has symptoms apparently due to inhalation or contact with skin or eyes

Additional information provided by manufacturer or sender :

HUNT CHEMICAL N.V.
EUROPARK NOORD 21-22
2700 SINT-NIKLAAS
BELGIUM

TELEPHONE

03/776.85.11

Prepared by CEFIC (CONSEIL EUROPEEN DES FEDERATIONS DE L'INDUSTRIE CHIMIQUE, EUROPEAN
COUNCIL OF CHEMICAL MANUFACTURERS' FEDERATIONS) Zürich, from the best knowledge available;
no responsibility is accepted that the information is sufficient or correct in all cases.

Acknowledgement is made to V.N.C.I. and E.V.O. of the Netherlands for their help in the preparation of this card.

Applies only during road transport English

Dangerous goods by rail

The Reglement International Dangereux (RID) is the rail freight equivalent of ADR and dates back to 1893. The requirements are very similar to the ADR because of the deliberate co-operation between the two regimes. In the UK RID is entitled *'The Regulations concerning the International Carriage of Dangerous Goods by Rail'* and has force of law through the ratification of the 'Convention concerning the International Carriage by Rail' (COTIF).

As the UK is an island (ignoring the Channel Tunnel for now) then it can be argued that there are only two possible modes of transport for an export, that is sea or air freight. In fact international rail and, particularly, road journeys are very common from the UK and the contracts of carriage, under the Convention des Merchandises par Route (CMR) for road and the Convention International des Merchandises par Chemin de Fer (CIM) for rail, commence from the time the goods are loaded until off loading at final destination (see chapter 5). However the road trailers and rail wagons do depend on roll on/roll off (RO/RO) ferries to cross the North Sea or the Channel. The contract of carriage remains CMR or CIM, even though the trailer or wagon are at sea, but it is important to note that the dangerous goods regulations will change. The sea freight element of the journey is subject to the IMDG which takes precedence over ADR and RID for the sea part of the transit.

Definitive rules for dangerous goods carried through the Channel Tunnel, which commences operation mid-1994 are not yet finalized, but it has been indicated that the scope for carriage of dangerous goods will be severely limited. It is almost certain that high hazard and bulk consignments will remain dependent on the ferry companies.

Dangerous goods by air

In the UK the Air Navigation Order and Air Navigation (Dangerous Goods) Regulations ratify the *'Technical Instructions for the Safe Transport of Dangerous Goods by Air'* which are published by the International Civil Aviation Organisation (ICAO) which is the air version of the International Maritime Organisation (IMO). However, in practice, the operational manual is the

International Air Transport Association's (IATA) Dangerous Goods Regulations which are published annually and which can be more restrictive than the ICAO in some areas.

The written declaration is not the Dangerous Goods Note, which is specific to surface freight, but the IATA 'Shipper's Declaration for Dangerous Goods' which **must** be signed by the shipper and not the agent.

Figure 4.8: Air freight hazard warning labels

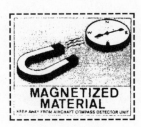 

The nine hazard classes also apply to air freight, with special additions such as Magnetised Material, and a distinction between cargoes which can be carried on passenger aircraft and those that are only permitted on pure freight flights. Specific packing and marking conditions are also specified in the regulations, particularly a restriction on the size of packing units. There are even some hazard warning labels which are unique to air freight as shown in figure 4.8.

It has been mentioned earlier in this chapter that air freight poses unique problems, particularly with regard to possible changes in temperature and pressure which the goods may experience. This means that goods which are non-hazard or low hazard for surface freight may be declarable, and potentially high hazard, for air freight. Examples of this would include barometers, manometers and other electrical equipment which contains mercury, solid carbon dioxide (dry ice) which even makes bull's semen a dangerous cargo, and even toys if they are made from cellulose-based material.

The one other problem relating to air freight is that of security. Following the Lockerbie disaster the problem of cargo checking was addressed by the Aviation and Maritime Security Act 1990. Not only did this tighten up the definitions of 'known' and 'unknown' shippers but also required certifications as to the security of shipments.

In addition, the Aviation Security (Air Cargo Agents) Regulations 1992 makes it possible for agents, and regular shippers, to be 'listed', based on the quality of their security systems, and thus avoid the more stringent checks, and related delays, experienced by other cargo providers. The Department of Transport, Air Cargo Inspectorate, 2 Marsham Street, London SW1P 3EB can supply more specific information.

Conclusion

It will be clear from the above that the regulations controlling the identification, packing, marking and declaration of dangerous goods are by no means simple. This is inevitable when one considers the enormous range of goods which are carried on a variety of transport modes. Consider this in relation to the risks, not only to the carrier's equipment and other cargoes, but to the people involved in handling the goods and well defined regulations become essential.

We have established that the exporter has both a commercial and moral obligation to comply with all regulations. The worst possible situation is one in which the dangerous goods are not declared at all; second worse is a mis-declaration of goods. Any company in any doubt whatsoever as to whether goods are classed as hazardous, and if so how they should be declared, should consult the relevant carriers and ask their advice. It is as much in the carrier's interests as your own to ensure that regulations are applied correctly. As long as they are, then dangerous goods will move as easily as any other cargo. Figure 4.9 gives a final overview of the basic procedures.

We are now almost at the stage where we can at least get the export consignment off our premises and begin the journey to our overseas customer. The only other procedure which could now delay us is that of pre-shipment Inspection.

Pre-shipment inspection

It may be necessary for the exporter to obtain some form of certification, generally as to the standard of goods, prior to actual shipment. These may result from a specific buyer's requirements or may be needed to meet import regulations in the country of destination. Such requirements can actually obstruct

Figure 4.9: Overview of the basic procedures for declaring dangerous goods (Reproduced by permission of Derek Downs, Micor Freight Ltd, from *Understanding the Freight Business.*)

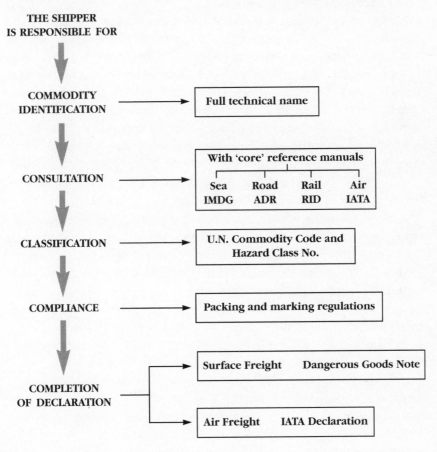

THE SHIPPER
IS RESPONSIBLE FOR

COMMODITY
IDENTIFICATION → Full technical name

CONSULTATION → With 'core' reference manuals

Sea	Road	Rail	Air
IMDG	ADR	RID	IATA

CLASSIFICATION → U.N. Commodity Code and Hazard Class No.

COMPLIANCE → Packing and marking regulations

COMPLETION
OF DECLARATION → Surface Freight   Dangerous Goods Note

→ Air Freight   IATA Declaration

sales into a particular market or, more likely, increase the cost, in view of the expense of testing and certification and potentially, the cost of product modifications to meet the required standards. Collectively they are prime examples of what are known as 'non-tariff barriers' to trade, which operate in addition to the more obvious 'tariff barriers' such as duty, tax, excise and licensing restrictions.

The particular inspection requirements will differ enormously from market to market, and from product to product. Not only may the actual standards differ from market to market, but also the organizations authorized to test and certificate will also change. It is sometimes the case that the exporter cannot self-certify and is obliged to obtain independent certification, which could be in the importer's country.

An important aspect of the development of the Single European Market is the 'New Approach to Technical Harmonisation' which has gone a long way towards removing these non-tariff barriers, and the mutual recognition of testing authorities. (See chapter 14). In fact one of the cases which led to the Single Market proposals concerned the standard for the noise level of diesel lawnmowers. The situation was that every member of the European Community imposed a different standard and the only manufacturer producing a product which met all standards happened to American.

Whilst the problem may be partially solved within the European community, it is still a major consideration in other world markets. Reference to published information, particularly product specific items from the appropriate Trade Association, are essential. The organization in the UK which offers specialist help in this area is Technical Help to Exporters (THE), which is part of the British Standards Institution. They offer:

1 a technical enquiry service;
2 consultancy;
3 a library and information service;
4 standards update;
5 technical translations; and
6 pre-shipment inspections including detailed reports.

In addition to the above technical inspections the exporter may also be faced with the need for a more general pre-shipment inspection, based on a visual examination of the goods and documents, which must be performed by inspection authorities, in the exporter's country, appointed by the government of the importer. This is particularly common with African countries, although not exclusive to them, and, in the UK, the majority are carried out by Société Général de Surveillance (SGS Inspection Services Ltd.) and Cotecna International Ltd, on the exporter's premises. They physically verify the quantity, dimensions and quality of the goods and, increasingly, the fact that the price is at market level, and will issue a Clean Report of Findings, assuming, of course, that the inspection results are acceptable.

Pre-shipment inspection gives the importers, and their governments, specific protection against:

1 non-conformity to samples;
2 non-conformity to specifications;
3 unsafe or hazardous products;
4 non-conformity to safety regulations;
5 incorrect quantity or size; and
6 short shipments.

These are extremely important when the importing country has taken some care to issue import licences for specific quantities of specific goods, as is the case in many developing countries as we saw in chapter 3. It is also very common that the markets which require such inspections are making payment by Letter of Credit and the Clean Report of Findings will be one of the documents required under the Credit.

All the above requirements apply to goods for export even while they are still in the exporter's warehouse and well before we actually get them loaded and on their way. It is not enough to manufacture and pack goods before we worry about getting them there. In fact the compliance with procedural requirements has to be carefully considered right from the quotation stage, and continues throughout the order processing. What subsequent chapters of this text will address is the actual movement of international consignments from the exporter's premises to their final destination.

Questions for Discussion

1 Correct packing and marking are vital aspects of the inter-national movement of goods.
   (a) Outline the factors that influence an exporter when deciding on the most appropriate packing and marking for an export consignment.
   (b) What sources of information are available to an exporter who wishes to obtain advice and information on correct packing and marking?
   (c) Which organizations are responsible for the regulations for the carriage of dangerous goods by road, rail, sea and air?
2 Regulations exist which affect and control the packaging and transport of substances which are not classified as harmless.
   (a) Name two of the principal international organizations directly concerned with such regulations for goods carried by sea or air.
   (b) What information must be furnished and what action must be taken by the shipper before hazardous goods are tendered for carriage?
   (c) Describe the object of current procedures and regulations.

5

International Transport Modes (I)

In the dim and distant past the UK exporter had an easy job in choosing the mode of transport for an international consignment. It went by sea, or it didn't go.

The modern exporter is now faced not only with a range of modes of transport (sea, air, road or rail) but with a wide variety of specialized services within each mode. It is no longer enough to simply decide to send the goods by sea, or air, but decisions need to be made regarding the use of unitized systems, FCL or LCL services, RO/RO or LO/LO, LASH or BACAT, and so on. An understanding of the wide range of modern freight services is essential to the exporter attempting to compete competitively in world markets.

Freight Forwarders

Most exporters, and nearly all importers, use freight forwarders, often referred to as shipping agents. Some use only one, others use dozens, but clearly the freight forwarder plays an essential part in the UK's international trading activities.

The role of the freight forwarder is shown in figure 5.1, which illustrates their function as intermediaries between shippers, with goods to send, and carriers with space to be filled.

Figure 5.1: Role of the freight forwarder

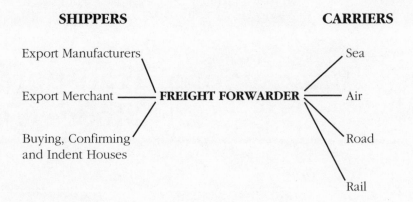

SHIPPERS   CARRIERS

Export Manufacturers   Sea

Export Merchant ———— **FREIGHT FORWARDER** ←—— Air

Buying, Confirming   Road
and Indent Houses

                                              Rail

The traditional situation represents a clear cut distinction between the range of organizations providing cargoes, either as pure manufacturers, or by merchanting other people's goods, or as representatives of overseas buyers, and the freight forwarder acting as an agent between them and the various shipping and air lines, and road and rail carriers.

However, over the last decade the distinction has become somewhat blurred. The exporter is now more likely to become involved in **own account** operations, that is, they will carry their own goods. This is perfectly feasible for road freight movements, although much more difficult for other modes of transport, and reflects the increase in the UK's trade with Western Europe, which now represents some 65 per cent of our total exports. Also the increase in containerized movements, and the growth of Inland Clearance Depots, has made it easier for the carriers to move their operations inland and offer their own groupage and documentation services. Finally, and most importantly in terms of future developments, the Customs & Excise are proceeding ever faster towards the collection of trade information direct from the trading companies through computerized systems which provide Customs declarations periodically, and the collection of European Community trade statistics via the Intrastat system from January 1993 has reduced the role of the forwarder. (See chapter 8).

All of these developments have caused the freight forwarder

to do one of three things; go out of business, get bigger or become more specialized. There are less forwarding agents than there were but the range of services which they offer has expanded in to almost every area related to the movement of goods or people.

The Services of the Forwarder

Advice

As a service industry the major function of all agents is to provide specialist advice. In the case of the forwarding agent this advice will be specific to the complex procedures of international trade. The good agents will have detailed knowledge of Transport and Customs procedures in particular, and can save the trader much time and money, both in terms of legal compliance with systems and the selection of optimum procedures.

Documentation

Much of the day-to-day work of the forwarder is concerned with the completion of a range of documents to do with international physical distribution. Some exporters produce nothing but an invoice and leave all other documents to their agent. Others subcontract the more specialized documentation, particularly Customs, but complete the rest in-house.

Customs clearance

In relation to the above, the role of the fowarder in arranging Customs clearance of both export and import consignments is extremely important, and most declarations are completed by agents on behalf of traders. As will be mentioned later, this does not mean that the exporter or importer can abdicate the responsibility for the accuracy of these declarations.

Transport booking

Exporters can approach carriers directly and book space on their own behalf, but many find it more convenient to use forwarders who can perhaps make more efficient arrangements for carriage. The agent will also be able to accurately predict the carriage charges for particular transits.

Groupage

The expression 'unitization' describes the growing trend towards the movement of goods in standard size units, the most obvious example of which is the 20 ft container. As many exporters are not able to produce Full Container Loads then, to take advantage of containerisation, they deliver Less than Container Loads to forwarders who group a number of different exporters consignments into one full load. Containerization and groupage are covered in more detail later in this chapter.

In addition to the main services mentioned above the larger forwarders will also be involved in many other functions, which could include:

1 packing and marking;
2 storage;
3 personal and business travel;
4 personal effects;
5 exhibition goods; and
6 courier services.

As most traders make use of forwarding agents to a lesser or greater extent then it is clear that they are seen to offer advantages to the trade.

Advantages

Expertise

As previously stated, the forwarder operates within a service industry which offers specialized knowledge in certain areas. All forwarders should have a good grasp of basic international trade procedures, and be able to give advice in a wide variety of areas, not just physical distribution. Some will also specialize in certain market areas (often having contacts and offices at destination), or types of transport (refrigerated, large indivisible, and so on) or types of goods (hazardous, foodstuffs, livestock and even antiques).

Contacts

The contacts forwarders have at destination have been mentioned and are extremely valuable, particularly when the exporter is arranging Delivered contracts. The contacts they have in the UK are also very important for both exports out and imports in to the UK These may be official ones with carriers, Customs & Excise, Receiving Authorities, warehouse keepers and other agents, but just as important are the personal, and informal, contacts individuals have with other individuals which should not be underestimated in terms of avoiding problems, and finding quick solutions when they happen.

Facilities

Most forwarders can offer, or arrange, a wide range of physical facilities for traders' goods, including storage, packing and repacking, sorting and checking, as well as the actual movement of goods, However, of increasing importance are the computer facilities of the forwarders which take advantage of the growing computerisation of Customs systems and the concept of Direct Trader Input, which give access to the Customs computers to authorized agents. Also, the developments in Electronic Data Interchange, and the use of electronic messages rather than paper, require more sophisticated computer systems.

Convenience

Whilst convenience may not seem to be such a powerful advantage of the use of forwarders, it has to be said that for many traders it is the main reason they use agents rather than do it themselves. The point is that many exporters and importers choose to do what they do well, which is manufacture, or procure, goods and sell them overseas, and are very happy to subcontract the physical distribution problems to third parties. As we will see below, not every company is of this opinion.

Disadvantages

To be perfectly equitable it has to be said that the use of forwarders may also involve some disadvantages.

Increased cost

Because a third party is involved, which is attempting to be a profit making organization, then it must cost more for a trader to use intermediaries rather than do it themselves. It can be argued that the savings agents can generate more than compensate, but there is still no doubt that a trader, doing the job properly, would reduce costs.

Loss of control

Some exporters find it difficult to accept that a third party should have such control of, and access to, their business, and endeavour to keep everything in-company. It cannot be avoided that the typical forwarder will represent a very large number of traders and bottlenecks can sometimes happen.

Security of information is, however, rarely a cause for concern.

The situation in practice is very varied. Some companies do not use forwarders at all and keep all procedures within the company. In some cases this is the result of them selectively employing experienced forwarding staff from outside the company. Other companies decide to put their shipping business out to tender and award an annual contract to just one forwarder. That forwarder attempts to function as the equivalent of the shipping department of that company, at a profit, and it may involve the allocation of, for example, 2.5 staff to that trader's business. This may also involve the forwarder's personnel working actually on the trader's premises.

The most typical situation is one in which traders use a small number of regular forwarders, the choice depending on the mode of transport (a distinction between surface and air freight being very common) or on the countries of destination or origin.

Finally, a situation which exists but is in no way ideal, is that of a small number of traders who have so little control over their physical distribution that they can find themselves using, literally, dozens of different forwarders. It is almost as if the agents pick them rather than them picking the agents.

The British International Freight Association (BIFA) acts as a trade association for forwarders in the UK, and its educational arm, the Institute of Freight Forwarders, organizes professional examinations in co-operation with The Institute of Export.

A final point regarding the use of freight forwarders should be emphasized. The exporter or importer has a perfect right to delegate the business of physical distribution, and documentation, to an agent but it should never be forgotten that the forwarder is an agent, and the trader remains the principal in any dealings. This is particularly important when one considers the mandatory obligations to comply with Customs & Excise requirements which cannot be abdicated to an agent. The Customs will always hold the trader liable for the accuracy of any declarations, even if they are made by an agent on the trader's behalf.

Whether the exporter chooses to use a freight forwarder or not, there is still a wide range of specialized transport modes which need to be negotiated and the following is something of an expanded glossary which attempts to classify the range of services.

Sea Freight Services

There are very many different types of vessels plying their trade on the high, and not so high, seas throughout the world. Figure 5.2 highlights only those vessels which carry goods, and that is quite a collection in itself.

Figure 5.2: Sea freight vessels

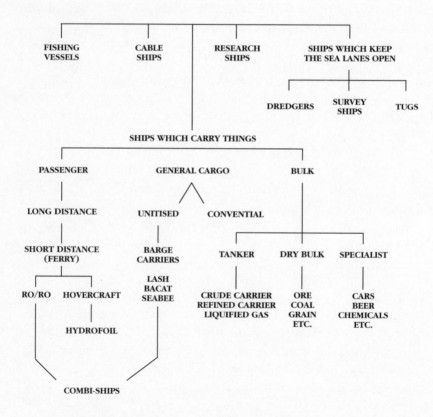

As a broad overview it is possible to divide all sea carriers into one of two categories, they are either:

LINERS	or	**TRAMPS**
General cargo and passengers		Mostly bulk cargo
Regular Sailing Schedules		No Schedule (React to Demand)
Regular Routes		No Fixed Routes
Firm Freight Rates		Rates subject to negotiation
BILL OF LADING		**CHARTER PARTY**

The distinction between liners and tramps is based on the nature of the service and not the type of vessel. Tramp vessels are not so called because they are rather scruffy, but because they have no fixed abode. Perhaps the most appropriate analogy is that the liners are the buses of the shipping world, whilst the tramps are the taxis.

Liners offer regular schedules, between the same ports, based on an advertised sailing schedule, and carry the majority of international sea transits (certainly in terms of the number of consignments). Tramps will carry, generally bulk, cargoes from almost anywhere in the world to anywhere else, and negotiate a rate for the job.

Many liner services, operating on the same routes, voluntarily form together into Freight Conferences. The members of a typical Conference are shown in figure 5.3. They co-operate on both rates and schedules and are, of course, illegal, both in terms of UK Monopoly & Mergers legislation and European Competition law. However, whilst the lines do not compete on rates, they do benefit the shipper in terms of their co-operation on schedules and the exporter is virtually guaranteed a regularity of service. Just like buses there will be one vessel for a particular destination, receiving cargo every seven days, rather than three all at once and then receiving nothing for a month.

Figure 5.3 also shows the form of contract which shippers can sign to obtain freight discounts (see overleaf).

Figure 5.3: A typical Freight Conference

Conference
Reference No. R.U.K. _____

United Kingdom/Far Eastern Freight Conference

GENERAL CARGO CONTRACT

SHIPMENTS FROM UNITED KINGDOM & EIRE

(Alternative to Deferred Rebate System)

This Agreement is for signature by Principals only and not by firms acting as Forwarding Agents.

WHEREAS:-

(A)

Ben Line Steamers Ltd.	Korea Shipping Corporation
Blue Funnel Line Ltd.	Malaysian International Shipping Corpn. Berhad
(The Ocean Steam Ship Co. Ltd.	Neptune Orient Lines (Singapore) Ltd.
The China Mutual Steam Navigation Co. Ltd.)	Nippon Yusen Kaisha
Cho Yang Shipping Co. Ltd.	Orient Overseas Container Line/Orient Overseas Line
Compagnie Generale Maritime	(Chinese Maritime Transport Ltd., Taipei)
Ellerman & Bucknall Steamship Co. Ltd.	A/S Det Østasiatiske Kompagni (The East Asiatic Co. Ltd.)
Glen Line Ltd. (Glen & Shire Joint Service)	Peninsular & Oriental Steam Navigation Co.
	The United Thai Shipping Corporation Ltd. (Unithai)

(members of the United Kingdom/Far Eastern Freight Conference) and

Ben Line Containers Ltd.
Ben Ocean
Overseas Containers Ltd.

all of which Lines are hereinafter together called "the Carriers", together provide services sufficient for the ordinary requirements of the trade from the United Kingdom and Eire ("Conference Shipment Areas") to the States of Malaya and Singapore, Thailand, Hong Kong, Taiwan and Korea ("Conference Destinations") and seek to maintain stable rates of freight for such services.

(B)   The Carriers offer a discount to all shippers who agree to give their entire support to the Carriers, and

(C)

NAME AND FULL ADDRESS OF THE SHIPPERS TO BE INSERTED

("the Shippers") wish to benefit from such discount and to give their entire support to the Carriers,

    IT IS AGREED between the Carriers and the Shippers as follows:–

    1. The Shippers agree that during the currency of this Agreement they will give the Carriers their entire support (in the sense defined in Clause 3 hereof) in respect of Conference Cargo (as defined in Clause 5(a) hereof).

    2. The Carriers agree to accept Conference Cargo for carriage:–

        (a)   by vessels operated by the Carriers, subject only to their ability to carry the cargo and to agreement between the Shippers and the carrying Line concerned as to the quantity to be carried in each vessel;

        (b)   at the Conference Tariff rates ruling at the time of shipment, or at such special rates as may be quoted by the Carriers in the case of large parcels of cargo not being ordinary berth cargo, less a discount of $9\frac{1}{2}\%$ on the amount of freight so calculated except in so far as such rates are nett; and

        (c)   subject to the provisions of the Conference Tariff Conditions and to the terms and conditions of business of the carrying Line.

    3. For the purposes of this Agreement, unless otherwise agreed by a Conference Representative, the Shippers are deemed to give their entire support to the Carriers in respect of Conference Cargo if, but only if, the Shippers:–

        (a)   ensure that all contracts for the carriage of Conference Cargo made by the Shippers, whether as principals or as agents, or by others as agents for the Shippers, are made with one or more of the Carriers;

        (b)   refrain from participating directly or indirectly in any arrangements relating to the carriage of Conference Cargo by any vessel not operated by one of the Carriers;

        (c)   procure that each Associate (as defined in Clause 5(b) hereof) of the Shippers conducts its business as if it were bound by this form of Agreement and, if and when a Conference Representative (as defined in Clause 5(c) hereof) so requires, signs this form of Agreement with the Carriers;

        (d)   refrain from any action which would enable persons who are neither parties to an Agreement in this form nor their Associates nor consignees of goods sold by such parties or their associates to obtain like benefits as are conferred upon the Shippers hereunder; and

        (e)   refrain from acting as agents for competitors of the Carriers in respect of the carriage of Conference Cargo.

There may also be Non-Conference lines operating on some routes, in competition with the Conferences, and this means that the exporter has, basically, three choices – Conference line, Non-Conference line and tramp.

The cheapest freight rate per ton of these three will invariably be the tramp, but very few exporters can produce cargoes of sufficient size to interest even small tramp steamers. The choice between Conference and Non-Conference lines is influenced by the fact that the Conferences offer immediate discounts, usually 9.5 per cent, off the freight invoice to shippers who contract to use Conference vessels only. Alternatively, deferred rebates, usually 10 per cent, are given following periods of loyalty to the Conference. It may also be the case that Non-Conference services are either not available on certain routes, or are seen as being less reliable than the Conference services.

What this leads to is the simple fact that the great majority of exporters use Conference lines for all of their sea freight consignments.

The equivalent in terms of air freight would be the distinction between schedule and charter, and tramping is also an expression used to describe road haulage operations across national frontiers.

Charter Party

Before we examine the range of liner services available to the exporter, it is sensible to briefly look at the arrangements which could be made with a tramp operator, and which could be relevant to larger traders.There are basically three types of charters which can be arranged.

Voyage charter

The vessel is chartered for one specific voyage between specified ports. This may involve more than one port of call but is nevertheless just one voyage.

Time charter

The vessel is chartered for a period of time. During that period the charterer might have a degree of freedom regarding the use of the vessel, or it may only allow a number of repetitive voyages.

Bareboat (Demise) charter

Both of the previous charters depend on the vessel owner operating and crewing the ship, and it will be the vessel owners own Master in control. A Bareboat charter is almost self-explanatory in that the charterer takes over the vessel, often for periods of time as long as 15 years, and operates the vessel as if it were their own. This is not uncommon in, for example, the oil industry, where the tankers carrying oil company's cargoes are crewed by oil company staff, but will revert back to the vessel owners at the end of the charter period.

In all these cases the contract will be based on the Charter Party, and a Charter Party Bill of Lading will be issued. It should be noted that such Bills are not acceptable to banks against Letters of Credit requiring Shipping Company's Bills, as the bank have no knowledge of the contract of carriage conditions. The reason for this is that there are some 50 standard Charter Parties and the parties can agree any conditions they like in addition to, or instead of, a standard Charter Party. As is detailed in chapter 7 this is not the case with a Liner Bill of Lading which evidences a standard contract. The majority of charters in the UK are arranged through the Baltic Exchange in London.

On the assumption that the average exporter will be using liner services for most, if not all, shipments the following describes the basic range of services available.

Types of Sea Freight Services

Conventional

The traditional, but now less common, service carrying break-

bulk, that is non-unitized cargoes. The development of containerisation over the last 30 years has severely reduced the
number of conventional vessels in operation.

Containerized

By far the most common sea freight service used by the average
exporter. The principle was first developed in the mid 1950s
and is based on the concept of moving goods in standard sized
units, as opposed to the traditional three dimensional jigsaw
offered by non-unitized break-bulk cargoes. Sometimes referred
to as Lift On/Lift Off (LO/LO) in that the container is lifted from
one mode of transport onto another.

The majority of containers are built to the International Standards Organisation specification, that is 8 ft 6 in x 20 ft or
40 ft, and a wide range of different designs are now in common
use. These include insulated and/or refrigerated (Reefers), open
topped, curtain sided, liquid and powder tanks, half height
(Donkey) and even hazardous cargo tank containers. There are
few cargoes which cannot be containerized, except for the very
large indivisibles.

It is also important to note that the standard container is
suitable for all surface freight, and not just sea, and this leads to
one of its major advantages.

Advantages

Multi-modal
The risk of loss or damage to the goods is much reduced
because he goods are not handled as they transfer from one
mode of transport to another, for example road trailer to vessel.
This allows an exporter who can fill a container, that is supply
Full Container Loads (FCL), to actually arrange door to door
deliveries during which the goods will not be handled at all.

Through documentation
Because containers move goods door to door, or depot to depot.

then the documentation covers more than just the sea freight part of the journey. This also means that 'through freight rates' are used which cover the greater part of the journey. The use of Combined Transport Bills of Lading is described in chapter 7.

Vessel efficiency

There are a number of advantages to the vessel owner, notably the ease of segregation of cargoes which require separation from others.

Also the 'turn-round' time of the vessel, that is the time spent in discharging and receiving cargo, is minimized because of the speed with which the container units can be handled. Finally the use of space above the main continuous deck to stack containers is a very efficient method of operation, as much of the vessel operating costs are based on its Gross Registered Tonnage, that is the space below the main continuous deck. The container vessel makes great use of free air. (See figure 5.4.)

Figure 5.4: A typical container ship

Specialist barge services

There is a growing use in mainland Europe, if not in the UK, of vessels which are designed to carry floating lighters or barges. These units are like floating containers but carry up to 600 tonnes of cargo, and their main advantage is that they make use of inland waterway systems, the cheapest means of inland transport. The barges are floated into ports such as Antwerp, Rotterdam and Zeebrugge and the ocean going vessels load them for the deep-sea movement. The most common versions are Lighter Aboard Ship (LASH) and Barge Aboard Catamaran (BACAT) but sea going barges known as SEABEEs, which move as large pontoons of barges, are also available.

Whilst this list does not exhaust the range of sea freight services, others are more appropriate to road or rail modes and are covered below.

Road Freight

The function of the international road haulier has become increasingly important to the UK's export business in that some 65 per cent of our exports are to western Europe (about 55 per cent to the European Community) and a very large proportion of that (approximately 80 per cent) is moved by road freight. As we are an island then these road trailer loads are dependent on Roll On/Roll Off (RO/RO) services to cross the North Sea or Channel. In fact RO/RO vessels also offer deep sea services. The load may be Accompanied by the driver who continues the journey, or be Unaccompanied and a 'subsequent' carrier will collect the trailer and continue the transit to destination. Modern RO/RO vessels are also able to carry containerized and break-bulk cargoes. (See figure 5.5.)

Figure 5.5: Roll On/Roll Off vessels

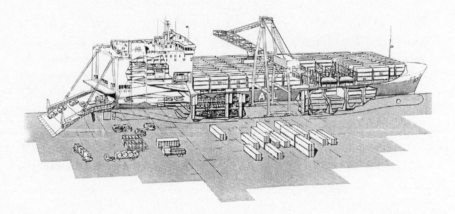

The operation of Customs approved TIR vehicles is covered in chapter 9, and the use of the CMR Consignment Note in chapter 7.

It should also not be forgotten that the Channel Tunnel, whilst being a rail link, will be carrying anything up to 28 trailers between 27 and 50 times per day.

Rail Freight

Only a small proportion of UK exports are shipped by rail freight and those that are use the rail equivalent of RO/RO, that is a Train Ferry service, particularly from Dover to Dunkirk. However the environmental problems of the increased use of road freight and the opening of the Channel Tunnel do mean that rail does offer great potential for growth, which it is hoped Railfreight Distribution, and perhaps its privatized elements, will be prepared to take advantage of.

Apart from the specific operation of the Channel Tunnel, European rail freight has, for many years, operated road-rail services, often referred to as 'Piggyback', based on road trailers being carried on specially designed rail wagons.

In particular, French railways have operated so called Kangaroo services all over Europe. There is also a growing use of 'Swapbodies' which are flat bed wagons, without wheels, carried on rail wagons.

Air Freight

The traditional use of air for high value, low volume, cargoes will always exist but there is now a clear trend towards the use of air transport for many other cargoes. The benefits of speed and security, very competitive rates and the appreciation of the Total Distribution Cost of a transit rather than just the freight cost (see chapter 6) have persuaded many exporters that air freight is a genuine and viable option.

Much of this cargo is carried on scheduled passenger aircraft rather than dedicated freight flights and there has also been an increase in combined services, which link either sea or road transits with air freight legs, using combined transport documentation.

Just as many of the shipping lines form together into Freight Conferences, then some 80 per cent of scheduled air traffic is operated by members of the air freight equivalent which is the International Air Transport Association (IATA). The IATA Traffic Conferences operate in the same way in terms of co-operation on rates, but also attempt to promote safe, regular and economical air commerce. Whilst IATA deals with the commercial aspects of airline operations, the International Civil Aviation Organisation (ICAO), which is a branch of the United Nations, governs relationships between member countries.

Groupage

This applies to all modes of transport and describes the grouping of a number of distinct export consignments into one unitized load. The most typical unit is the ISO container, carrying Less than Container Loads (LCLs), but road trailers and rail waggons are also units which require certain quantities of cargo to fill. In air freight the expression more commonly used is Consolidation and the standard unit is referred to as a Unit Load Device (ULD), sometimes called an Igloo because of its distinctive shape (see figure 5.6). These services may be offered by the carriers themselves or by specialized Groupage operators which are often general Freight Forwarders. The documentary consequences of the exporter dealing with a Groupage operator rather than direct with the carrier are covered in chapter 7.

Figure 5.6: Unit Load Device (or Igloo) being loaded (By permission of TransGlobal Air Ltd.)

Express Operations

Express operations are also an area of rapid development, particularly within continental Europe. They specialize in relatively small consignments, up to 35 Kilos, and use large networks of vehicles and aircraft to guarantee deliveries within specified time limits. Within Europe this will be between one and three days for UK exports.

They may also be linked with courier services which specialize in documents and very light items, again guaranteeing fast and personal delivery.

It will be clear from the above that the international trader has a very wide choice as to the specific transport mode and nature of service for each consignment. The following chapter will examine those factors which need to be considered when making that choice.

Questions for Discussion

1 The introduction of modern transport and handling methods of cargo have affected the work of all parties concerned with international trade. Summarize these changes and discuss.

2 The services offered to exporters by freight forwarders and carriers have become increasingly similar over the past ten years. Outline the functions of a freight forwarder today and indicate any services they provide which are not normally offered by carriers.

6

International Transport Modes (II)

The previous chapter has presented us with an almost bewildering choice as to the methods of international transport available to the average exporter. Clearly not all of them are appropriate to every consignment, in fact quite the reverse, and certain types of services will be far more commonly used than others.

A brief summary of the choices the exporter has for moving goods internationally, which were examined in the previous chapter, would include:

SEA	**Carriers**	Conference Line
		Non-Conference Line
		Tramp
	Offering:	Conventional Break Bulk
		Containerized Bulk
		Roll On/Roll Off (RO/RO)
		Train Ferry
		LASH and BACAT

Of the above choices the average exporter will use Conference Container Lines almost exclusively for genuine sea freight journeys, and RO/RO for road transits.

AIR	**Carriers**	Schedule
		Charter
	Offering	Break Bulk
		Containerized (ULD)
		Freight only
		Freight/Passenger
		Road/Air

Once again the most typical would be the air freight equivalent of Conference Liner, that is **Scheduled** services, and much of that is now containerized.

ROAD	**Carriers**	Hire and Reward
		(freight earning)
		Own Account
	Offering	Break Bulk
		Specialized Bulk
		Containerized
		High Street Delivery
		Express

RAIL	**Carriers**	Nationalized (British Rail,
		French Railways (SNCF)
		Privatized
	Offering:	Break Bulk
		Specialized Bulk
		Containerized
		Road/Rail (Piggyback)

In addition, all of these modes will operate either on a full load basis, the full load being a container (Full Container Load, FCL) or road trailer or rail wagon, or, more commonly, as Groupage operators carrying Less than Container Loads (LCL) or the equivalent.

So, given such a wide choice, what factors should the exporter consider in choosing a particular mode of transport and type of service?

Selection of Transport Mode

Export contract terms

As shown in chapter 3 the exporter can become involved in a wide variety of Contracts of Sale as defined in the International Trade Term agreed by the two parties. These range from the Ex Works contract, in which the exporter does no more than make the goods available to the buyer, to Delivered Duty Paid, in which the exporter is responsible for the whole of the transit, usually right into the buyer's premises. There are also eleven other trade terms (*Incoterms 1990*) which the parties may choose, each with varying degrees of responsibility for buyer and seller.

The relevance of this to the question of which transport service will be used simply relates to 'who decides?'. The trade term used will clearly define which party will be responsible for arranging the international movement. Figure 6.1 illustrates who chooses the transport for each Incoterm.

Figure 6.1: Choice of transport

Buyer chooses	Ex Works	(EXW)
	Free Carrier	(FCA)
	Free Alongside Ship	(FAS)
	Free On Board	(FOB)
	Cost and Freight	(CFR)
	Cost, Insurance and Freight	(CIF)
	Carriage Paid To	(CPT)
Seller chooses	Carriage and Insurance Paid to	(CIP)
	Delivered at Frontier	(DAF)
	Delivered Ex Ship/Ex Quay	(DES/DEQ)
	Delivered Duty Unpaid/Paid	(DDU/DDP)

It may seem inappropriate to include FOB as a term which involves the buyer arranging the transport but this is the actual situation. In a 'strict' or 'classic' FOB, that is one defined in *Incoterms 1990*, the seller simply delivers to the carrier nominated by the buyer. The reason this may seem strange to many exporters is that it is very common, in FOB contracts, for the seller to arrange the shipment on behalf of the buyer simply because it is more convenient. In such a case the seller will attempt to arrange a 'Freight Forward' or 'Freight Collect' contract in which the carrier will collect the freight charge at destination from the consignee (buyer). This is logical in that, in an FOB contract, the buyer is responsible for payment of any charges after the 'ship's rail port of shipment'. In the event that the seller is unable to arrange Freight Forward contracts, because the carrier insists on freight 'in advance', then the freight charge must be invoiced to the buyer. This should be done on a separate invoice from the basic FOB invoice. Technically the FOB contract in which the seller arranges shipment is known as an 'FOB with services'.

The second point to be made is that the buyer may request that a particular mode, route, and even carrier, should be used. This is often referred to as a 'routing order' and can be included as a condition of the buyer's order even on contracts where the transport is solely the concern of the seller. Such routing orders will often favour the buyer's national carriers or those which have offered promotional benefits to the buyer. The exporter, having agreed a contract which includes the choice of carrier, has to decide whether such routing orders should be complied with, or ignored. It may be that the desire for customer satisfaction means that the requested carriers are used, but the exporter must consider the possible consequences in terms of cost, quality of service and reliability. It must not be forgotten that the seller's calculated price, under a CIP contract for example, is based on freight calculation for the seller's chosen carrier and any changes would have to operate at similar cost levels.

The final point to make is that if a buyer were to open a Letter of Credit which specified that a Shipping Company's Bills of Lading were required then the exporter has very little choice, short of an amendment to the Credit, but to comply.

Destination

The final destination of the goods will clearly have a direct influence on the transport service used. It is not surprising that almost 90 per cent of the UK's exports to western Europe (65 per cent of total exports) are by road, and that the most common transport mode for our markets in developing countries is sea freight, although there is a growing use of air freight into those countries. Certain modes of transport become a logical 'rule of thumb' for particular markets, unless there are reasons why other modes should be used.

Availability

In relation to the above comments it is generally the case that the most available transport services, in terms of number, regularity and quality, will be those most commonly used for certain destinations. It is again not surprising that there are few deep-sea carriers offering cross channel services, or road hauliers specializing in the Far East, from the UK. There are, however, other factors which might distort this simple picture regarding the availability of carriers to the exporter.

There is potentially a reduction in choice because of the restrictions on **cabotage** operations. This describes the situation in which an international carrier performs domestic movements. In road haulage, for example, it would describe a French haulier moving goods from Milan to Naples, that is, a non-Italian carrier performing a domestic Italian delivery. This should not be confused with a perfectly legal **tramping** operation such as a French carrier moving goods from Milan to Berlin. Until 1992 road cabotage has been illegal in the UK but the Single European Market developments have led to a situation in which Community registered hauliers, subject to the allocation of an ever increasing number of licenses, may operate between any points within the Community. In effect a legalisation of road cabotage has taken place.

In terms of sea freight, the UK has always permitted coastal cabotage, allowing foreign registered vessels to pick up and drop at UK ports. Not all Community countries allow this, although the Single Market is gradually liberalising the service.

It has to be said that at the time of writing we are a long way from permitting cabotage in air and rail transport, principally because of the complex relationships between carriers and certain national monopolies which enjoy protection. However, it is the European Commission's intention that even these modes should be opened up to free competition across the whole of the Community.

The above comments have highlighted developments within the European Community, which are examined in more detail in chapter 14, but, outside the Community, the situation is not so liberalized. Cabotage is still illegal in many non-Community markets and does limit choice to a certain extent. Also many countries impose unilateral obligations on importers, particularly in the mandatory use of national, as opposed to foreign, carriers.

The final potential restriction on availability concerns the nature of the goods and any special requirements they have regarding stowage and movement. In fact this is so important we will treat it as a separate criteria.

Type of goods

There are many factors to do with the nature of the goods to be shipped which will affect the mode used, and indeed its availability. These include:

Size
Large indivisibles (which cannot be 'broken down') require very special treatment and routing. It may also be that very dense cargoes cannot be moved as full loads because they will exceed legal weights.

Segregation
Some goods are liable to taint others, or be easily tainted themselves. That is to say they impart on other goods, or pick up themselves, odours or flavours which are not desirable. Careful segregation, often from particular types of cargo, is essential.

This may preclude the use of a normal groupage service.

Fragility
Not only does this affect the nature of packing but also leads to modes of transport which minimize handling and maximize speed of transit (see below).

Value
Likewise, highly valuable goods will require minimum handling and maximum speed. It is also the case that certain services, for example express, can provide greater levels of security and personal care than others.

Perishability
Perishable goods need maximum speed of transit and often special stowage.

Special Requirements
Apart from the above there are many other special needs which the transport method must accommodate. These include refrigeration, insulation, ventilation and even heating. Plus all the packing, marking and stowage requirements of hazardous goods (see chapter 4).

Speed of transit

It is not only perishable or high value goods which are appropriate to fast transit times, but also those for which there is an urgent demand. This would include items such as replacement components for broken down equipment, or vehicles off the road. The cost of lost production due to a faulty component can far outweigh any freight costs involved in getting replacements there. It should also be borne in mind that a faster transit invariably leads to earlier payment with calculable financial benefits. More on this later.

Cost

A factor which is always of concern whenever choices must be made in business. In the case of international transport it is pretty obviously the case that the freight rate charged will differ from one service to another, and that the fastest method, that is, air freight, will be the most expensive, and the slowest, usually sea freight, will be the cheapest. It is extremely important that the exporter is able to make accurate predictions of the freight costs, not only as an aid to choice of mode of transport, but also to ensure that the quoted prices adequately cover all costs. Chapter 3 examines the importance of correctly calculated quotations and the consequences of mistakes.

However, the exporter who uses only the freight cost as a means of comparison is being rather shortsighted, in that this ignores a number of other cost elements of the transit which should also be considered. The attempt to predict all of the costs related to a particular shipment, and compare one option with another is referred to as calculating the **Total Distribution Cost**. This is one of the most important elements of the growing science of Physical Distribution Management which attempts to take an integrated view of, in our case, international physical distribution, and consider all aspects of the movement. Before we examine this there are still two aspects of the selection of transport mode which we should clarify. One is the beginning of the process of Total Distribution Cost Analysis, that is the accurate calculation of the freight charge for an individual consignment. But first, a look at how an exporter might find out specifically what services are available, and where and when, once the decision as to the particular mode of transport has been made.

Carrier Selection

Sea

The two major sources on information on shipping line schedules are contained in *Lloyd's Loading List* and *The Handy Shipping Guide*, both of which are produced weekly. They list most of the information an exporter would need to check on the availability of an appropriate service. The schedules are based on an alphabetical listing of the ports of destination and the following illustrates a typical listing.

(1) **PORT KELANG, Malaysia (MY). 00 03N., 101 24E.**
(2) **AMBASSADOR BRIDGE** (3) **(R /Cs)** ... (4) **L Ja** (5) **45643**
(6) **FELIXSTOWE ...** (7) **... WALTON CONT TERM** (8) **FCL -**
(9) **/Ap 15 Ap 17** (10) **OOCL (UK) LTD**

(1)   Destination ... Country, Customs Country Code, Latitude and Longitude.
(2)   Vessel Name.
(3)   Type of service ... In this case specifying refrigerated space and container. Other common codes include Ro (Roll on/ Roll off), Cv (Conventional), P (Conventional Palletised).
(4)   Type of carrier ... L (Shipping Line), F (Freight Forwarder), C (Consolidator), N (Non Vessel Owning Carrier) and Flag ... Ja (Japan).
(5)   Dead Weight Tonnage. The weight of cargo which can be carried. Calculated by the difference between the Loaded Displacement Weight (vessel fully loaded) and the Light Displacement Weight (empty vessel).
(6)   Port where cargo is being received.
(7)   Address of cargo receiving point.
(8)   Description of container service ... FCL (Full Container Load), LCL (Less than Container Load).
(9)   Receiving dates for cargo.
(10) Name of carrier.

Air

Direct air services are also listed in *Lloyd's Loading List* and, bi-annually, in *Air Cargo Numbers* supplement. A more regular source of current schedules is the *ABC Air Cargo Guide* which is published monthly.

Road and rail

Lloyd's Loading List also includes regular international road services. British Rail will provide freight timetables on request.

In addition to all of the above there are many publications concerned with international trade, which contain advertisements for transport services, and many of the carriers will circulate exporting companies with regular promotional material detailing current schedules. The international transport sector is a highly competitive one and carriers are not known for keeping quiet about their services.

Freight Calculation

As mentioned earlier, cost is a major factor which affects the exporter's choice as to transport services, and is a core element of the Total Distribution Cost. Whilst many exporters method of calculating a freight cost is to telephone a freight forwarder and ask them to do it, it is clearly something that every company should have control of, without abdicating the responsibility.

Some exporters, unfortunately, have only a vague idea as to the true cost of international movements, and operate on rough, and often outdated, figures. It is not uncommon that a percentage of the value of the goods is used as an estimate of freight for various destinations. This could work, but not when the percentage has not been checked for the last few years. Also 'guestimates' of a cost per ton, with no reference to current tariffs, represent another way of taking the easy way out, and another way of losing money. Companies must have an accurate and up-to-date grasp of the ancillary costs which they face in order to produce price quotations which actually include a profit margin.

There is no reason why every exporter cannot calculate the freight charge for each individual consignment, without the need to rely on a third party, such as the freight forwarder, and get it right every time. All carriers operate on the basis of firm tariffs for the whole of their service, and the principle which governs the calculation is the same for all modes of transport.

Sea freight calculation

An enquiry to a shipping line for a specific freight rate could elicit a response such as **US $285.00 per freight ton . . . Weight or Measure**. Quite what is meant by a 'freight ton' or 'weight or measure' we will look at soon, but first we should examine the criteria which affect the actual base freight rate quoted. The rate quoted by carriers is based on:

Destination
Logically enough, the carrier offering a range of services to different destinations will charge different rates depending on the final point of delivery. Typically lines will operate regular (scheduled) services to specified destinations, and will special-ize in certain geographic areas. Naturally the larger carriers may be involved in a wide range of routes covering much of the globe, and charter, or tramp, services exist which operate 'one-off' routes subject to demand, but, as we have established earlier in this chapter, the average exporter is using scheduled (liner) services which offer regular and repetitive services to specified destinations.

Clearly, the further away the destination then the higher the freight rate is likely to be, but distance is not the only criteria affecting rates. The carrier must also consider other operating costs related to specific destinations such as routing costs (canal and inland waterway links), port or harbour dues, berthing fees, lighterage and/or handling charges, and any other costs specific to a particular route and destination.

Many carriers will therefore operate on a tariff which contains a number of basic freight rates per freight ton for the specific points of delivery on their schedule.

Commodity
In addition to the differing destination rates, which is perfectly logical, carriers also charge a range of different rates dependent on the nature of the goods themselves, which might appear to

be somewhat less logical. It is not unusual for lines to have anything up to 22 different commodity rates for each destination. The explanation is partly to do with the fact that higher value goods do increase the carrier's liability for loss or damage (although, as can be seen in chapter 7, the carrier's liability does have a ceiling) but is mostly to do with the range of cargoes carried by sea, Imagine the situation if all goods attracted the same freight rate. Freight as a percentage of the value of the goods would differ enormously in that high value goods would pay very low percentage freight, whilst low value goods would be paying very high percentages of their value as freight. What the commodity rates do is to redress the balance somewhat so as not to penalise low value goods. It could therefore be argued that this is a form of subsidy financed by the higher value commodities.

A final consideration regarding commodity rates is the carrier's need to accommodate the **Stowage Factor** of goods. This refers to the weight of a commodity in relation to its volume, that is the density of the goods. Clearly the stowage factor would differ greatly from, say, stainless steel sheet to foam rubber, and this affects the available capacity of the carrier. As we shall see when we actually look at the calculation of a freight charge for a particular consignment, the method of calculation does directly relate to the Weight and the Measure (or volume) of goods, but some carriers use a tariff which ignores the nature of the commodity but contains perhaps eight classes based on the weight to measure ratio of the goods.

In these cases the rate may be based on a scale such as:

Up to 2 CBM per tonne
2 to 4 CBM per tonne
4 to 6 CBM per tonne and so on.
(Where CBM = Cubic Metre and Tonne is a Metric Ton of 1,000 Kg.)

Box rates

Because of the predominance of containerized movements for modern ocean freight it is not surprising that there is a move towards the calculation of freight based on the standard container load, as opposed to the weight or measure of its contents. The typical situation is that the carrier will apply a small number of broad commodity bands and calculate a 'lump sum' charge for the box. In this case any shortfall in terms of the capacity usage of the container by the shipper may incur an extra charge, based on the highest rated commodity in the container, in other words a minimum Full Container Load charge will apply. By definition this FCL 'box rate' can only apply to exporters able to supply Full Container Loads as opposed to Less than Container Loads, but it does also allow for large shippers to negotiate very favourable rates for sufficient FCL shipments.

It is also possible that so called Freight of All Kinds (FAK) rates can be obtained. This represents a situation in which a relatively large number of containers, composed of a wide range of different commodities, are shipped as one consignment. The carrier may be prepared to charge an 'averaged' rate rather than be involved in a complex breakdown of the individual commodities. Whilst this is not a common method of charge it can be seen that it has a clear relevance to Grouped or Consolidated consignments and could be negotiated by the groupage operators rather than the exporters.

Ad valorem

In rare cases the freight rate may be calculated as a percentage of the value of the goods. A quoted rate per freight ton may be followed by a comment such as 'or 3 per cent ad valorem', in which case if 3 per cent of the value of the goods is greater than any weight or measure charge then that percentage is charged. It serves to reflect the increase in the liability of the carrier but is quite unusual in practice.

Whatever the basis of the freight rate the carriers will also operate a Minimum Rate which will be charged should the calculated freight fall below the specified minimum. This clearly applies to relatively small consignments and can be avoided by the use of groupage (LCL) services.

Unfortunately, finding the appropriate freight rate for a particular commodity is not the end of the exporter's problems in that there are often adjustments to the basic rate which have to be taken into account. Typical adjustments would include:

1 Conference Discounts or Rebates (see chapter 5). Either 9½ per cent Immediate Discount (for contract signatories) or 10 per cent Deferred Rebate. A typical Conference contract is shown in figure 5.3.

2 Currency Adjustment Factor (CAF). As most shipping lines use the US $ as the basis for their tariffs they make adjustments to allow for fluctuations in the value of the $ against the currency in which they earn their revenues, £ sterling in the case of the UK exporter. The actual £ sterling rate used will be based on the agreed conversion rate on the sailing date.

3 Bunker Adjustment Factor (BAF). Bunkerage is the expression used to describe the fuel used by the vessel and derives from the coal bunkers used on the original steam ships. The BAF therefore reflects any changes, generally increases, in the cost of fuel to the carrier.

Having considered all of the above we should now have a basic freight rate per freight ton which can be applied to an individual consignment to calculate the specific freight charge. As we saw earlier this would often be expressed as **US $285.00 per freight ton ... Weight or Measure**, for example.

The shipping line will charge either on the weight of the consignment or its volume, whichever gives them the greatest return. This is still sometimes referred to as 'W/M Ship's Option'. This is perfectly reasonable as the carrier's capacity is limited both by the space available for cargo and the maximum weight (deadweight) which can legally be carried. A vessel fully loaded with steel sheet will still have volume unused, and a vessel full of foam rubber would not use anywhere near its deadweight capacity. The process of freight calculation takes into account the different stowage factors of the wide range of commodities carried.

For sea freight the units used are:

Metric Tonne	or	Cubic Metre
(1,000 Kg)		(CBM or M3)

These have applied since the metrication of the lines in the early 1970s and replaced the traditional Imperial units of the ton (2240 lbs) and its volume equivalent, 40 cu ft. This balance, established over centuries, between the ton and 40 cu ft, was lost in the conversion in that the metric tonne is very close to the imperial ton (that is, 2,205 lbs) but the Cubic Metre is only 35.3 cu ft. Because of this it was not unusual for the carrier to charge Dual Rates such as:

$240 per tonne   or $215 per cubic metre

However many rates are now rationalized into one rate, weight or measure, and the exporter has to calculate whichever is the greater for a particular consignment, It should be said that the majority of sea consignments are charged on a volume basis, but the exporter must calculate both units to be sure.

The weight unit is 1,000 kg, commonly known as the metric ton or tonne, and the freight will be calculated on the gross weight of the consignment. That is to say that the weight of the packing (Tare weight) will also be included for freight purposes. As an example, a consignment of 2 cases each 4,000 Kg would generate a total of 8 freight tons.

The volume, or measure, unit is the cubic metre and is calculated by a multiplication of the length by breadth by height. Thus if our two cases above where each 200 cms x 200 cms x 150 cms then each would be 6 cubic metres (CBM), giving a total of 12 CBM. This can be calculated by a multiplication of the cms to give cubic centimetres, and then a division by 1,000,000 (1 CBM = 1,000,000 cubic cms) or, more easily by converting cms into metres, by dividing by 100, and then multiplying. Thus, in our example we actually have 2 cases which are 2 m x 2 m x 1.5 m, that is 6 CBM per case.

Given that the freight rate for these two cases was, for example, $285.00, then the freight cost would be:

12 CBM x $285.00 = $3,420.00
NOT 8 tonnes x $285.00 = $2,280.00

the carrier charging on volume, not weight.

It should also be noted that the volume must be calculated on the extreme dimensions of the goods, including any projections. Also for irregularly shaped objects the carriers will require a rounding out of the widest dimensions. In this respect drums and rolls would be calculated as oblongs for freight purposes. However allowances may be given for handling aids such as pallets, hooks and rings.

The Appendix contains a fully worked example of a sea freight calculation, including insurance premium and duty, which is actually a model answer from the International Physical Distribution examiner of The Institute of Export.

Road/rail freight calculation

The other two modes of surface freight are based on exactly the same method of calculation, that is Weight or Measure, but there does tend to be a greater range of rates applied, particularly in the highly competitive area of road haulage. Also it is very common that the ratio of weight to measure changes, the most common being **1,000 Kg** or **3.3 CBM**. Sometimes, because the average consignment size may be smaller than 1,000 Kg, the carriers will quote rates based on smaller units of **100 Kg** or **0.33 CBM**. It is also possible that similar ratios will be applied to Short Sea shipments, in particular to Scandinavia.

Air freight calculation

Just as with surface freight, the principle of weight/volume is applicable to air freight, but the structure of the carrier's tariff is different.

The typical airline will base its tariff on:

General Cargo Rates (GC)
These apply to non-unitized consignments of mixed commodities.

Specific Commodity Rates (SC)
Shippers of large quantities of specific commodities between

specific ports can apply for SC rates which will be much lower than the GC rates.

In the case of both GC and SC rates the lines will often offer quantity discounts once a certain level of business is achieved.

Classification Rates
Certain categories of goods, for example live animals, cadavers and bullion attract charges based on a discount or surcharge on the GC rate.

Unit Load Device Rate (ULD)
Chapter 5 examines the unitization of international movements and ULDs are the air equivalent of the ISO container. The ULD rates ignore the nature of the goods and charge for a specific unit up to a specified maximum weight. They are the air equivalent of the 'box rates' which may be available for sea shipments.

Freight of All Kinds (FAK)
There is a growing use of FAK rates as a means of simplifying the rate structure and avoiding SC rates. A rate per kilo is charged subject to a minimum weight requirement.

The actual calculation of air freight charges is based on a ratio of weight to volume which is somewhat different from sea freight. The most common method is **1,000 Kg** or **6 CBM**.

It will be clear that volume does not become relevant to air consignments unless the cargo is extremely voluminous. So whilst the majority of sea shipments are charged by volume, it is more usual for air cargoes to be calculated on the basis of weight.

In practice the ratio of 1,000 Kg or 6 CBM is somewhat too large for the average air consignment and it is therefore more usual for rates to be quoted **per kilogram** or **per 6,000 cubic cms**, that is the volume unit is one thousandth of 6 CBM. A 6,000 cubic cms unit is referred to as a 'volumetric unit' or a 'chargeable kilo'.

Take as an example a case of 50 kilos, 100 cms x 100 cms x 50 cms, at a rate of £9.00 per chargeable kilo.

The freight charge will not be 50 kilos x £9.00 = £450.00
but will be   **83.33 volume units x £9.00 = £750.00**.
(The volume units being the product of 100 cms x 100 cms x 50
cms = 500,000 cubic cms, divided by 6,000 cubic cms.)

In conclusion, each transport mode will generate its own basic
tariff, based on factors such as destination, commodity, value
and standards units, and will apply that basic rate to the weight
or volume of the cargo in order to maximize revenues in relation
to the carrier's limits on deadweight and space available. The
ratio of weight to volume will differ from one mode of transport
to another, but the principle of W/M (weight or measure) is one
which applies to all modes.

More specialized applications of a carrier's freight charge
include:

Back Freight

The charge made for the return of goods which have not be
taken up at destination. As long as the carrier is still in possession of the goods then the shipper has the right to give
further instructions regarding their disposal.

Dead Freight

In the situation where the shipper, or their agent, has made a
verbal booking of shipping space but does not subsequently
take up the booking, the carrier has a right to charge for the
space booked and not used. Dead freight is reduced by any
other cargo which is obtained to take up the available space.
(See chapter 7.)

Total Distribution Cost

Assuming that we are now in a position to calculate an accurate
freight cost we still must accept that the freight itself is not the
only cost item which should be considered in comparing one
mode of transport to another. The concept of Total Distribution
Cost, mentioned earlier in this chapter, is based on the fact that
a number of other, transport related, factors can be quantified,
in addition to freight cost, in order to make a more realistic

choice as to transport mode and route.

A simple comparison of freight costs will always reveal air freight as being far more expensive than surface freight, but a consideration of other cost factors could change that perception.

Elements of the Total Distribution Cost, other than the freight charge, would include:

Packing

The need for protection is reduced where the transit time, and level of handling, is reduced.

Documentation

A simplified documentary regime, which is offered by air freight, and to a lesser extent road and rail, can lead to savings in administrative costs.

Inland carriage

It is often the case that there are major differences between the costs of transport into the port of departure, and from the port of destination, which will depend on the mode, and specific ports, involved.

Insurance

It may be the case that the cargo insurance premiums will differ depending on the mode of transport, the most common distinction being between air and surface freight.

Unpacking and refurbishing

With some goods, following surface movements, extensive

renovation of the goods and packing is necessary. This can be minimized by fast transits such as air freight.

Speed of transit

Many of the points raised lead to a conclusion that air ship-ments provide a number of advantages as compared with surface freight, many of which are related to the reduction in handling time and the speed of transit. Perhaps the most obvious conse-quence of a faster transit time is the fact that, whatever the terms of payment, then payment will be received sooner. The higher the interest rates faced by exporters then the greater are the savings from quicker payments.

Taking all these factors into consideration it is possible to prepare a **Total Distribution Cost Analysis** which compares the transport options available to the exporter for a particular consignment. A simplistic comparison of sea and air freight might look something like figure 6.2.

Figure 6.2: Comparison of sea and air freight costs

	AIR £	SEA £
Ex Works value	26,000	26,000
Freight	1,170	220
Packing	190	530
Inland transport . . . UK	50	200
Overseas	130	430
Insurance	60	70
Total	27,600	27,450

If we were to assume that the reduction in transit time between air and sea transits was 42 days (which would be perfectly reasonable for any dispatch to a developing country) and that interest rates were, for example, 7 per cent, then the additional saving from faster payment of the delivered price would be:

	SEA £	**AIR** £
Delivered price	27,450	27,600
Interest saved	–	222
Total Cost	27,450	27,378

Whilst this example is not representative of all consignments, it does illustrate the point that a consideration of all the quantifiable factors of physical distribution may well lead to a more objective choice of transport modes which takes into consideration more than just the freight costs. The narrowing of the gap between air and surface freight cost is typical of a genuine and comprehensive comparison which all exporters should attempt.

The calculation of a true Total Distribution Cost can provide great advantages to all exporters and could lead to a more professional approach to the whole area of Physical Distribution Management. This would involve the consideration of all aspects of the physical movement of goods, from the receipt of raw materials, through the whole internal handling and storage , through to the actual delivery to the end-user.

It is not the purpose of this text to examine Physical Distribution Management (PDM) in any detail but perhaps the example of Toyota's success in PDM could be instructive. Toyota (allegedly) have achieved the ultimate level of efficiency by making Just In Time (JIT) principles actually work. They claim to hold zero inventory, that is, no stock at all. Components arrive from suppliers JIT to be fitted, JIT to be tested, JIT to be packed, JIT to be dispatched, JIT to be shipped, JIT to arrive and JIT (it is hoped) to be sold.

Well, it is worth thinking about, and is certainly an improvement on the more common British version known as JTL (Just Too Late!).

Questions for Discussion

1 Explain what is meant by 'Total Distribution Cost Analysis' and outline the factors an exporter or freight forwarder will need to consider when using this technique. Illustrate your answer with a detailed example.
2 When deciding between which mode of transport is to be used for the dispatch of an export consignment, what factors must be considered by the exporter? Justify your answer with a detailed example showing calculations.

7

International Transport Documentation

Perhaps the biggest problem for companies involved in international trade is the number of bits of paper which are essential to the performance of their export contracts. That is to say that the documentation involved in the administration of their overseas business is perceived as being abundant in quantity, complex in character and designed to hinder rather than help their export effort.

Whilst there is an element of truth in this perception it has to be said that many companies suffer from the consequences of this complexity because they make very little effort to understand the purposes and functions of the range of documents with which they deal. There is often an element of negligence in their own management, in particular in terms of staff training, which translates itself into a continuous saga of documentary errors and their, sometimes disastrous, consequences. The fact that something like 60 per cent of document sets, presented to banks against Letters of Credit, are rejected on first presentation due to documentary discrepancies does serve to prove this point.

It is an unfortunate fact that many personnel involved in export documentation have only received what is sometimes referred to as 'standing next to Nellie' training. The administrative procedures are passed on to new operatives by the more experienced ones, so that it is often clear **what** is to be done, but very rarely is it so clear **why** it needs to done. Not only is this an extremely boring way to perform office functions for the personnel involved, but it is also an extremely error prone process, simply because there is no real understanding of the consequences of procedures and documents are simply completed or produced by rote. Also the systems become very inflexible and unable to accommodate anything out of the ordinary, and, just because something works does not make it right, and it can often be the case that company systems incorporate mistakes which become almost 'carved in stone', because they work despite being incorrect practice.

It could be said, with some validity, that because of the use of forwarding agents and of computerized systems, such an understanding is of less value in modern offices, but agents have to be instructed, monitored and, most importantly, paid; and computer systems have to be set up on the basis of a clear understanding of procedural requirements, all of which work much better with a knowledgeable principal.

What the following chapters will attempt to do is to look at the 'why' of documentary procedures rather than just the 'what', and to show how logical the procedures are (yes, even Customs procedures) once it is clear exactly what they do.

An Overview of Export Documentation

As has already been mentioned, the range of documents encountered by exporters is often seen as intimidating and confusing, and those involved directly in the procedural elements can find it difficult to take a step back and see the wood for the trees, as it were.

This is aggravated by the, perhaps obvious, fact that it takes more than one piece of paper to move an international consignment. A set of documents is required which may be relatively simple and involve only three or four or may be extremely complex and include a number of specialized documents. Also the set will differ from one consignment to another depending on the specific collection of variables including the type of goods, method of transport, destination, method of payment and the buyer's requirement.

Over the next six chapters a wide range of documents will be examined individually and in isolation in terms of their specific functions, but first it is possible to take what is a veritable 'mountain' of documents and to rationalize them into four smaller 'hills'. As was mentioned in chapter 2 it is possible to categorize any document used in international trade into one of four types depending on its origin or application. The four categories are:

1 Transport.
2 Customs.
3 Insurance.
4 Payment.

With a little flexibility all international trade documents can be listed under these headings and figure 7.1 list these documents which will be described in the following chapters.

Figure 7.1: International trade documents

Transport
Bill of Lading (B/L)
Air Waybill (AWB)
Road Waybill (CMR Note)
Rail Waybill (CIM Note)

Customs & Excise
Single Administrative Document (SAD)
Export Invoice
Certificate of Origin
ATA Carnet

Insurance
Policy
Certificate
Declarations

Payment
Letters of Instruction
Bill of Exchange
Letter of Credit

If any of the titles or abbreviations or not clear or familiar rest assured that they will be explained in full in the following chapters.

Thus an international consignment will require a set of documents which can be selected from those listed in figure 7.1. As an example, a simple document set could be composed of a Bill of Lading, an Export Invoice, a Certificate of Origin, a Cargo Insurance Certificate and a Single Administrative Document. This could also be supplemented by a wide range of more specialized documents, depending on each consignment's specific requirements.

Chapter 5 looked in some detail at the various modes of international transport, and this chapter will examine the range of transport documents which relate to those modes.

The Transport Conventions

There is a fundamental problem associated with international trade which is so obvious that it is often missed. It is the fact that there are always at least two nationalities involved in the export transaction. This is most obvious when one considers the Contract of Sale (see chapter 3) in which the buyer and seller are of two different nationalities, and where the law governing the contract must be established. These problems are compounded by the fact that the international carrier is often a **third** nationality.

The problems that this could cause to the exporter can be divided into two areas: the contract of carriage; and the bill of lading.

That is, do the carriers impose their conditions of carriage (dependent on nationality) on the shipper, in which case the exporter will potentially be involved in many different contracts of carriage; or do the shippers impose their conditions on the carrier, in which case the carrier, working for a range of different nationalities of shipper, has the same problem?

The same complexities could apply to the transport document, in that many different Bills of Lading could exist depending on the nationality of the shipper or the carrier. The situation in practice is that a range of international conventions address, and solve, the problem of the mix of nationalities involved in the Contract of Carriage.

Each mode of international transport operates within the scope of a Convention which standardizes the documentation and the Contract of Carriage and which, in practice, mean that the exporter can generally ignore the nationality of the carrier.

The International Transport Conventions are (briefly):

Sea	Hague-Visby or Hamburg rules
Air	Warsaw
Road	CMR
Rail	CIM

These are the titles of the major Transport Conventions which have been ratified in many countries, including the United Kingdom's Carriage of Goods Acts, and which standardize the conditions of carriage and the documentation. In practice they mean that an exporter can deal with a variety of nationalities of carrier and still operate with standard documentation. (See Clause Paramount below.)

The Bill of Lading

Procedure

1 The exporter, or their agent, completes a set of blank Bills of Lading, for the appropriate Shipping Company, and provides them at the carrier's offices. Alternatively the Bills are raised from the carriers computers against a Cargo Shipping Instruction form from the exporter or agent.

2 The goods are delivered into the port or depot with a Standard Shipping Note (see chapter 4).

3 Goods are recorded by Tally/Port clerks, compared with the Stowage Plan and Booking References, and entered on to the Ship's Manifest.

4 Once the goods are in the possession of the carrier the Bills of Lading are signed on behalf of the Ship's Master and returned to the exporter/agent. Computer produced Bills may be pre-signed, but are still issued on behalf of the Ship's Master.

Whilst the layout of Bills differs from one carrier to another the great majority are now produced with very similar A4 size layouts and contain broadly the same information. This would include:

1 the parties involved (shipper, consignee and notify party);
2 ports / depots of loading and discharge;
3 vessel name/s and voyage number;
4 number of original Bills;
5 marks and numbers;
6 description of goods;
7 type of packages;
8 gross weight (Kg) and measurement (M3);
9 received and/or shipped dates; and
10 reference to payment of freight, that is prepaid or forward.

And, of course, the important signature on the original Bills on behalf of the Ship's Master. All Bills will contain most of these items and all operate in the same way.

Functions

The Bill of Lading has three major functions:

1 A receipt for the goods.
2 Evidence of the Contract of Carriage.
3 A Document of Title.

Receipt for goods

A Bill of Lading will contain the words 'apparent good order and condition' thus obliging the carrier to deliver the goods in the same condition. Such a Bill is known as a **clean** Bill and acts as a clean receipt for the goods. However there may be situations in which the shipping line does not think that the goods are in good order and condition and will say so on the face of the Bill. Such a reference is known as a **clause** on the Bill which overrides the 'good order and condition' reference. These **Claused Bills** are sometimes referred to as 'dirty' or 'foul' Bills of Lading and cause great problems to exporters. The clauses can be stamped or handwritten and typical examples might be: 'Inadequate packing'; 'second hand packing'; 'one case short'; 'five cases short shipped'; and even 'five cases thought to be short shipped ... if on board will deliver'; or 'three drums leaking'.

The final example may seem somewhat ridiculous but is nevertheless a genuine clause. This reflects the, justified, attitude of the Shipping Lines, that they will honour their part of the Contract of Carriage if at all possible, and earn their freight, but protect themselves from the misconduct of the shipper.

The problem for the shipper is that a Claused Bill of Lading clearly provides no evidence of contract performance to the buyer, in fact quite the opposite, and will never be acceptable to a bank against a Letter of Credit.

This is a problem which is rarely seen with other transport modes as the carriers either reject the goods, rather than ship them, or issue clean receipts for the quantities actually received.

Evidence of the Contract of Carriage
The first point to be made is that the Bill of Lading is not the Contract of Carriage itself, but merely evidence of it. The actual contract is a verbal one made at the time the space is booked and the Bill is produced part way through the performance of the contract. In practice it is a rare situation in which the conditions expressed on the Bill do not represent the Contract of Carriage conditions.

As the contract is a verbal one made at the time the space is booked this also means that the carrier is able to charge freight for space booked even if it is not used by the shipper. This is known as **dead freight** and is reduced should the carrier obtain alternative cargo to take up that space.

The second point is that the Bill evidences the conditions of the contract and will contain, on its back, a wide range of contract clauses. As has already been mentioned the majority of contracts for the carriage of goods by sea are carried out by shipping lines whose national legislation has ratified the appropriate convention (either the Hague-Visby or the Hamburg Rules) and the clause which specifies this is known as the **Clause Paramount** or **Paramount Clause**. Thus the carrier is committed to the standard rules, which specify important elements such as the carrier's liability, which will take precedence over the rest of the carrier's conditions should there be a conflict. The fact that these rules are ratified in legislation also means that carriers cannot contract out of such obligations. A typical Clause Paramount is shown in figure 7.2.

Figure 7.2: A typical Clause Paramount

The Hague Rules contained in the International Convention for the unification of certain rules relating to Bills of Lading, dated Brussels 25th August 1924, or in those countries where they are already in force the Hague-Visby Rules contained in the Protocol of Brussels dated February 23rd 1868, as enacted in the Country of Shipment, shall apply to all carriage of goods by sea and, where no mandatory international or national law applies, to the carriage of goods by inland waterways also, and such provisions shall apply to all goods whether carried on deck or under deck.

Document of title

This is the most relevant, and unique, feature of the Bill of Lading and one which has important implications in terms of its functions and applications in practice.

The first point to make is that Bills are issued in sets containing two or three originals and any number of Copies. The Originals are signed on behalf of the Ship's Master and are referred to as **negotiable** as they contain, and are able to transfer, property in the goods. The copies are unsigned, and non-negotiable, and merely convey information. The availability of at least two Original Bills means that they can be dispatched to the destination port separately to ensure that at least one is available .

The reason why this is so important, and an explanation of the practical importance of the Bill of Lading's status, is the fact that one Signed Original Negotiable Bill must be presented back to the Shipping Line at destination in order for them to release the goods. The Bills may be sent direct, or through the banks, and once one is **accomplished** (by presentation to the Line) the others are void. Facsimile or photocopy versions are not acceptable.

The relevance of this to the exporter should not be under-estimated in that it is possible to restrict the buyer's access to the goods at destination, by withholding the Bills of Lading. Thus payment terms can be arranged which require buyers to pay not for goods but for documents, and this does create some security for the seller.

We should also be grateful that there is often a correlation between high risk markets and deep-sea transits which means that the security of the Bill of Lading is often available when it is needed. The relationship between documents and methods of payment is examined in chapter 12.

The negotiability of the Bill is effected by the manner of its completion, in that the title may be addressed to a specific consignee, in which case it is not freely negotiable. The consignee may then **endorse** the back of the Bill which can then transfer title. More commonly the Bill is made out to **order**, rather than to a named consignee, endorsed by the exporter, and naming a **notify party** which the carriers will advise of the arrival of the goods. In this case the Bill is drawn up as a negotiable instrument. See figure 7.3.

It is clearly important for an exporter to be careful in the handling of Bills of Lading as a 'To Order Blank Endorsed Bill of Lading' confers title in the goods to the bearer.

The face of the Bill will always show how many Signed Originals there are and the banks will invariably require the Full Set of Bills, which may be expressed as 2/2 (that is, two of two) or 3/3.

145

Figure 7.3: Bill of Lading completion

	EITHER	**OR**
SHIPPER:	Exporter (or Agent)	Exporter (or Agent)
CONSIGNEE:	Importer	'Order' or 'To Order'
NOTIFY PARTY:	———————	Importer or Agent or Bank etc:
	Title addressed to a specific party. No endorsement. Named consignee may endorse and transfer.	Title open to bearer; Endorsement needed.

From a purely practical point of view it is obviously necessary to ensure that Bills are available at destination in order to clear the goods on arrival. Should the goods have arrived but not the Bills, they are then known as **Stale** Bills of Lading, and this will inevitably lead to delays in clearance. In some cases extra charges for such a delay may be imposed which are known as **Demurrage** and can be expensive, particularly in congested ports and depots.

Banks dealing with Letters of Credit will describe a Bill as being Stale when it is presented outside of the days allowed for presentation of documents against the credit. This will often be seven or 15 days, and if no time period is specified, the bank will assume 21 days.

Types of Bills of Lading

Received

Confirms that the goods are in the possession of the carrier, but not that they have been loaded. The increase in containerized, depot to depot, movements has led to the increased use of Received Bills which are issued as the goods arrive at the Inland Container Base.

Once the goods are loaded the Received Bill can be stamped with a 'Shipped on Board' notation and date and therefore become a Shipped Bill of Lading.

Combined Transport

This refers to the fact that the typical, containerized, sea freight consignment will move from one inland depot of departure to another at destination. The whole transit will be organized under one contract of carriage evidenced by the Bill of Lading, and therefore covers, for example, a road-sea-road transit. Most Bills issued by container lines are Received Combined Transport Bills of Lading. (See figure 7.4.) A Bill showing an inland destination may also be referred to as a Through Bill of Lading.

Transhipment

In the case where the goods are not shipped direct to the port of discharge, but via a third port, using two vessels, it is possible to obtain a Bill covering both vessels. These may be refereed to as the Feeder vessel and the Ocean vessel and the transhipment port will be shown as well as the ports of shipment and destination. Letters of Credit may not allow transhipment.

Many UK exporters have found that it may actually be cheaper to tranship through a European port than to ship direct from the UK.

Figure 7.4: Received Combined Transport Bill of Lading

Shipper

BILL OF LADING No.:
FOR COMBINED OR PORT TO PORT TRANSPORTATION

Consignee

ALIANÇA

EMPRESA DE NAVEGAÇÃO ALIANÇA S/A

Av. Pasteur 110, CEP 588, 22290 BOTAFOGO/R.J.
B R A S I L
Telephone: (21) 546.11.22, Infotec: (21) 541.56.49
Telex: 21.23.778 or 21.22.811
General agents for EUROPE:
Maritime Services ALEUROPA GmbH,
Oberhafenstrasse 1, Fruchthof, 2000 Hamburg 1
tel. (40) 33 96 10 – telex 211187 al d
cable address: Aleuropa
Infotec: (40) 33 73 87

Notify address (Carrier not liable for failure of notification)

Voyage No.	* Place of receipt (if pre-carriage)				
(Ocean) vessel	Port of loading		FREIGHT	origin	destination
			Pre-carriage payable at		
Port of discharge	* Place of delivery (if on-carriage)	No. of original Bs/L	On-carriage payable at		
			Ocean freight payable at		
Marks and Nos./ Container No.	Quantity and description of goods		Gross weight, kg	Measurement, m3	

ORIGINAL

Cargo value:

Particulars above declared by the Shipper.

The cargo destined to Brazil may only be released at the place of destination after payment of the additional to the freight for the renewal of the Merchant Marine in accordance with the Brazilian legislation.

Freight and charges shall be paid in the currency in which the goods are freighted or at Carrier's option in the currency of the country of the place of loading or place of delivery in each case converted at the highest rate of exchange on the date of shipment or date of payment whichever the higher.

FREIGHT

RECEIVED the goods in apparent good order and condition and, as far as ascertained by reasonable means of checking, as specified above unless otherwise stated. The Carrier, in accordance with the provisions contained in this document,
a) undertakes to perform or to procure the performance of the entire transport from the place at wich the goods are taken in charge to the place designated for delivery in this document, and
b) weight, measure, quality, contents and value if mentioned in this bill of lading is to be considered unknown unless the contrary has been expressly aknowledged and agreed to.
The signature on this bill of lading is not to be considered an agreement.
One of the Bs/L must be surrendered duly endorsed in exchange for the goods or delivery order.
IN WITNESS wereof number of original B/L, all of this tenor and date have been signed as stated above, one of which being accomplished the others to be void.

Place and date of issue

Signed as agent (s) only

* Applicable only when this document is used as a combined transport bill of lading.

International Transport Documentation

Figure 7.5: Certificate of Shipment

(AS6153)

| CERTIFICATE OF SHIPMENT | NUMBER BM2321263
DATE   6/01/94 |

NATIONAL STARCH & CHEMICAL
LAING NATIONAL LIMITED
ASHBURTON ROAD EAST
TRAFFORD PARK,
MANCHESTER   M17 IJ

Davies Turner

Davies Turner Northern Ltd
(A Division of Davis Turner & Co Ltd)
Telephone: 061-872 7651 Telex: 668093 Fax: 061-848 0539
International Freight Terminal, Westinghouse Road, Trafford Park, Manchester M17 1DP

TRAILER NO	HUL 1	LOADING DATE 16/12/93	DEPOT	
FROM	DOVER	VIA ZEEBRUGGE	CONVEYANCE	EUROPE
SEWAY				
SHIPPED	17/12/93	TO ISTANBUL CUSTOMS		

CONSIGNEE
IS TICARET VE SANAYI
TURK A.S, YILDIZ POSTA
CADDESI YENER SOKAK NO 3
BESIKTAS / ISTANBUL
TURKEY

MARKS
UN
CF
ISTANBUL

| | | | KG | M3 |
| S | PALLETS: 200 BAGS COLFLO 67 | | 5100 | 9.158 |

WE HEREBY CERTIFY that the above mentioned goods have been shipped in apparent good
order and condition, except as shown (contents and description measurements weights
quantity and condition quality and value as declared by shipper) Subject to conditions
of carriage as shown on the back of this certificate.

FREIGHT FORWARD   DAVIES TURNER & CO LTD
Despatch through our correspondents
UNATSAN ULUSLARARASI NAKLIYE
TIC. VE SAN. LTD.
EVREN MAHALLESI, GULBAHAR   MANCHESTER
CADD, GUROL SOK, GUNESLI
ISTANBUL, TURKEY

NOTE: THe only conditions on which we transact business are shown on the back.

REGISTERED IN ENGLAND No. 62270 BELLEVUE HOUSE, ALTHORP ROAD, LONDON SW17 7ED

Figure 7.6: FIATA Ocean Bill of Lading

Consignor

FBL

FBL No.

Customs Reference/Status

G
B

Shipper's Reference

B I F A

Forwarder's Reference

Consigned to order of

**NEGOTIABLE FIATA
COMBINED TRANSPORT
BILL OF LADING**

issued subject to ICC Uniform Rules for a Combined
Transport Document (ICC publication 298)

ICC

Notify address

IFF REGD NO. 0255

HW GROUP

WATSON-SEAKING LINE

Herbert Watson Freight Services Limited

Furness House,
Trafford Road,
Manchester M5 2RJ
Telephone: 061-872 8181
Fax: 061-872 5466

4 Kitson Road
Bankfield Ind. Estate
Leeds LS10 1NT
Telephone: 0532 423200
Fax: 0532 425118

Place of Receipt

Ocean Vessel | Port of Loading

Port of Discharge | Place of Delivery

Marks and Numbers | Number and Kind of Packages | Description of Goods | Gross Weight | Measurement

according to the declaration of the consignor.

The goods and instructions are accepted and dealt with subject to the Standard Conditions printed overleaf.

Taken in charge in apparent good order and condition, unless otherwise noted herein, at the place of receipt for transport and delivery as mentioned above.

One of these Combined Transport Bills of Lading must be surrendered duly endorsed in exchange for the goods. In Witness whereof the original Combined Transport Bills of Lading all of this tenor and date have been signed in the number stated below, one of which being accomplished the other(s) to be void.

Freight Amount | Freight Payable at | Place and date of issue: Stamp and signature

Cargo Insurance through the undersigned | Number of Original FBL's

☐ not covered ☐ Covered according to attached Policy
For delivery of goods please apply to

Text authorised by FIATA Copyright Reserved FIATA/Zurich - Switzerland 8-87 (BIFA 8 89)

VERDI BUSINESS FORMS 07708 732046

A 229875

Groupage

As described in chapter 5, it is common that exporters who cannot provide full loads, for either containers and/or road trailers, will make use of Groupage operators. The Groupage operator will group or consolidate a number of exporter's consignments into one shipment will be covered by a set of Groupage Bills of Lading issued by the Shipping Line.

The Groupage operator may issue a Certificate of Shipment (figure 7.5) which simply acts as a Freight Forwarder's receipt or a **House Bill of Lading**, which is often referred to as a Non-Vessel Owning Common Carriers Bill (NVOCC) and is inferior in status to a Shipping Company's Bill of Lading.

FIATA

Issued on behalf of the Federation Internationale des Associations de Transitairies et Assimiles (International Federation of Freight Forwarders Association) and acceptable as an Ocean Bill of Lading against a Letter of Credit. It is perceived as being issued by an agent of the Shipping Line. (See figure 7.6.)

Common

Sponsored by SITPRO (Simpler Trade Procedures) and intended to replace the range of individual Bills produced by the Lines. The carrier's name is not preprinted on the Bill but a space is left for the name to be added. Unfortunately the Common Bill of Lading is uncommon in use.

Short Form

The detailed clauses on the reverse of many Bills are omitted and instead the carrier's 'standard conditions of carriage' are referred to along with the Clause Paramount on the face of the Bill.

Figure 7.7: Common Short Form Bill of Lading

Shipper	VAT no.	**COMMON**	B/L no.

**COMMON
SHORT FORM
BILL OF LADING**

Shipper's reference

Forwarder's reference

Consignee	VAT no.

Name of Carrier

Notify party and address

The contract evidenced by this Short Form Bill of Lading is subject to the exceptions, limitations, conditions and liberties (including those relating to pre-carriage and on-carriage) set out in the Carrier's Standard Conditions applicable to the voyage covered by this Short Form Bill of Lading and operative on its date of issue.
If the carriage is one where the provisions of the Hague Rules contained in the International Convention for unification of certain rules relating to Bills of Lading, dated Brussels on 25th August, 1924, as amended by the Protocol signed at Brussels on 23rd February, 1968 (the Hague Visby Rules) are compulsorily applicable under Article X, the said Standard Conditions contain or shall be deemed to contain a Clause giving effect to the Hague Visby Rules. Otherwise, except as provided below, the said Standard Conditions contain or shall be deemed to contain a Clause giving effect to the provisions of the Hague Rules.
The Carrier hereby agrees that to the extent of any inconsistency the said Clause shall prevail over the exceptions, limitations, conditions and liberties set out in the Standard Conditions in respect of any period to which the Hague Rules or the Hague Visby Rules by their terms apply. Unless the Standard Conditions expressly provide otherwise, neither the Hague Rules nor the Hague Visby Rules shall apply to this contract where the goods carried hereunder consist of live animals or cargo which by this contract is stated as being carried on deck and is so carried.
Notwithstanding anything contained in the said Standard Conditions, the term Carrier in this Short Form Bill of Lading shall mean the Carrier named on the front thereof.
A copy of the Carrier's said Standard Conditions applicable hereto may be inspected or will be supplied on request at the office of the Carrier or the Carrier's Principal Agents.

Pre-carriage by *	Place of receipt by pre-carrier *
Vessel	Port of loading
Port of discharge	Place of delivery by on-carrier *

Shipping marks; container number	Number and kind of packages; description of goods	Gross weight	Measurement

Applicable only when document used as a through bill of lading

Particulars declared by shipper

ORIGINAL

Freight details; charges etc.

RECEIVED FOR CARRIAGE as above in apparent good order and condition, unless otherwise stated hereon, the goods described in the above particulars.

IN WITNESS whereof the number of original bills of lading stated below have been signed, all of this tenor and date, one of which being accomplished the others to stand void.

C of S
CSF
BL
1987

Ocean freight payable at	Place and date of issue
Number of original Bs/L	Signature for carrier; carrier's principal place of business

BL03

Export Trade Connections, SITPRO approved licensee No 10

Both Common and Short Form Bills are acceptable against Letters of Credit, unless the Credit says they are not. (Figure 7.7.)

Lost or destroyed

In this case delays are inevitable but can be reduced by the use of a Letter of Indemnity. This will allow release of the goods at destination without presentation of a valid Bill. The original, or replacement, set will be produced at a later date. The indemnity is invariably required to be countersigned by a bank and should not be accepted at destination without the approval of the shipper.

Waybills

Waybills, used for Air, Road and Rail transits, have a number of characteristics in common with the Ocean Bill of Lading but have one very important difference as shown in figure 7.8.

Figure 7.8: Comparison of Ocean Bill of Lading and Waybills

BILL OF LADING	WAYBILL
Receipt for the goods	Receipt for the goods
Evidence of the contract of carriage	Evidence of the contract of carriage
Document of Title	Goods released to named consignee

Where Waybills are issued the carriers will release the goods at destination. It is not necessary to produce a transport document to obtain possession of the goods. The advantage of this is

Figure 7.9: House Air Waybill

			HOUSE AIR WAYBILL NO.
Shipper's name and address	Shipper's account number	Not negotiable **Air Waybill**	
		Issued by	
			Member of IATA
		Copies 1, 2 and 3 of this Air Waybill are originals and have the same validity.	
Consignee's name and address	Consignee's account number	It is agreed that the goods described herein are accepted in apparent good order and condition (except as noted) for carriage SUBJECT TO THE CONDITIONS OF CONTRACT ON THE REVERSE HEREOF. THE SHIPPER'S ATTENTION IS DRAWN TO THE NOTICE CONCERNING CARRIER'S LIMITATION OF LIABILITY. Shipper may increase such limitation of liability by declaring a higher value for carriage and paying a supplemental charge if required.	
Issuing carrier's agent name and city		Accounting information	
Agent's IATA code	Account no.		
Airport of departure (addr. of first carrier) and requested routing			

to	By first carrier	Routing and destination	to	by	to	by	Currency	Chgs Code	WT VAL PPD COLL	Other PPD COLL	Declared value for carriage	Declared value for Customs
							GBP					

Airport of destination	Flight/date	For carrier use only	Flight/date	Amount of insurance	INSURANCE - If carrier offers insurance and such insurance is requested in accordance with conditions on reverse hereof indicate amount to be insured in figures in box marked Amount of insurance
				NIL	

Handling information

No. of Pieces RCP	Gross weight	kg lb	Rate class / Commodity item no.	Chargeable weight	Rate / Charge	Total	Nature and quantity of goods (incl. dimensions or volume)

Prepaid	Weight charge	Collect	Other charges
	Valuation charge		
	Tax		
	Total other charges due agent		Shipper certifies that the particulars on the face hereof are correct and that insofar as any part of the consignment contains dangerous goods such part is properly described by name and is in proper condition for carriage by air according to the applicable Dangerous Goods Regulations.
	Total other charges due carrier		
			Signature of shipper or his agent
Total prepaid	Total collect		
Currency conversion rates	cc charges in dest. currency		
			Executed on (Date) at (Place) Signature of issuing carrier or its agent
For carriers use only at destination	Charges at destination	Total collect charges	

ESC4

Original 3 - (For Shipper)

convenience in that the availability of a document at destination is not related to the release of goods. However it should be realised that a Waybill is not a Document of Title and cannot be used to transfer property in the goods as part of the payment procedures. The most obvious problem area is associated with air freight into high risk markets.

Air Waybill

Procedure

The exporter, or agent, completes a Letter of Instruction to the Airline. In the great majority of cases air freight is arranged through agents rather than direct with the Airline. Because of this it is not uncommon that House Air Waybills are issued as opposed to the carrier's Air Waybill (figure 7.9). However, as long as the carrier countersigns the House Air Waybill, it will be accepted as a carrier's receipt against a Letter of Credit.

The Air Waybills are issued in sets of anything up to 12 copies but will contain at least three originals:

1 retained by Airline;
2 forwarded to consignee;
3 returned to exporter;

and any number of copies for internal control and information.

The Air Waybill does not protect ownership of the goods but it may be possible to arrange Cash on Delivery (COD) in certain markets.

In the cases where the exporter perceives a risk and is looking for some security then it is possible for a party other than the buyer to be named as consignee. If you do not entirely trust the buyer, then do not name the buyer as the consignee, name a party that you do trust, that is, a bank. It is not uncommon that banks are named as consignees for air, road and rail shipments, and, subject to specific instructions, will collect payment against release of the goods, as opposed to release of the documents.

International Transport Documentation

Figure 7.10: Road Waybill

LETTRE DE VOITURE INTERNATIONALE (CMR) INTERNATIONAL CONSIGNMENT NOTE	
Sender (Name, Address, Country) Expéditeur (Nom, Addresse, Pays) 1	Customs Reference/Status Référence/désignation pour mise en douane 2
	Senders/Agents Reference Référence de l'expéditeur/de l'agent 3
Consignee (Name, Address, Country) Destinataire (Nom, Addresse, Pays) 4	Carrier (Name, Address, Country) Transporteur (Nom, Addresse, Pays) 5
Place & date of taking over the goods (place, country, date) Lieu et date de la prise en charge des marchandises (Lieu, pays, date) 6	Successive Carriers Transporteurs successifs 7
Place designated for delivery of goods (place, country) Lieu prévu pour la livraison des marchandises (lieu, pays) 8	This carriage is subject, notwithstanding any clause to the contrary, to the Convention on the Contract for the International Carriage of Goods by Road (CMR) Ce transport est soumis nonobstant toute clause contraire à la Convention Relative au Contrat de Transport International de Marchandises par Route (CMR)

COPY 1 SENDER
COPY 2 CONSIGNEE
COPY 3 CARRIER

*NB FOR DANGEROUS GOODS

INDICATE

1. CORRECT TECHNICAL NAME (PROPER SHIPPING NAME)

2. HAZARD CLASS

3. UN NUMBER

4. FLASHPOINT (IF ANY) IN °C.

Approved by FTA/RHA/SITPRO UK 1981

Marks & Nos. No & Kind of Packages: Description of Goods* Marques et Nos. No et nature des colis, Désignation des marchandises* 9	Gross weight (kg) 10 Poids Brut (kg)	Volume (m³) 11 Cubage (m³)

Carriage Charges Prix de transport 12	Senders Instructions for Customs, etc.... Instructions de l'Expéditeur (optional) 13
Reservations Réserves 14	Documents attached Documents Annexés (optional) 15
	Special agreements Conventions particulières (optional) 16
Goods Received/Marchandises Recues 17	Signature of Carrier/Signature du transporteur 18	Company completing this note Société émettrice 19
		Place and Date: Signature Lieu et date, Signature 20

Printed by Systemforms Ltd. 01-505 6125

730

Road Waybill

Covered by the CMR Convention (Convention des Merchandises par Route) and provides a standard, non-negotiable, consignment note used by most nationalities of international road haulier. (Figure 7.10.)

Rail Waybill

Covered by the CIM Convention (Convention Internationale des Merchandises par chemin de Fer) and again acts as a standard consignment note for international rail carriers. In the UK this is the British Rail Consignment Note BR 20105. (Figure 7.11.)

Both of these documents act as receipts and evidence of the Contract of Carriage but not as a Document of Title.

As will be seen from an examination of the sample documents, they all contain their equivalents of the Clause Paramount in terms of the references to the Warsaw Convention (Air), CMR (Road) and CIM (Rail).

Sea Waybill

As we have seen, the Bill of Lading is specifically a sea freight document and is unique in that it operates as a Document of Title. This confers great advantages in terms of the security afforded to the exporter in controlling physical access to the goods, but can be very inconvenient where the Bills become **stale** due to late arrival at destination. This is a particular problem where short sea transits are concerned, in which case it is very difficult to get Bills to destination before the goods arrive. In these cases it is not unusual for a Sea or Liner Waybill to be issued by the Shipping Line. This document (figure 7.12) serves as a receipt for the goods and evidence of the Contract of Carriage but **not** as a Document of Title. Such Waybills are now being used for deep-sea transits to low risk customers and markets such as the United States of America and are sometimes referred to as Express Bills in that the goods are subject to

International Transport Documentation

Figure 7.11: Rail Waybill

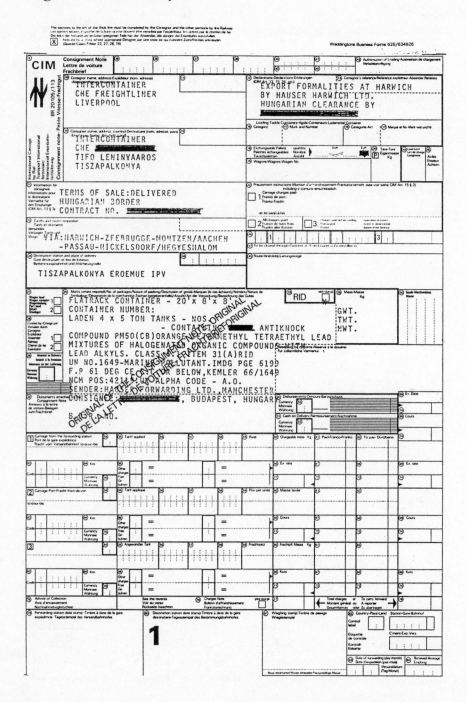

Figure 7.12: Sea or Liner Waybill

Shipper	**LINER WAYBILL**	**LWB No.** 5613
	NON-NEGOTIABLE for Port to Port Shipment or Combined Transport	Reference No. RO 59202

WELD ROAD
SOUTHPORT PR8 2LY

LWB

Finanglia Ferries

FF

Oy FINANGLIA FERRIES Ltd.

Consignee (not to order)

SF 00100 HELSINKI
FINLAND

Notify address

	Head Office Etelaranta 8 00130 HELSINKI 13	Telex 122882 FCRS SF Phone 90-1781 Cable FINNCARRIERS

Pre-carriage by ROAD	Place of receipt WINSFORD	
Vessel WESTON	Port of loading HULL	**Branch Office** 17A & 18 Bevis Marks, London EC3A 7JB — Telex 887002 FINLDN G Phone 01-623 9441 Cable Finanglia London EC3
Port of discharge HELSINKI	Place of delivery QUAY	

Marks and Nos. &/or Unit Nos.	Number and kind of packages: description of goods	Gross Weight kilos	Measurement CBM
UBCU9640165	1 40FT JUMBOCONTAINER S.T.C. 18 PALLETS YELLOW ROCKIES 1)	21000	

Particulars furnished by the Merchant

Freight details, charges etc.	

RECEIVED the goods as specified above according to Shipper's declaration in apparent good order and condition – unless otherwise stated herein – weight, measure, marks, numbers, quality, contents and value unknown for carriage from the place of receipt or port of loading to the port of discharge or place of delivery, whichever is respectively applicable.

The goods covered by this Liner Waybill will be delivered to the Party named as Consignee or its authorised agent, on production, of proof of identity without any documentary formalities. Carrier to exercise due care ensuring that delivery is made to the proper party. However, in case of incorrect delivery, no responsibility will be accepted unless due to fault or neglect on the part of the Carrier.

This Liner Waybill which is not a document of title to the goods is deemed to be a contract of carriage which is subject to the terms, conditions, exceptions, limitations and liberties set out in the Carrier's Standard Conditions of Carriage applicable to the voyage covered by this Liner Waybill and operative on its date of issue. Except for live animals, and goods which are stated herein to be carried on deck and as so carried, these Standard Conditions of Carriage incorporate, insofar as no provisions contained in any international convention or mandatory national law apply to the carriage by sea, in respect of the sea portion of the transit, the Hague Rules contained in the Brussels Convention dated 25th August 1924 and any compulsorily applicable national enactment of either the Hague Rules as such or as amended by the Hague-Visby Rules contained in the Brussels Protocol dated 23rd February 1968, which would have been applicable if the Carrier had issued a Bill of Lading instead of this non-negotiable Liner Waybill.

A copy of the Carrier's Standard Conditions of Carriage applicable hereto (which are, as regards the performance of the Contract and basic liability with respect to combined transport, based on Combiconbill adopted by BIMCO in January 1971) may be inspected or will be supplied on request at the office of the Carrier or of the Carrier's principal agents. The Shipper accepts these Standard Conditions on his own behalf and on the behalf of the Consignee and/or the Owner of the goods and warrants that he has authority to do so.

The Shipper agrees to indemnify the Carrier for any liability incurred by the Carrier to any party in connection with the goods in excess of the Carrier's liability under the Standard Conditions.

Without prejudice to the above, the Carrier may process, and settle, claims from any party entitled to bring such claims and any such settlement or payment shall be a complete discharge of the Carrier's liability to the Shipper.

Freight payable at ORIGIN	Place and date of issue HULL 8 JAN 85
	Signature

O R I G I N A L

OV FINANGLIA FERRIES LTD.

express release without the presentation of a Bill of Lading.

Carrier's liability

It is not the intention of this book to examine the complex articles of the Transport Conventions but it is important to highlight a potential problem regarding the liability of the carrier for loss or damage to the goods whilst in their charge.

The Conventions basically define liability as 'the value of the goods at place and time of collection', but it should be noted that this is subject to a maximum which protects the carrier. The ceiling will differ from one convention to another but the current versions all use a unit of account known as a Special Drawing Right (SDR), the value of which is published in the national financial press.

Very approximately the **maximum** carrier's liability for the current conventions (based on an SDR of £0.80) are:

SEA (Hague-Visby) £530 per package or £1,600 per tonne

(Hamburg) £670 per package or £2,000 per tonne

AIR (Warsaw) £13,500 per tonne

RAIL (CIM) £13,500 per tonne

ROAD (CMR) £6,600 per tonne

It should be noted that these figures represent the maximum liability of the carrier, but exporters of high value goods may well find it worthwhile to negotiate higher limits with the carrier. The relationship between carrier's liability and the use of cargo insurance cover is examined in chapter 11.

Questions for Discussion

1 Describe the characteristics of the following documents:
  (a) a Common Short Form Bill of Lading;
  (b) an Ocean Bill of Lading;

(c) a Common Short Form Sea Waybill;

(d) a Combined Transport Bill of Lading.

2 The Common Short Form Bill of Lading is being increasingly used.

(a) Why is this?

(b) Does it have equal status with the Long Form Bill of Lading?

(c) When is its use inappropriate?

8

International Customs
Controls (I)

Having examined one important area of export documentation, that of transport, in our last chapter, the next category of documents we identified in figure 7.1 were those associated with Customs & Excise procedures specific to international movements.

All exporters and importers must comply with Customs regulations and cannot abdicate that responsibility to a third party. That is not to say that agents cannot be used, and in fact the great majority of Customs declarations are made by agents on behalf of traders, but that the exporter and importer always bears the ultimate responsibility for the accuracy of the information provided. It is this fact, coupled with the need to instruct and pay agents, that should persuade traders generally to at least attempt a basic understanding of Customs requirements.

It is because this understanding is often vague or even non-existent that the coverage of this area of International Physical Distribution will cover three chapters.

It is vital to understand that compliance with Customs requirements is mandatory and the consequences of non-compliance can be very expensive, in terms of time as well as money. Ally this to the fact that ignorance is **never** an excuse and it is obvious that all traders should be concerned with understanding those procedures which apply to them.

It may seem hard to believe but there is a logic to Customs controls. There is no document or procedure which is there simply to make your life more difficult. They all exist for good reasons and, in many cases, they actually simplify rather than complicate. As we will see in chapter 10 it is probable that an improved understanding of Customs procedures will actually present great opportunities to reduce the time spent and the costs of compliance. The Customs even give money back on occasions.

An Overview of Customs Controls

Just as it is possible to rationalize the range of export documents into four basic categories (see figure 7.1) so it is possible to take the wide and complex range of Customs procedures and to rationalize them into three categories, or, more accurately, sources. These are:

1 Export (departure);
2 Transit; and
3 Import (destination).

A little simplistic, but it does allow some logical rationalization of the 'mountain' of Customs procedures into three smaller 'hills'. It also makes an important, although perhaps obvious, point that goods moving internationally must move through Customs controls for the whole of the journey. The same, of course, applies to people.

Goods depart from their country of export from a Customs post of departure (where some form of export declaration will be required) through Customs posts of transit (if applicable) and into a Customs post of destination (where an import declaration will be needed). For some international movements only the departure and destination posts will be relevant, such as a sea or air freight movement between two ports or airports. However for road and rail movements it is perfectly possible that the goods will cross a number of countries of transit, in between the departure and destination countries, and therefore move through posts of transit into and out of these countries.

So what sort of controls result from these movements?

Export

All countries are interested in goods leaving their territory but invariably it is only because they wish to count them. Developed countries operate highly sophisticated systems designed to collect trade statistics, such information being considered, quite rightly, as being vital to economic planning. Whilst less sophisticated levels of collection may operate in other parts of the world, all countries still count and analyse their exports. The great majority of exports are, in fact, only of statistical interest and are described by Customs as 'Non-Controlled' goods (even sometimes as 'innocent 'goods). However certain types of goods are subject to export controls as well as being of statistical interest. Thus you cannot send your Chieftain tanks off to Iran without encountering some controls; in such a case, export licensing control. The range of Customs regimes which could apply controls to exports are examined later in this chapter (see Pre-entry).

Import

Just as logically, Customs authorities throughout the world are interested in goods entering their territories. In fact they are invariably a lot more interested in their imports than their exports. This is due to the fact that, whilst most exports do not attract controls, there is no such thing as a 'Non-Controlled' import. Imports are of statistical interest in the same way as exports but many other controls may also apply. These can briefly be broken down into:

1 Tariff barriers
   (a) Duty;
   (b) Tax;
   (c) Excise;
   (d) Levy;
   (e) Licensing;
   (f) Quotas; and

2 Non-Tariff barriers

(a) Standards . . . technical, health and safety.

These will be examined in greater detail in chapter 10, but it should be quite clear that all imports will be affected by a number of these control regimes. Even if goods are entering duty free they are probably subject to VAT. We should also remember that when the first teams of Excise men were formed in the 17th century to collect revenue on behalf of Parliament on, for example, French brandy, the UK coastline was divided up into 'Collections' and, to this day, each Customs region in the UK is referred to as a Collection. Their job is to **collect** and it is imports which generate revenue, not exports.

Transit

As mentioned earlier, it is not unusual for goods to actually move through other Customs territories between their departure and destination points. This is, in fact, quite common for inter-national road and rail movements. In such a case it would be nice for the road trailer driver to say to the first Customs post en route that he was only passing through their country and did not intend to stop, and for the Customs to take his word for it and allow the goods to enter. It would be nice, but you can guess that it cannot happen. We have to remember that those goods, if they remain in that country, are potentially subject to all of the import controls mentioned above. The countries of transit need some way to ensure that goods allowed in actually leave, or that they collect whatever revenues are due if they say. Also consider the fact that the vehicle is quite a valuable commodity in its own right, irrespective of the goods. A driver allowed in simply on the promise that he would leave, could sell the goods, sell the vehicle, even sell the diesel in the tanks, and there is a lot of revenue, in the form of duty, tax and excise, at stake. It may even be that the goods are subject to other controls in addition to these fiscal ones. The result of all this is that Transit procedures have been established to protect the countries of transit and these are examined in chapter 9.

Therefore, over the almost 400 years that the Customs have existed, procedures have developed which control all these areas and this and the following chapters will examine them in some detail.

The European Community/Union

Before we can actually look at these procedures there is one other broad overview necessary to put them into context. The UK is a member of not just a free trade area but a Customs Union. The distinction is of great significance. A simple free trade area such as the European Free Trade Area (see later) or the North American Free Trade Area (NAFTA comprising the USA, Canada and Mexico), is based on an agreement between its members that they will give duty free entry to each other's goods. Thus goods of Canadian origin will be allowed into the USA duty free, but UK origin goods will attract tariff controls. However the controls which UK goods attract into the USA will not necessarily be the same as those applicable if the same goods were to enter Canada or Mexico. They do not co-operate on the treatment of non-member country's goods, only on each others. The distinction is that the European Community not only has free trade between it members but also operates a **common** Customs Tariff against non-members.

A useful map of the Community, although clearly not a geographic one, is shown in figure 8.1.

This reveals some very interesting facts regarding the UK as a Customs authority.

1 The distinction between **internal** and **external** frontiers. The borders between member states being internal and those with non-members being external.
2 Goods entering the Community from outside, that is, from non-members, cross a common Customs frontier which means that they attract broadly the same tariff controls whichever member state they enter, in particular the duty rates will be identical in every member state.

Figure 8.1: Map of the European Community

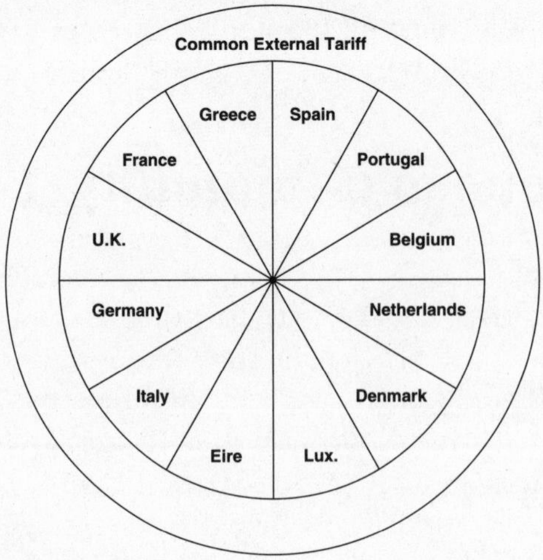

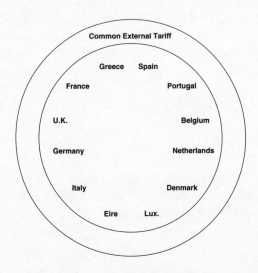

The changes which occurred on the 1st of January 1993 in creating a Single European Market are clearly based on this distinction and the situation now is basically that the internal frontiers have been removed allowing the free movement of not just goods but people, services and capital. However the Common External frontier remains intact.

Figure 8.2: Customs Union

The structure of the Community's Integrated Tariff (TARIC) is examined in chapter 10 and the broader ramifications of the Single European Market in chapter 14. But for now our picture of the UK as a member of a Customs Union is illustrated in figure 8.2.

What happens in the future regarding the Common External Tariff is very much dependent on the on-going negotiations under the General Agreement on Tariffs and Trade (GATT) which may allow a further lowering of duty rates worldwide or, unfortunately, generate a 'Fortress Europe' scenario in which the Community raises barriers against non-member goods.

Which country?

In terms of basic Customs procedures it is clearly vital for the UK trader to distinguish between EC and non-EC customers and suppliers. We have established that the current member states of the European Community are (in the order in which they joined):

France
Germany
Italy
Belgium
Luxembourg
Netherlands
United Kingdom
Ireland
Denmark
Greece
Spain
Portugal

These 12 member states have also come to very specific trade agreements with a number of other western European countries, predominantly providing for bilateral free trade, which are often referred to as the ex-EFTA (European Free Trade Association) countries. These are:

Austria
Sweden
Switzerland
Finland
Norway
Iceland
Liechtenstein

These countries (with the exception of Switzerland) formed the European Economic Area (EEA) in 1991, strengthening the commercial links and almost forming a 'waiting room' for full membership of the Community. It is likely that by the end of the century most of these countries will be full members of the single Market. In this context it is entirely feasible that, over the next 20 years, the Community will also expand to include Cyprus, Israel, Malta, Turkey, Poland, Hungary, the Czech and Slovak Republics and, who knows, even Russia.

It should also be noted that since the 1st of November it is actually technically correct to refer to the European Union as opposed to the European Community. This is due to the ratification of Maastricht Treaty which is examined, along with the Single European Act, in chapter 13.

The complex picture of EC preferential trade agreements with non-member states is examined in more detail in chapter 10, but for now we can make an important distinction between three categories of trading partners, they are either:

1 EC Member States, for example Germany, Belgium;
2 Ex-EFTA Member States, for example Austria, Sweden; or
3 Non-Members, for example Japan, USA.

Figure 8.3 shows the procedures which would apply to each element of control (export, transit and import) for each category of overseas country.

Figure 8.3: Customs control procedures

		EXPORT	**TRANSIT**	**IMPORT**
UK	→ EC	Intrastat	.....	Intrastat
UK	→ EFTA	SAD	SAD	SAD
UK	→ non-EC non-EFTA	SAD	TIR or TIF	?

The terms used above will all be explained as we proceed to examine these procedures, beginning, quite logically, with the export of an international consignment.

Export Procedures

The first point that should be made is that, since the 1st of January 1993, trade between the UK and other member states of the Community should not be referred to as export or import. In terms of trade statistics we are dealing with **dispatches** and **arrivals**, and in terms of VAT, **supplies** and **acquisitions**. For the sake of simplicity we will continue to use the words Export and Import when describing general procedures, and the technically correct descriptions when referring to specific VAT or Trade Statistics applications for Community trade.

Perhaps the best way to examine current Customs procedures for export clearance is to engage in a brief history lesson. Since the early 1980s there has been a continuous development of Customs procedures, all of which have genuinely served to simplify the administrative burdens on traders (honestly).

Let us take, as an example, a consignment of washing machines from the UK to, say, Italy, by road, in the mid 1980s. The exporter, or their agent, would have had to complete and present a full export declaration to UK Customs, primarily for statistical purposes. This would have probably been a C273 form or, if

Figure 8.4: Single Administrative Document

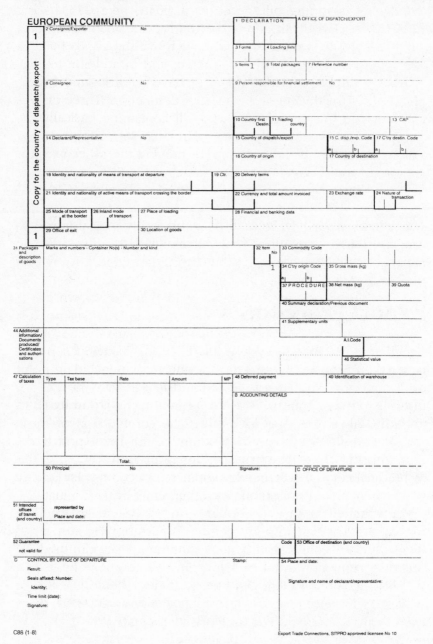

the goods were subject to specific export controls then one of a range of 'shipping bills' such as a C63A, or a C1334, or a C1172, or a GW 60. In addition, a transit document, such as a T1 or T2 or T2L, would be needed to move the goods through the countries of transit, that is, France, and in addition to that, an Italian import declaration would have been lodged by the importer, or their agent, at the post of destination. Three distinct and separate Customs declarations, all containing basically the same information, and all operating in what was, supposedly, a Common Market. If the goods were moving the other way the situation would have been the same; an Italian export declaration, plus a T form, plus a UK import declaration (C10, C11 or C12).

The next major development was the totally logical introduction of a single document which combined the three distinct areas of Customs controls, export, transit and import. Known as the Single Administrative Document (SAD) (see figure 8.4), this was introduced on the 1st of January 1988 and is known as the C88 in the UK. The important point is that the SAD was not just introduced in the UK but in every other member state of the Community. It actually replaced something like 150 separate Customs documents throughout the Community, including every one mentioned for our Italian job. Not only did the EC co-operate in the adoption of the SAD but also the seven ex-EFTA countries also agreed to its use. As the combination of these countries represents some 65 per cent of the UK export trade, then it can be seen that this was quite a step forward.

The final, and most recent development, was on the 1st January 1993 when, amongst a number of other Single Market initiatives, the Intrastat procedures where introduced which replaced the use of the SAD for intra-Community trade, but did not affect its use for EC trade with the EFTA countries. Therefore the SAD is now no longer relevant to trade within the Community.

We now have a situation, which is illustrated in figure 8.3, in which the Intrastat procedure operates alongside the SAD, there use being dependent on the country of destination.

Figure 8.5: Supplementary Statistical Declaration

INTRA EC TRADE STATISTICS — Supplementary Declaration

Trader VAT No. Branch ID

Agent VAT No. Branch ID

H M Customs and Excise

INTRASTAT

DISPATCHES Period No. of Items

For each numbered item (1–9):

1. Commodity Code	2. Value £'s Sterling	3. Delivery terms	4. Nature of transaction	5. Net mass (kg)
6. Supplementary units	7. Country of dest.	8. Mode of transport	10. No of consignments	11. Trader's reference

When complete return to:-
HM Customs and Excise, Tariff and Statistical Office,
Sort Section, Portcullis House, 27 Victoria Ave.,
Southend-on-Sea,
Essex, SS2 6AL
Your declaration must be received by the 10th working
day after the period end.

Place and date

Name of signatory (in BLOCK LETTERS)

Signature

1501

174

Intrastat

The collection of trade statistics on intra-Community trade is now accomplished via three levels of declaration by exporters, depending on their level of business.

1 All traders must complete normal VAT returns which, on the current VAT 100 form, require information on total **supplies** to EC customers and **acquisitions** from EC suppliers, in boxes 8 (Ex Works out) and 9 ((Delivered in).

2 Those organizations which are conducting EC business of less than £60,600 need only to supply an annual listing of their business specifying individual VAT numbers for customers and/or suppliers. Those traders above that level but below £135,000 total value of dispatches or arrivals must supply an EC Sales Listing (ESL) usually on a quarterly basis, on form VAT 101.

   (It is important to note that any figures quoted here are correct at the time of writing but are subject to alteration by the Customs & Excise authorities at any time. Please check with your local Customs office).

3 All traders above these levels must also supply Supplementary Statistical Declarations (SSD) (see figure 8.5) on a monthly basis within 10 working days of the end of the month. These will take precedence over the need for ESLs and the SAD is **not** acceptable as a SSD. It is not necessary to declare Temporary Exports, Packing, Samples or Exhibition Goods.

Whilst these might appear to be very complex arrangements the fact is that for smaller traders (some 150,000 of them) the requirements are actually easier than they were, in that they no longer have to make individual SAD declarations for each consignment. For the larger companies (approximately 30,000) then the situation is no worse, it is simply a different form of statistical declaration. It is estimated that some Customs offices, technically referred to as Entry Processing Units, will lose up to 95% of the Customs entries previously handled. This also reflects the growing use of electronic methods to make the necessary declarations.

Submission of declarations

The introduction of Intrastat has not changed the option that the trader has to use an agent to make declarations on their behalf, and many have continued to do so. One of the potential problems is that, as the information is presented in an aggregated format, then the use of a number of different agents can make the compilation of information more difficult. It, perhaps, means that the use of a single agent or forwarder does have advantages. There is, however, no reason why traders cannot make the ESLs and SSDs on their own behalf.

The second point to make is that the Customs are keen to encourage traders and agents to provide information in other than paper format. This involves the use of computer discs or tape as a means of declaration, or even what is known as Direct Trader Input, in which case the information is keyed straight into the Customs computers, invariably by clearance agents. The development of Electronic Data Interchange (EDI) even reduces the information keying requirements. Chapter 13 examines these systems from the exporter's point of view.

VAT and the Single Market

It will be clear from the above that the collection of intra-Community trade statistics is now closely linked to the VAT regime which operates throughout the community. The current situation is that UK sales to member states are still covered by a zero-rated invoice and subject to proof of export if required. In addition, the buyer's VAT number must appear on the invoice. Thus, what is known as the 'destination principle' still applies, in that Community VAT will be collected at the time of the acquisition (import) in the buyer's country. The only change here is that from the 1st of January, 1993, for UK acquisitions from EC suppliers, we reverted to the Postponed Accounting System (PAS) which allows importers to account for VAT on the 'Tax Due' side of their VAT returns. The requirement to pay, or defer, VAT on non-EC supplies remains.

However, the intention is that the Community will move

towards a system based on the 'Origin Principle', to take effect, it is planned, in 1997. This will mean that sales invoices to EC buyers will include UK VAT just as a home sales invoice. It will, in fact, be regarded as a 'home' sale. The anomaly which results is that the VAT will be paid into the UK whilst the goods will actually be used in, for example, France. This requires a clearing system to adjust the revenue balances, bearing in mind that VAT will also be being paid into France for goods which are used in the UK. Simple really. It is hoped that this will encourage a greater harmonization, or convergence, of VAT rates across the Community.

As a brief summary, UK sales to EC buyers and purchases from EC suppliers are subject to Intrastat procedures, and will be based on zero-rated invoices until 1997 when VAT will then be charged by the seller. The SAD has no relevance to this intra-Community trade.

The Single Administrative Document

As we have seen, the SAD was introduced on the 1st of January, 1988 and replaced almost 150 Customs documents within both the EC and ex-EFTA countries, combining the requirement for export, transit and import declarations into one document used by 19 western European nations. (See figure 8.4.)

Since the 1st of January 1993 the SAD became irrelevant to Community trade, but it is still extremely important for trade with non-Community members. These can be divided into the ex-EFTA countries and the rest, in that the Ex-EFTA adopted the SAD on the 1st of January 1988 and have continued its use despite the EC moving over to Intrastat on the 1st of January 1993. Thus the SAD still operates as a full eight page document for trade between the Community and Austria, Sweden, Switzerland, Finland, Norway, Iceland and Liechtenstein. As we will see later for trade outside of these countries then only elements of the SAD will be relevant.

The combination of functions within the SAD can be simply expressed as:

Pages 2 and 3   Export
Pages 1, 4, 5 and 7   Transit
Pages 6 and 8   Import

As an example, a consignment from the UK to Austria could be export declared, pass through posts of transit and be import declared at destination by just one completed SAD. By the same token an import from, say, Finland, could complete all Customs controls with one SAD.

In practice it is actually more common that the so-called 'split use option' is used. This allows the distinct elements of the SAD to be separated so that the export declarations can be made separately from the transit documents and the import declarations. The separation of the import declaration from export and transit is very common, as the importer often lodges the import entry prior to the arrival of the goods. For non-EC/EFTA countries there is no option but to separate the export or import elements of the SAD depending on the direction of movement.

The UK exporter has two choices in making the export declarations for goods destined for outside the Community. The SAD declaration can be made before the goods are actually shipped, **pre-entry**, or the goods are shipped and the declaration is made later, **post-entry**.

SAD post-entry

If goods are only of statistical interest to the UK Customs, that is they only want to count them, then it is possible to ship the goods before making the full statistical declaration. This is known as the **Simplified Clearance Procedure** and requires the person responsible for making the declaration to be registered with Customs and posses a Customs Registered Number (CRN) which also identifies the address at which records are kept. The goods will be accepted for loading against any one of a number of approved commercial documents. These include a Standard Shipping Note (chapter 4), Air Waybill, CMR or CIM Note (chapter 7) or a partially completed SAD. The full SAD export declaration must be provided within 14 days from outward clearance and bear a unique **Export Consignment Identifier** made up of the CRN and a unique shipment reference number.

Prior to the introduction of the Simplified Clearance Procedure described above, in October 1981, the vast majority of UK exports were post-entered. Since then many exporters, and particularly agents, have found that it is more efficient to produce full statistical declarations before shipment and thus comply with all Customs requirements without the need for any subsequent procedures. This is known as **voluntary pre-entry** in that the goods could be post-entered but the trader chooses to make a full pre-entry.

However, we must also consider the fact that not all goods are only of statistical interest, and therefore able to be post-entered, in that certain categories of exports are also subject to specific controls. In such case it would clearly be inappropriate for Customs to allow shipment, and a post-entry within 14 days after, and then attempt to apply the necessary controls. Therefore if exports are **controlled** then the exporter has no choice but to **pre-enter** and allow Customs to exercise such controls.

SAD pre-entry

It is possible to identify a number of specific control regimes which may affect certain categories of UK exports to certain overseas destinations, and which would make a full pre-entry declaration mandatory. Knowledge of the application of these regimes is extremely important to exporters because of the point made earlier in this chapter, that 'ignorance is never any excuse'. It is not the responsibility of Customs & Excise to advise traders that certain controls apply, but for the trader to ensure that whatever regimes are appropriate are actually complied with.

Export licensing control

The Export of Goods (Control) Order, issued regularly by the Department of Trade and available from HMSO, contains

Schedule 1 which is a lengthy list of goods which require an export licence before they will be allowed out of the UK. This is commonly referred to as the Prohibition List and whilst detailed reference is necessary in practice it is possible to identify certain types of goods which are likely to attract such controls.

1 Goods of **strategic** value (to our enemies?). These include military equipment, ships, aircraft, weapons and navigation systems.
2 Goods of **technological** value. These include computer hardware, specialist testing and measuring equipment and so on.
3 Goods of **cultural** value. These include antiques, works of art, the family china, London Bridge.

Application must be made to the Export Licensing Branch of the DTI and the granting of licenses will be dependent on the proposed country of destination. The license must be presented to Customs to support the export pre-entry. For goods subject to Common Agricultural Policy controls there is an equivalent licensing regime operated by the Intervention Board for Agricultural Produce and the Ministry of Agriculture, Fisheries and Food.

Exports from bonded warehouses

All imports into the UK enter into bond. This describes premises which are operated under a bond, or guarantee, to Customs. Should the warehouse keepers allow goods to be cleared from the bond without the approval of Customs, given via an 'Out of Charge' message, then the guarantee safeguards Customs revenues. It is however unusual for goods to be exported out of bond. Those which are are subject to **Excise Duty** if they are consumed domestically. As we have seen Excise, or Revenue Duty, is payable on certain imports, and has been for 350 years. The goods which are subject to this very specific charge include:

1 Alcohol – Spirits, beer, wine and even toiletries.
2 Tobacco – Cigarettes, cigars, smoking tobacco.

3 Mineral oils – Petrol, diesel, lubricants.

These goods attract excise on import into the UK and, this is where pre-entry comes in, are excise free if exported. Thus whisky, for example, is excisable if consumed in the UK but free from excise if exported. The Customs are therefore very concerned to ensure that any goods for which excise has not been paid do leave the country. This is particularly important as excise represents 25 per cent of central government revenue in the UK, (VAT actually represents 37 per cent) and the UK has the second highest excise rates in the Community, second only to Denmark. The UK charge of 2,660 ECU per 100 litres on spirits compares with the Greek equivalent of 171 ECU. The requirement for a full pre-entry for these goods exported out of bond is designed to protect revenues.

Whilst on this subject we should note that since the 1st of January, 1993 the movement of excisable goods between bonded warehouses will be supplemented by the addition of a new type of approved trader known as Registered Excise Dealers and Shippers (REDS) who will be approved to receive excisable goods from other member states of the Community. A freight forwarder, acting for a number of importers, may be a REDS.

Duty frees?

As far as our major concern, that is, exports, is concerned, then there has been no change in the nature of the pre-entry controls but it is relevant to mention the future of duty-free purchases. They originate from the export of goods excise free which are not subsequently imported. The duty free shops operate in the limbo between the export and import and can sell cheaper because the goods are zero rated for VAT and excise free. As the actual tax free cost of a bottle of Scotch is not much over £2.00 then duty free shops are not that cheap. It is obvious that there need to be limits on the amount of duty free purchases travellers can bring back into a country because of the loss of revenue from duty paid sales. The current situation regarding duty frees within the EC will continue until 1999 when duty free sales will disappear in the absence of internal frontiers. The extension, from the 1st of January 1993 as originally intended, has been purely to do with UK protestations. What happened on the 1st of January 1993 was the removal of duty paid limits on purchases for personal consumption made in other member states of the Community. The removal of internal frontiers means that cross-border shopping is likely to increase and that the differences in excise rates between member states are likely to be reduced, as the high charging countries will lose revenue to the low excise members. The convergence of both VAT and excise rates within the Community is one of the developments generated by the Single Market.

To conclude this section we should remind ourselves that in terms of the production of a full SAD export declaration goods subject to **Export Licensing** and those subject to **Excise Duty** must be exported under cover of a full pre-entry. In the case of such goods being destined for another EC member then we already know that the clearance will comply with Intrastat requirements and not be based on the SAD. In such cases the controls will be exercised on the trader's premises and the new Administrative Accompanying Document (AAD) will allow the Customs control at the departure and destination points. Once again the distinction between EC and non-EC trade becomes very important.

There is one other Customs regime, or more accurately range of regimes, which require full pre-entry on the SAD, and which, in fact, can only apply to non-EC trade. These are situations in which the Customs grant relief from duties and fall into two categories Inward Processing Relief (IPR), and Outward Processing Relief (OPR).

Inward Processing Relief

If goods are imported from outside the EC and subsequently re-exported then it is possible to obtain relief from the duty payable at import. The duty may be avoided by suspension at the time of import, in which case all the goods must be re-exported, usually within six months, or the duty is paid and whichever goods are subsequently re-exported claim a **drawback** of duty. It should be emphasized that the expression re-export applies only to goods which are destined for a non-EC country, that is, they must leave the Community. This procedure applies where the re-export is simply a repacked version of the import or, more importantly, where the re-export is the result of processing of the import. Complex manufacturing processes can be approved for relief as long as it can be proved that the imported commodities are genuinely re-exported. As an example, the import of printed textiles from the Far East and subsequent re-export of garments to the USA could qualify for relief.

Outward Processing Relief

This describes the equivalent procedure where goods are exported, out of the Community, for processing and subsequent re-import. Again subject to prior approval, the Customs will allow relief on the value of the goods before the process and charge only for the 'added value' of the processing. This procedure therefore also applies to repair or replacement situations where, if it is free of charge to the importer, then no duty is payable at all. There is a further procedure known as Returned Goods Relief where duty and VAT may be avoided for goods returned in the same state as at export, which often applies to defective goods.

Finally, it is perfectly feasible to combine these two procedures. For example goods could be imported and processed under IPR and re-exported and re-imported under OPR. Discussions with your local Customs collection are essential to investigate the possibilities.

SAD Summary

The SAD is relevant to non-EC trade only. Where goods are moving between EC members and an ex-EFTA country the export, transit and import declarations are combined in the one document. For exports outside the EC and EFTA then the export element of the SAD must be used for the export declaration but the transit and import elements are irrelevant. For imports from outside the EC and EFTA then the import element of the SAD is the import declaration but the export and transit elements are irrelevant.

If the exports are only of statistical interest and attract no Customs controls it is possible to post-enter the goods under the Simplified Clearance Procedure (SCP) making the full SAD declaration within 14 days. If the exports attract controls the goods must be pre-entered. The basic export control regimes are Export Licensing, Exports from Bond and Goods Re-exported under Duty Relief Schemes.

It is also possible for Full Container Loads to be export cleared under the Local Export Control (LEC) in which control may be exercised at the exporter's premises and the full declaration made later on the SAD. In the case of goods below £600 value and 1,000 Kg in weight a range of commercial documents, acceptable under the SCP procedure, are sufficient without the full SAD declaration.

CHIEF

Customs Handling of Import and Export Freight (CHIEF) is the successor to the Departmental Entry Processing System (DEPS) and describes the UK Customs development of computerized systems for the clearance of exports and imports. Some 95 per cent of imports are cleared by Direct Trader Input involving mostly clearing agents having direct access to the Customs computers. CHIEF envisages an extension of this system into exports but it is taking some time to implement and covers few exports at the moment. This does not preclude the possibility, encouraged by customs, that statistical information is supplied on computer tape or disk.

The ultimate aim is the provision of all information by Electronic Data Interchange (EDI) using electronic messages, rather than bits of paper, between compatible computer terminals. Chapter 13 returns to this view of the future.

Export Declarations Summary

As we saw in figure 8.3 earlier in this chapter, the UK exporter must make a very clear distinction between trade with EC and non-EC customers. The export element of that diagram hopefully makes a little more sense now and is reproduced in figure 8.6.

Figure 8.6: Customs export control procedures

UK Exports to EC members   Intrastat, ESL and SSD

UK Exports to EFTA members   SAD (Pages 2 and 3)

UK Exports to non-EC/EFTA   SAD (Pages 2 and 3)

The next stage of the international movement, following the export clearance, involves the second important category of Customs controls, that which affects the transit of goods through intermediate Customs posts between departure and destination. These transit procedures are covered in the next chapter.

Questions for Discussion

1 The role of HM Customs & Excise with regard to exports is varied as they perform an agency role for a number of other government departments or bodies. Describe what these functions are when exporters and freight forwarders declare goods to Customs on exportation from the United Kingdom.

2 The export of goods is zero-rated for VAT purposes, that is, the exporter does not charge VAT on his commercial invoice to the overseas buyer. One of the conditions which Customs lays down in support of this zero-rating is that the exporter has to have proof that the goods left the UK. List the various transport documents that are acceptable to Customs and who issues them.

9

International Customs Controls (II)

In the previous chapter we identified the fact that Customs controls could be divided up into three main areas: export; transit; and import. Having covered the procedural requirements related to UK exports it is logical for us now to proceed to the next stage of the international movement which may involve the goods passing through Customs posts of transit on the way to their final destination. The words 'may involve' are used advisedly as not all international consignments will pass through posts of transit.

In the case of a sea or air movement then the goods will not actually transit any Customs territory during the journey. The goods on the vessel or aircraft will export clear out of a port of departure and import clear into a port of destination. They may call at other ports on route but they will not enter a country at one point and pass through to leave at another point, which is the essences of a true transit. It is perfectly feasible for goods to be transferred from one ship or aircraft to another at a port part way through the journey, but this is actually a transhipment, not a transit. This transhipment will be done under Customs control, invariably through bonded warehouses, and the goods will not be imported and re-exported as long as they stay within the bonded premises. The ultimate example of this type of transhipment is the use of Freeports in which case the goods could even be processed before the re-loading (see chapter 10). Therefore true transit, in which the goods enter a country at one point and leave at another, applies only to international road and rail transits.

Another look at figure 8.3 in the previous chapter will reveal that the distinction between EC , EFTA and non-EC/EFTA trade, which makes such a difference to the methods of export clearance used, is just as important when we consider transit procedures. The element of that diagram which is relevant to us now is reproduced in figure 9.1.

Figure 9.1: Customs transit control procedures

UK → EC	No transit controls
UK → EFTA	SAD Transit
UK → non-EC non-EFTA	TIR or TIF

It can be seen that the current situation within the EC is the result of developments over many years and once again a history lesson might be useful. In fact we will examine these procedures from the first establishment of Customs transit systems through to the current regimes which have applied since January 1st, 1993.

Why Transit Controls?

But first a brief reprise on why transit systems should exist in the first place. The example we used in the previous chapter was a road consignment travelling from the UK to Italy and crossing France en-route. The problem the French Customs have is that they are allowing goods into their territory which may be subject to duty, tax, excise and levy, as well as other restrictions such as quota or licensing controls. The promise of the driver that the goods are not stopping in France is hardly likely to give the French Customs the security they need in order to allow the goods in free from such controls. To add to the problem they would also consider the vehicle to be of value, sometimes more than the goods, and even the fuel in the tanks. The solution for the Customs authorities, all of them, not just France, was to insist on **duty deposits** being lodged to cover the potential Customs revenues. Such deposits were refundable as long as the haulier could prove that the goods actually subsequently left the country. Thus if the goods were to stop in France the Customs simply kept the payments. The problem for the haulier was that every country en-route would also require the same form of deposit and on a journey to Saudi Arabia, for example, there could be anything up to 10 customs posts of transit.

The second major problem was the fact that, in order to asses the level of deposit necessary, the Customs would invariably examine the goods in order to determine their tariff classification and therefore the level of charges and controls appropriate. This would clearly be very time consuming on a journey involving a number of posts of transit and greatly increased the possibility of damage, and even pilferage, during the journey.

The growth in international road freight since the Second World War served to highlight the need for a solution to the dual problems of duty deposits and examination and the solution was TIR.

Transport Internationaux Routiers

The familiar white and blue plates that can be seen on many heavy goods vehicles represent the title of an international convention, established by the Economic Commission for Europe, which has been ratified by a very large number of Customs authorities throughout the world. It was ratified in the UK in 1959 and includes the USA, Japan and most of the Middle East and Eastern Europe. So how does TIR solve the problems?

Duty deposits

A TIR Carnet (figure 9.2) must be issued by an approved

Figure 9.2: TIR Carnet

No du passeport du conducteur
....

IRU Union Internationale
des Transports Routiers

CARNET TIR*

THIS CARNET MUST BE
RETURNED TO THE
ASSOCIATION WITHIN
10 DAYS OF USE OR
EXPIRY

20 volets   I.R.U. **No** 0618512

1. **Valable pour prise en charge par le bureau de douane de départ jusqu'au** ___17 FEB 1982___ **inclus**
   Valid for the acceptance of goods by the Customs office of departure up to and including

2. **Délivré par** _FREIGHT TRANSPORT ASSOCIATION LTD._
   Issued by

   (nom de l'association émettrice / name of issuing association)

3. **Titulaire** Lucas International Transport, Modermay
   Holder Mills, Mytholmroyd, Hebden Bridge, W. Yorks. U.K.
   (nom, adresse, pays / name, address, country)

4. **Signature du délégué de l'association émettrice et cachet de cette association:**
   Signature of authorized official of the issuing association and stamp of that association:

   17-2-82

5. **Signature du secrétaire de l'organisation internationale:**
   Signature of the secretary of the international organization:

(A remplir avant l'utilisation par le titulaire du carnet / To be completed before use by the holder of the carnet)

6. **Pays de départ** ___GREECE___
   Country of departure

7. **Pays de destination** ___ENGLAND___
   Country /Countries of destination (')

8. **No(s) d'immatriculation du (des) véhicule(s) routier(s)** (')
   Registration No(s). of road vehicle(s) (')
   RCM·543 T — GA·0002

9. **Certificat(s) d'agrément du (des) véhicule(s) routier(s)** (')
   Certificate(s) of approval of road vehicle(s) (No. and date) (')
   CP· 552564.   2.9.81

10. **No(s) d'identification du (des) conteneur(s)** (')
    Identification No(s). of container(s) (')
    GA 0002 -   Tony Brownlee

IMPRIME EN SUISSE – PRINTED IN SWITZERLAND – 1990 – GESSLER & CIE SA, CH-COLOMBIER (NE) authority and accompany the goods throughout the journey. First a brief word about these documents called 'Carnets'. There are a number of different forms of Carnets used in international trade including ATA Carnets and Carnet de Passage en Douane (both covered in chapter 10) and even Carnets for the Paris Metro. The word simply describes a booklet of vouchers (or volets). In the case of TIR the Carnet is issued in the UK by either the Freight Transport Association (FTA) or the Road Haulage Association (RHA) on behalf of the International Road Transport Union.

Duty deposits are avoided by the provision of a guarantee by the carrier to the issuing authority, usually countersigned by a bank or insurance company. The carrier must undertake to abide by all TIR regulations. In simple terms this guarantee acts as a duty deposit, lodged in the country of departure, and replaces the need for such deposits at each post of transit. The Customs authorities in transit accept Volets from the Carnet, on entry into and exit from their Customs territories, rather than a duty deposit. Should the evidence of exit from a country not be available, that is, the Volet 2 (exit) to match the Volet 1 (entry), then the financial guarantees provide the Customs revenues. The whole journey is controlled by the stamping of counterfoils, left on the Carnet when the volets are removed, by the Customs posts, producing a record of the journey which must be returned to the issuing authority after completion of the movement. Carnets are available as 14 or 20 page documents, dependent on the number of transit posts involved.

Vehicle examination

The regular, and very time consuming, examination of vehicles and goods at posts of transit is avoided by the requirement for TIR vehicles to be approved. The approval, in the UK, is given, following inspection of the vehicle, by the Department of Transport (Vehicle Inspectorate) who act on behalf of Customs. This takes the form of a GV60 approval certificate and is issued on the basis that:

Figure 9.3: TIR TABAC Carnet

IRU Union Internationale
des Transports Routiers

CARNET TIR*
20 volets   I.R.U. **No** 1064073

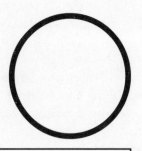

1. Valable pour prise en charge par le bureau de douane de départ jusqu'au _____ inclus
   Valid for the acceptance of goods by the Customs office of departure up to and including

2. Délivré par _____
   Issued by

   (nom de l'association émettrice / *name of issuing association)*

3. Titulaire _____
   Holder

   (nom, adresse, pays / *name, address, country)*

4. Signature du délégué de l'association émettrice et cachet de cette association:
   Signature of authorized official of the issuing association and stamp of that association:

5. Signature du secrétaire de l'organisation internationale:
   Signature of the secretary of the international organization:

   de Gotthan

(A remplir avant l'utilisation par le titulaire du carnet / *To be completed before use by the holder of the carnet)*

6. Pays de départ
   Country of departure

7. Pays de destination
   Country / Countries of destination (')

8. No(s) d'immatriculation du (des) véhicule(s) routier(s) (')
   Registration No(s). of road vehicle(s) (')

9. Certificat(s) d'agrément du (des) véhicule(s) routier(s) (No et date) (')
   Certificate(s) of approval of road vehicle(s) (No. and date) (')

10. No(s) d'identification du (des) conteneur(s) (')
    Identification No(s). of container(s) (')

11. Observations diverses
    Remarks

12. Signature du titulaire du carnet:
    Signature of the carnet holder:

(') Biffer la mention inutile
Strike out whichever does not apply

TABAC ALCOOL TOBACCO ALCOHOL

IMPRIME EN SUISSE – PRINTED IN SWITZERLAND – 1990 – GESSLER & CIE SA, CH-COLOMBIER (NE)

IRU – CH-GENEVE – REPRODUCTION INTERDITE

* Voir annexe 1 de la Convention TIR, 1975, élaborée sous les auspices de la Commission économique des Nations Unies pour l'Europe.
* *See annex 1 of the TIR Convention, 1975, prepared under the auspices of the United Nations Economic Commission for Europe.*

1 the vehicle can be sealed so that it is not possible to add or remove goods without breaking the seal/s; and

2 there are no concealed areas.

The purpose of the approval is to enable Customs, at the point of departure, to seal the goods in the vehicle with one or more seals. The Customs of transit then need to examine the seal/s only and, as long as they are intact, will waive their right to examine the goods.

Thus approved vehicles, carrying a TIR Carnet, are able to pass through any number of Customs posts of transit without the need for examination or the payment of duty deposits.

TIR TABAC Carnets

On the 1st of January, 1993 a new form of TIR Carnet was introduced specifically to cover the high value movements of tobacco and alcohol (figure 9.3). The problem in this case is that if goods are illegally diverted en-route then the Customs revenues lost are much greater than usual because such goods are subject to significant Excise Duties; the specific problem being the disappearance of such goods as they transit into some Eastern European markets. The new Carnets require higher guarantee levels which reflect the greater risk and greater values.

So TIR was the first solution to Customs Transit problems and remains extremely important now. It should also be noted that the equivalent system exists for the movement of rail wagons and is known as TIF (Transport International par Chemin de Fer) and operates in the same way as TIR.

Whilst TIR is still very important to UK exporters it has to be said that the UK's membership of the European Community in 1973 made us part of a Community Transit system which replaced TIR for intra-Community movements, and therefore reduced its scope to a great extent.

Community Transit System

When the UK joined the European Community in 1973 we became part of a Transit system unique to the Community which
the original six member states had developed during the 1960s.

The Community Transit system, which replaced TIR for goods
destined for Community states, centred on the use of Transit
documents, known as 'T' Forms, and on the concept of 'free
circulation'.

Goods are regarded as being in free circulation within the
Community if:

1 they are wholly produced within the Community; or
2 are imported duty paid.

It will be clear from the above that the vast majority of goods
moving within the Community are free circulation goods
because they either started here or, if imported from outside,
the duties and other Customs charges have been paid. Free
circulation goods were referred to as 'T2 status'. The only way
goods could be moving through the EC which were not in free
circulation is if they were to be imported into the EC duty
unpaid and then moved to another member state where the
duty and other charges would be met. In such a case the Customs
charges should be the same, wherever they are paid, but there
would be a consignment of goods for which charges were still
outstanding and which would therefore not be in free circulation. The goods would be referred to as 'T1 status'.

The document actually used, which replaced the TIR Carnet
within the Community, was a four page Transit form (the 'T'
form), which bore the T1 or T2 reference, whichever was
appropriate. Guarantees needed to be lodged, just as with TIR,
mostly by the road hauliers or forwarders, and the document
attempted to ensure that the planned journey was completed by
the return of copy 3 from destination. The arrival of goods
accompanied by a T2 form would allow clearance at destination
duty free, or, if accompanied by a T1, would indicate that
Customs duties are still outstanding. In this respect the T Form
acted as a Status document as well as a Transit form for the

intermediate Customs posts.

In the cases where the goods were an intra Community movement with no posts of transit, that is, a sea freight from London to Piraeus or an air freight from Manchester to Milan, then the only requirement would be for a Status declaration. In this case a 'Limited' version of the T Form was used, known as a 'T2L', which was composed of only two pages.

Thus from 1973 to the end of 1992 goods were moved within the Community with either a T1 or a T2 or a T2L. However, as we have seen in chapter 8, the 1st of January 1988 saw the introduction of the Single Administrative Document (SAD) within the 19 countries of the EC and EFTA. Not only did the SAD become the basic export declaration for all of those countries, but it also replaced the T Forms. In fact pages 1, 4, 5 and 7 of the SAD became the new Transit Form, retaining the concept of T1 and T2 status, but with a clearly different format. The equivalent of the T2L was pages 1 and 4 of the SAD.

It is now possible to identify the functions of each page of the SAD as follows:

Pages 2 and 3   Export
Pages 1 and 4   Status (T2L)
Pages 1, 4, 5 and 7   Status and Transit (T1 or T2)

and the only pages left are 6 and 8 which represent the Import Declaration at destination.

The situation since January 1st, 1993 is that the SAD acts as part of a Transit system only for the trade with the EFTA countries, the transit requirement within the Community having been removed. Thus for movements from the UK to an EFTA member the relevant parts of the SAD act as an export declaration and status and transit, just as they have since the 1st of January 1988. It should be noted that the requirement for SAD T forms will also apply for goods which transit an EFTA state on the way to a final destination within the Community. In such a case the T2 requirement would only attach at, for example, the Austrian frontier, but it is likely that the document will be made out at the beginning of the journey.

There is also the probability that transit and status T2ES and

T2PT will remain in use for Spain and Portugal as long as some transitional duties remain, which could be up to 1995.

The above has dealt with the situation of genuine free circulation goods moving from the UK to another EC member state, in which case there is no Transit documentation at all, or to, or through, an EFTA member, in which case the SAD, T2 or T2L equivalent, will still apply.

However, what about goods which are imported into the Community and are therefore **not** in free circulation? From the 1st of January 1993 the T1 document was still officially required for goods in transit and, for the first time, being transhipped, within the Community. So for example, a consignment of goods from Japan which arrive in Felixstowe for transhipment to Zeebrugge, would need T1 certification for the Felixstowe/Zeebrugge movement. The added complication is that there is a good chance that the ship out of Felixstowe will also contain goods which are in free circulation, and the equivalent of a T2L would be needed to prove their status. The solution is a Simplified Transit Procedure which allows the carriers themselves to make Transit Declarations by producing separate T1 and T2 manifests, rather than individual transit documents for each shipment. In some cases the carriers are approved to authenticate their own manifests in which case they do not even have to present them to Customs before departure. For approved airlines the information is simply made available within their computer systems.

The Single Market

As of 1993, the situation for intra-Community trade was that the development in the 1950s of TIR, followed by T Forms, followed by the SAD was followed by a removal of all transit requirements within the Community. Figures 8.1 and 8.2 in chapter 8 show the transformation which took place on the 1st of January 1993, with the removal of internal frontiers. Free circulation goods now move through the Community, as long as the destination is a member state and they do not leave the Community en route, with no transit controls whatsoever. If the destination is an EFTA country then SAD Transit documents are needed but it is unlikely that they would be examined until the goods actually leave the Community and enter the first non-EC state. A destination outside the EC and EFTA would use TIR but, once again, the Carnet would not be examined until the first non-EC country was reached.

It will be obvious that the removal of transit controls within the Community has severely reduced the role of internal Customs posts and the reality is that many posts are now defunct. The European Commission has actually sponsored the St. Matthew project which is designed to retrain redundant Customs officers. Why St. Matthew? Well, he is the patron saint of revenue collectors.

More seriously, for this change to work there had to be a major change in the attitude of Customs towards goods entering their territories. Traditionally, there has always been an assumption that goods, and people, are not in free circulation unless they can prove differently. The mandatory check on documents such as T Forms, and passports, is necessary to provide the proof that the goods and people are not subject to specific controls. One might, quite properly, regard this as an assumption of guilt until innocence is proved. The very important change in the philosophy of Customs is that they now work on entirely the opposite assumption that goods are '**regarded as Community goods in the absence of anything to the contrary**'. This also applies to people and means that the mandatory checks on T Forms and passports are no longer needed. The number of T Forms used is about ten per cent of the previous number and we are very close to the removal of all passport checks for Community citizens.

Whilst estimates vary there is no doubt that major savings are already being made in avoiding the frontier delays which affected the majority of freight movements throughout the Community. We should not forget, however, that none of these developments have reduced the power of Customs authorities to stop and examine people and goods, but only changed the regular and mandatory checks which previously affected all movements.

Summary

We have established that the UK exporter must make a clear distinction between EC trade, EFTA trade and business outside of those 19 countries. In the case of both transit and export procedures the destination of the goods is the major deciding factor. The choices have been illustrated in earlier figures but it may be that figure 9.4 now makes a little more sense.

Figure 9.4: Customs control procedures

	EXPORT	TRANSIT
UK → EC	Intrastat	No transit controls
UK → EFTA	SAD Export	SAD Transit/Status
UK → non-EC non-EFTA	SAD Export	TIR or TIF

Questions for Discussion

1 Write brief notes on the following:
 (a) T1 status;
 (b) TIR Carnet.
2 The Single European Act removed the need for transit controls within the European Union, but they still apply to non-EU trade. Describe the different transit systems which affect exports from the UK to:
 (a) EU countries;
 (b) ex-EFTA countries;
 (c) third countries (that is, neither of the above).

10

International Customs Controls (III)

This third chapter in our coverage of Customs controls will examine the final area of specific controls, that of import procedures. However it should be pointed out that, as this book is specifically written to cover one of the syllabuses of The Institute of **Export**, then it may seem inappropriate for us to consider import controls. What we should always remember is that one company's exports are another company's imports, and all UK exporters should have a good knowledge of the controls which goods could attract at destination. We are therefore approaching the issue of Customs Import Procedures from the point of view of the UK exporter, rather than the UK importer. In reality the distinction is almost irrelevant to the modern international trader.

What we will also try to do is to identify the opportunities which may be available to UK exporters to minimise the costs and effects of Customs controls by prudent management of information and procedures. There are many opportunities missed by UK exporters because of the short-sighted perception that import clearance is the buyer's problem.

However it is worth just a few words regarding UK and EC import procedures if only to complete the picture we have built up in looking at export and transit procedures.

Community Imports

Goods which enter the UK from another member state actually require no immediate import declaration. Just as Intrastat procedures collect export statistics using the VAT returns, EC Sales Listing (ESL) and Supplementary Statistical Declaration (SSD), then import statistics are collected in exactly the same way. In addition the VAT which is due on such imports is now subject to the Postponed Accounting System (PAS) which actually operated in the early 1980s, which means it is simply accounted for on the 'Tax due' side of the trader's VAT return.

For imports from non-EC members then the import element of the SAD (pages 6 and 8) serves as the import declaration for all Community members. Such entries may be made by the importing company, periodically for large traders, but the great majority are made by Clearing Agents on behalf of the importers. In such cases it is probable that the declaration is made using Direct Trader Input (DTI) procedures. This describes the process which allows declarations to be made direct from the agent's computer to the Customs computers, the printed paper version of which will be a 'Plain Paper SAD', that is an import SAD with all the necessary information but no printed layout. This is simply because a computer does not need a boxed template to complete a document. In these cases the requirement for payment of VAT on import has not changed, although it is very likely that such payment is deferred until the 15th of the following month.

Just as Local Export Control (LEC) can simplify export clearances (chapter 8) then Local Import Control can allow large importers of full loads to actually bring the consignments right into their premises and make post-clearances to UK Customs.

Whilst it is difficult, or even impossible, to cover every country's import procedures outside of the Community, what we can do is to identify and explain the type and nature of import controls generally throughout the world. Outside of the EC there is very little, if any, standardization of import declarations but whichever particular document is required it will always fulfil the same basic purpose and apply the same range of controls.

Import Controls

It is possible to break all import controls into two broad categories – they are either Tariff or Non-Tariff barriers. The word tariff describes the product classification system which is the beginning of all countries import controls and which is examined later in this chapter. These controls would include:

1 Tariff controls
  (a) Duty;
  (b) Tax;
  (c) Excise;
  (d) Levy;
  (e) Licensing;
  (f) Quotas; and
2 Non-Tariff controls
  (a) Standards ... Technical, health and safety.
  (b) Political embargoes

Duty

Used as a specific fiscal control and selectively applied at a variety of levels by different countries. We already know that intra-Community trade is duty free and, as we will see later in this chapter, there are many situations where the origin of the goods may mean that they are not subject to duty. Such duties are usually ad-valorem, that is they are charged as a percentage of the (CIF) value of the goods. One of the great successes of the General Agreement on Tariffs & Trade (GATT) negotiations over the years is that the average worldwide duty rate of 24 per cent in the 1950s is now just over four per cent in the 1990s. However this does not preclude countries applying much higher rates on certain commodities, particularly when attempting to protect local manufacturers.

International Customs Controls (III)

Tax

Within the Community it is Value Added Tax (VAT), or its equivalent in each member state, which is the standard fiscal charge on all sales. As we have seen, in the UK, it is either accounted for on EC imports or deferred (to the 15th of the following month) for imports from outside the Community. Rates within the Community currently range from 15 per cent (ignoring the exempt and zero rates), to 38 per cent for certain luxury items. Other non-EC countries may impose similar charges on imports in the form of Purchase Tax or Turnover Tax.

Excise

Sometimes referred to as Revenue Duty, this accurately describes its purpose in that, rather than acting as a pure control, it is designed to collect government revenue. Chapter 8 examined the export controls relevant to excisable goods, chiefly alcohol, tobacco and mineral fuels, which are designed to ensure that excise is collected on such goods which are consumed domestically, that is, in the UK. Clearly such excise will be applied to imports of these goods into the UK and, of course, on entry into most overseas countries. These charges can be very high, they certainly are in the UK, and are often Specific duties in that they are expressed as a charge for a particular quantity or volume rather than as an ad-valorem charge. As an example, the excise on spirits imported into the UK is expressed as ECUs (European Currency Units) per hectolitre (100 litres). As these charges represent some 25 per cent of total UK government revenues it will be clear that the Customs & Excise prioritize their collection.

Levy

A specialized charge which, within the Community, generally only affects agricultural produce and items processed from them. Thus basic commodities like sugar and starch will attract levies as will most foodstuffs. This is not necessarily a charge that would be encountered in many overseas markets.

Licensing

We have, in previous chapters of this book, looked at both export and import licensing. Many overseas countries, particularly developing and under-developed countries, use specific import licensing to control every consignment. In fact, in chapter 3, we examined the role of the pro-forma invoice as a means of raising the import licence. The existence of the required licence must be certain before any shipments are made as the goods will not be import cleared without the appropriate licence.

Quotas

This describes quantitative restrictions which may be imposed on certain goods, usually to protect local manufacturers. The quota may be a quantity which is allowed in free from duty, subsequent imports being allowed but at the full rate of duty, or it may be that licences are issued only for that quantity and once used, no further imports will be allowed over the specified time period (usually 12 months). Some quota allocations are used in the first few days of the year.

Non-Tariff Barriers

Exporters will inevitably encounter an enormous range of different technical requirements across the world. The reason these may act as a barrier is that the exporter may actually not be able to comply with the standard or the certification requirements for that standard. Secondly, the cost of compliance, in terms of product modification, testing and certification, may make the product uncompetitive in the overseas market.

The above represent the range of common import controls which the UK exporter may encounter. We could also legitimately include Pre-Shipment Inspection (covered in chapter 4) and the use of Exchange Control as more indirect import controls, and we have to accept that in some overseas countries there have developed what might be termed 'unofficial' controls which can introduce significant compliance costs. It is an unfortunate fact but, in some countries, paying the right person can be the only import procedure that matters.

In order to decide which controls, and at what level, are to be applied to each consignment, there are three vital pieces of information which Customs authorities need:

1 description;
2 origin; and
3 value.

Whilst particular requirements differ from one country to another there is invariably an import declaration accompanied by supporting documents. One of the most important supporting documents is one which is always prepared by the exporter, that is the export invoice. This may also be accompanied by other statements, especially as to origin and value, all designed to provide the above elements of information to the Customs.

The Export Invoice

The UK exporter is faced with producing a wide variety of different invoices, involving a range of third party procedures, dependent on the country of destination. Because the export invoice is of such importance to the overseas Customs authorities, it is they who insist on a particular format. The exporter could bill the buyer with almost any document, from a standard commercial invoice to the back of an envelope; the more technical invoice requirements are purely the result of import Customs requirements.

Export invoices fall into five distinct types:

1 Commercial invoice.
2 Commercial invoice with a declaration.

3 Commercial invoice requiring third party verification –
  (a) Certified;
  (b) Legalised.
4 Consular invoice.
5 Specific Customs invoice.

Commercial invoice

The simplest situation is one where the importing country has no special requirements at all and the exporter uses the company's standard commercial invoice, just as for a home sale. The only difference will be the fact that the invoice is zero-rated for VAT (at the moment).

Commercial invoice with declaration

It is quite common for countries to require a specific declaration to be typed on the invoice. The wording differs from country to country, and is often in the language of the importing country, but invariably declares the origin of the goods and that the prices are correct export prices. A typical declaration would be: 'We hereby guarantee that this is a true and correct invoice and that the goods referred to are of the origin, manufacture and production of the United Kingdom.'

As we shall see later, the import Customs are concerned that the origin and prices are legitimate. The exact wording of such declarations is available from a variety of reference sources, most notably, Croner's *Reference Book for Exporters.*

Certified invoices

The above declarations sometimes require a third party to validate them and the most common requirement is for a UK Chamber of Commerce to Certify a set of invoices. They will stamp the documents with their own certification stamp an example of which is reproduced in figure 10.1. In theory they are certifying that the invoice and declaration are correct, but in practice they cannot validate the validity of the information. What they certify in practice is that the signatory of the invoice is one authorized by the company to make such declarations on behalf of the company. Exporting companies lodge the signatures of approved signatories with the Chambers for this purpose.

Figure 10.1: Chamber of Commerce certification stamp

THIS SIGNATURE IS AUTHENTIC

Authorised Signatory
Chamber of Commerce & Industry

THE MANCHESTER CHAMBER
OF COMMERCE & INDUSTRY
21 DEC 1993

CERTIFYING STAMP

Authorised by
Her Majesty's Department
of Trade & Industry 1991

Legalised invoices

In some cases, in particular the Middle East, there is a requirement for a further stage of third party verification. The Certified invoices are required to be legalised by the commercial section of the embassy of the importing country in the UK. Again it is often a rubber stamp or sometimes a more complex verification. The procedure is that the exporter arranges certification at the Chamber of Commerce and then presents the document set to the appropriate embassy, in London, for legalisation. In the case of the 20 plus Arab League countries, all of which require legalisation, a streamlined procedure exists in which the local certifying Chamber sends the documents to the Arab British Chamber of Commerce (ABCC) who make the presentations to the individual embassies. This reduces the time taken for the operation to an average of five to seven days. See figure 10.2.

Figure 10.2: Legalisation procedure for exports to Arab League countries

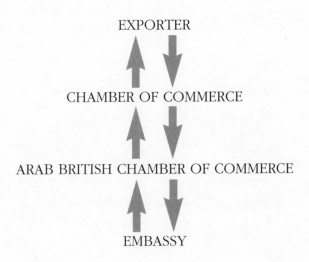

EXPORTER

CHAMBER OF COMMERCE

ARAB BRITISH CHAMBER OF COMMERCE

EMBASSY

It is not only the time delay that exporters must consider but also that charges are made for certification and legalisation. As an example, a set of documents certified and legalised through the ABCC will cost between £40 and £60.

In the case of Arab documents it may also be necessary to append a further declaration to the invoice certifying that the goods are not of Israeli origin or contain any Israeli materials.

Consular invoices

These are particularly common in Central and Latin American countries. They require their own, unique, consular invoice form to be completed and returned to the Consulate for **Consularisation**. The format of such invoices varies enormously and they are often in the language of the country of destination. Some examples are reproduced as figures 10.3 and 10.4. The Consulates, which are actually commercial sections of the embassy situated in regional centres, will check the whole set of documents before, what might be a very elaborate, consularising. Quite apart from the time delay it is possible that the consular

Figure 10.3: Example of a Consular invoice

FACTURE CONSULAIRE

SERVICE CONSULAIRE

CONSULAR INVOICE

DE LA REPUBLIQUE D'HAITI

A LONDRES

B.L. No

MARKS (Marques)							
	Merchandises Shipped on the S/S _____ Nationality _____						
	Marchandises expédiées sur le S/S			Name (nom) le		Date	
	Sailing from the Port of ...				for		
	Partant du Port de				pour		
	Name and Address of Sender (Shipper) _____						
	Nom et Adresse de l'expéditeur						
	Consigned to the order of _____			of _____			
	Consigné a l'ordre de			de			
	Notify to _____			of _____			
	Notifier			de			

Numbers	Number of Pieces	Description of the Packing	Country of Origin	Specification and details of each article (quantity, quality, measurement, yardage, etc.) in accordance with the conditions of Haitian Customs tariff	Weights in kilos Poids en K		Values in U.S. Currency
					Gross	Nett	Valeur en
Numéros	Nombre de Colis	Nature de l'emballage	Pays d'origine	Dénomination et détails de chaque article (quantité, qualité, mesure, yardage, etc.), dans les termes du Tarif Haitien	Brut	Net	Monnaie des E.U.

I state that the *Prices*, the Weights, the Specifications and the *Origin* of the above mentioned articles are true and correct and they are exactly the same as appearing on our Export Declaration No. _____ of the _____ made to the Customs Authorities of our country.

J'affirme que les *prix*, les poids les dénominations et *l'origine* des articles ci-dessus sont sincères et corrects et qu'ils sont exactement les mêmos qui figurent sur notre déclaration d'exportation No. _____ du _____ faits au Service des Douanes de notre pays.

Signature de l'Expéd.

I state that this invoice is corresponding exactly to the actual truth and that it is in every respect in accordance with our books and that nothing is changed of the usual description, and neither the weight, the quantity, nor the value of the articles specified therein have been altered.

J'affirme que cette facture est l'expression fidèle et sincère de la vérité, qu'elle est en tout conforme à mes livres, qu'aucune dénomination usuelle, ni le poids, ni la quantité des articles qui y sont portés ni la valeur n'ont été altérés.

_____ Date _____

Shippers

Expéditeurs _____

Per

Par : _____

_____

Signature

In any case when the goods are dutiable on the net weight basis the taxable weight of the said goods must include all the previous or immediate packing, including the cardboards (box) or objects made of cardboard not subject to a higher duty (Article 29 of the Act of 26-7-1926).

Dans tous les cas où les marchandises sont taxées au poids net, le poids imposable des dites marchandises comprendra tous les emballages antérieurs ou immédiats, y compris les cartons ou objets en carton, non soumis à un droft plus élevé Article 29, loi du 26 juillet 1926.

Value of the goods _____
Valeur des marchandises,

Packing (if it has not already been included in the value of the goods _____
Emballage (s'il n'est pas compris dans la valeur des marchandises

Freight and B/L., Embarking (Shipping) and Carriage charges _____

Frét et frais du connaissement, embarquement et camionnage

Total F.O.B. value _____

Brokerage Commission _____
Commission 'achat

Interest
Intérêts

Export Duties paid at the Port of origin _____
Droits d'exportation acquittés au port d'origine

Freight and B/L charges, including shipping and unloading charges _____

Frét et frais du connaissement, embarquement et debarquement compris

Insurance _____
Assurance

Consular Fees — 2% of F.O.B. value $ _____

Droits con- sulaires — Stamp on Inv. ($1 20) _____

B/L visa ($2.00) _____

Stamp on B/L ($1 20) _____

Surcharge :5·00

Other Expenses
Autre frais

Exact total of the Invoice _____
Exact total de la facture

UNDER $200 · THE FEE IS $3 00 $200 AND OVER 2, OF F.O.B VALUE

208

fees could be quite high, sometimes even a percentage of the invoice value, so it is important that exporters have a good idea of the costs right from the quotation stage. It is perfectly acceptable to show consular fees as a separate item on the pro-forma invoice quotation, along with the freight and insurance charges.

Figure 10.4: Example of a Consular invoice

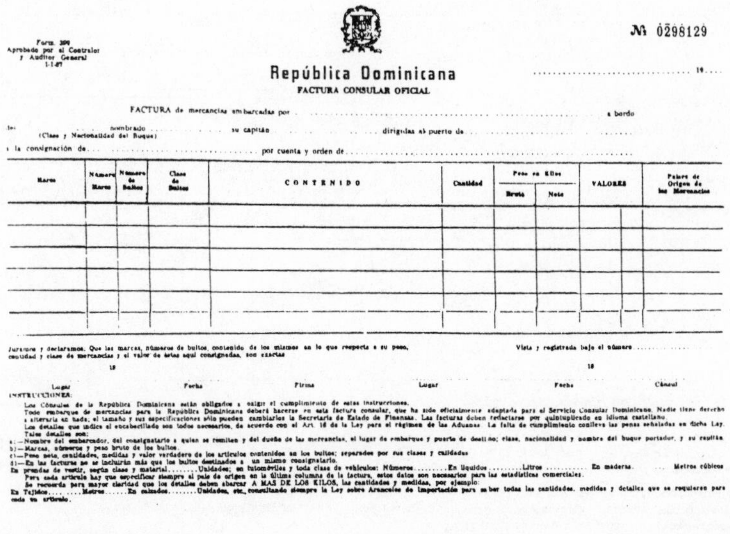

Form. 399
Aprobado por el Contralor y Auditor General 1-1-47

№ 0298129

República Dominicana
FACTURA CONSULAR OFICIAL

.... 19....

FACTURA de mercancías embarcadas por .... a bordo
del .... nombrado .... su capitán .... dirigidas al puerto de ....
(Clase y Nacionalidad del Buque)
a la consignación de .... por cuenta y orden de ....

Marca	Número Marca	Número de Bultos	Clase de Bultos	CONTENIDO	Cantidad	Peso en Kilos Bruto	Peso en Kilos Neto	VALORES	Países de Origen de las Mercancías

Vista y registrada bajo el número ....

The requirements detailed above for Certified, Legalised or Consularised invoices can be seen as an attempt, by the importing country, to impose some controls in the exporter's country, the logic being that if documents are not appropriately verified then the export shipment should not take place. Coincidentally, they also raise revenue for the overseas country's commercial sections in the UK.

Specific Customs invoice

These invoice forms are particularly related to ex-Commonwealth countries and are hangovers from the obsolete Commonwealth Preference System which, as we will see later, has been replaced by broader EC agreements. There are a lot less of these invoices

Figure 10.5: Example of a Specific Customs invoice

INVOICE AND CERTIFICATE OF VALUE FOR EXPORTS TO ZAMBIA   Page   of   pages

Insert full names and addresses

Exporter	Invoice no.
	Status of exporter (delete terms inapplicable)
	Manufacturer / Grower / Producer / Supplier
	Reference numbers and date
Consignee	Purchaser (if not consignee)
FOR OFFICIAL USE ONLY	Place and country from which consigned
	Country of origin
	Conditions of sale (e.g. F.O.B., C.I.F., consignment, etc. and details of discount and any other special arrangement)

Approved by Govt. of the Republic of Zambia (GRZ)

Ship/aircraft, etc.	Port of loading	Please state whether this is an open market sale (see clause 5 below).	NOTE: if this is an open market sale in terms of clause 5 below this column need not be completed	Open Market Value in currency of exporting country at factory/ warehouse/port of shipment* subject to cash discount already *deducted/not deducted	Selling price to purchaser State currency
Port of discharge	Final destination of goods		Quantity	RATE OF CASH DISCOUNT *Delete as necessary	

Marks and numbers; number and kind of packages; description of goods	(state units)	@	Amount	@	Amount
		Total		Total	

Enumerate the following charges and state if each amount has been included in the total selling price to purchaser	Selling price to purchaser		VALUE AND ORIGIN CLAUSES
	Amount (state currency)	State if Included	
1. Value of outside packages/containers			
2. Labour in packing goods into outside packages/containers			
3. Inland transport and insurance charges to dock/airport area			
4. Dock and Port charges			
5. Overseas freight			
6. Overseas insurance			
7. Details of any charges relating to delivery of goods			
8. Duty or taxes remitted on selling price			
9. Royalties (state full particulars)			
10. Commissions and similar charges (state full particulars)			

(1) This invoice is correct in all respects, and contains a true and full statement of the quantity and description of the goods, and of the price actually paid or to be paid for them, and of the country of origin.

(2) No different invoice of these goods has been or will be furnished to anyone.

(3) Unless otherwise declared, such or similar goods to those described in this invoice are sold for consumption in the country of exportation.

(4) No arrangement or understanding affecting the purchase price of these goods, by way of discount, rebate, compensation, or of any other nature whatsoever which is not fully shown in this invoice, has been or will be made or entered into by the said exporter and the purchaser, or by anyone on behalf of either of them.

(5) An open market sale is a sale in which price is the sole consideration whether or not there is common interest, or commercial, financial or other relationship between the buyer and the seller.

(6) The open market values shown in the column headed "Open Market Value in currency of exporting country" are those at which the said exporter would be prepared to supply identically similar goods in the country of exportation at the time of exportation, on a free sale in the open market to all independent purchasers trading at the same level of trade as that of the importer in Zambia and include any duty or taxes leviable in respect of the goods before they are delivered for home consumption. Any remission or drawback of duty or taxes which have been or will be allowed on exportation by the revenue authorities in the country of exportation are as shown in the table.

(7) "Exporting country" means the country where the goods are physically held prior to export to Zambia, but does not include any country through which such goods may pass in transit to Zambia.

I, THE UNDERSIGNED, being duly authorised in that behalf by the above exporter, and having made the necessary enquiries, HEREBY CERTIFY THAT THIS INVOICE, including continuation sheets, if any, IS MADE IN ACCORDANCE WITH THE VALUE CLAUSES SHOWN, and hereby declare that I will furnish to the Customs authorities of the importing country or their nominee, for inspection at any time, such accounts and other evidence as may be requested for the purpose of verifying this certificate.

Full name and business designation of signatory

Place and date

Signature of authorised signatory

ZAM1   Export Trade Connections, SITPRO approved licensee No 10 in existence than at one time, many countries going over to a commercial invoice with a declaration. Where they still apply the exporter must complete the appropriate invoice form for the country of destination, which are available from specialist printers. They are often in the form of Certificates of Value & Origin (CV/O) and may bear reference to Current Domestic Values (CDV) to control dumping of goods. It is not uncommon that the exporter also produces a commercial invoice as a bill to the buyer.

Whatever the form of export invoice required they will all contain basically the same range of information:

1 Seller and purchaser (who may not always be the same as the exporter and importer).
2 Goods description, quantity and value.
3 Trade terms (for example FCA, FOB, CIP, CIF).
4 Terms and methods of payment.
5 Ancillary costs (for example freight and insurance).
6 Shipment details (points of departure and destination).
7 Packing Specification – number and kind of packages, individual contents, sizes (in cms), weights (net and gross in Kg), marks and numbers. This may be included on the face of the invoice but it is just as likely that it is attached to the invoice as a separate Packing Specification. Sometimes it is referred to as a Packing List or Packing Note and is basically treated as an extension of the invoice.

We have now established that the country of destination will directly affect the type and format of export invoice used and that it represents an essential element of the buyer's import clearance declarations. As we saw earlier, the three vital pieces of information which the Customs authorities at destination need to apply import controls are:

1 description;
2 origin; and
3 value.

Description

This is the starting point for all Customs controls as the goods must first of all be very specifically identified in order to decide what particular controls apply to them. Customs authorities throughout the world are also wary about using words to identify commodities as there is clearly a language problem and also words can be vague and misleading. Therefore the means used by Customs to identify goods depends on the use of number classification systems, or **nomenclatures**, which translate vague words into the hard data of numbers which mean the same throughout the world. It should also be noted that exporters have a duty to declare their exports for statistical purposes based on accurate tariff numbers.

Such classification systems form the basis of Customs Tariffs and it would not be beyond the bounds of possibility that every nation state in the world were to develop its own unique nomenclature. Thankfully, this is not the case and in fact there is a marked degree of harmonization of classification systems across the globe. A potted history of the development of standardized classifications would start with the:

Brussels Tariff Nomenclature (BTN)

As the result of widespread discussions following the Second World War progress was made on the development of a standard product classification system. Not only was this seen as valuable in removing ambiguities in identification of goods from one country to another, but it also greatly facilitated the collection of meaningful international trade statistics. The classification was produced by the Customs Cooperation Council, in 1957, as a four digit nomenclature which was promoted as a standard throughout the world. In fact almost 150 countries used the BTN as the basis of their tariff. For developing countries the BTN gave sufficient level of identification but for the developed nations it was quite common for the four digit code to be extended to give a higher level of sophistication to the classification. As we will see later, the longer the number the greater the specificity of the identification.

The BTN was partially redrafted in 1965 and renamed the **Customs Cooperation Council Nomenclature (CCCN)** but remained a four digit code until the introduction of the:

Harmonized commodity description and coding System (HS)

The HS represents a wholesale update of the CCCN and is a six digit classification which has again been adopted by the majority of trading nations. The reason for the update was the fact that the BTN had been drawn up in the 1950s and it had become quite clear that it was no longer relevant to the needs of Customs in the 1980s. If one considers the range of goods which were traded in the 1980s which actually did not exist in the 1950s, it is quite clear that the original 9,000 or so numbers needed to be expanded to the current 15,000 plus. As an example, a company dealing in highly sophisticated optical fibres for computer applications was forced to classify the goods as Chapter 70 'glass ... others'; in the updated tariff such commodities are far more accurately identified in Chapter 90 as optical fibres. The predominance of 'others' as a safety net classification, for goods not specifically described in the old tariff, has been much reduced in the HS-based tariffs. Also the intention is that some trading nations, notably the USA, who have operated unique tariffs, will accommodate the HS and facilitate the further harmonization of tariff classifications.

The current situation, as far as the UK is concerned, is that it operates the EC Combined Nomenclature, which is based on the HS and came into force on the 1st of January 1988 as the Community Integrated Tariff (TARIC) and provides for eight digit harmonization within the Community and EFTA.

The structure of a tariff number for goods within the EC can be broken down into:

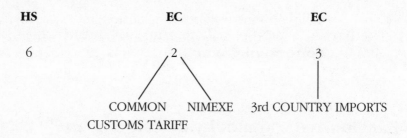

The six digit HS base is likely to be the same in most countries in the world and is extended by a further two digits common to all Community members. The seventh digit identifies the rate of duty applicable, which should be standard throughout the EC, and the eighth is the level of statistical collection of intra-EC trade figures (NIMEXE). For all UK exports and imports from other EC members the eight digit code is sufficient; for imports from non-EC members the full 11 digit classification is necessary to identify the appropriate EC import controls on such goods. In specialized cases such as agricultural produce, wine and where anti-dumping duties are concerned it is necessary to add a further four digits.

Finding a tariff number

We have established that the UK exporter has a duty to identify goods with the correct tariff number to the UK Customs for statistical purposes. Also the information supplied, for example on export invoices, could usefully identify the correct tariff number for the import Customs. In fact many overseas buyers may request that a particular description and tariff classification are included on the invoice.

It would be quite time consuming to start with the first line of the appropriate tariff and work through up to 15,000 lines until you reach one that seems right, and, of course there is a more logical way. It may be that the alphabetical index can immediately indicate the relevant part of the tariff. If not, then the logical process starts with finding the appropriate chapter. The HS is made up of 97 chapters listed from the most basic of commodities and gradually working through categories of products which become more and more sophisticated in terms of the amount of processing and technical enhancements. Thus a very broad breakdown would look like:

Chapter 1	Live Animals
Chapters 2-25	Agricultural Produce
Chapters 26-38	Chemicals
Chapters 39-49	Articles of Plastic, Leather, Wood and Paper
Chapters 50-63	Textiles
Chapters 64-84	Articles of Clothing, Ceramics, Glass, Iron and Copper
Chapters 85-97	Machinery, Locomotives, Aircraft, Ships, Furniture and so on

Once the correct chapter has been found it is then a matter of finding the appropriate sub-heading which identifies the goods more specifically and then the correct sub-sub-heading. As the classification number gets longer the identification of the goods becomes more and more exact.

Examples

A Riding Horse

01	Live Animals
0101	Horses, Asses, Mules and Hinnies (male horse/ female donkey, before you ask)
010119	Horses (Not for breeding) (HS Level)
01011990	Horses (Not for slaughter)

Thus 01011990 would describe a horse not for breeding and not for slaughter. Admittedly not a 'horse for riding' but there isn't much else you could do with a horse, is there?

X-ray tubes

90　　　　Medical and Surgical
9022　　　Apparatus based on the use of X-rays
90223000 X-ray tubes

It will be clear that the UK exporter would need detailed advice from the overseas buyer to assess the most appropriate tariff classification. What is meant by 'most appropriate'? The fact is that not only are tariff classifications highly complex, but also it may be that an exporter could legitimately describe goods in a variety of ways. Should this be the case it is potentially beneficial to consider carefully the description and tariff number quoted to importing Customs. However it must be made very clear that it is vital that the correct and most accurate tariff number is declared as mis-declaration is an extremely serious offence and the penalties can prove very expensive to all parties.

Thus it may be perfectly acceptable to describe parts for the diesel engines of tractors as either 'Agricultural equipment and parts thereof' or 'Diesel engines and parts thereof'. Even if the overseas Customs reject the latter description in favour of the former, it is unlikely that penalties would be imposed for mis-declaration (although there are never any guarantees). As an example of a clear mis-declaration, describing children's buckets and spades for the beach as 'Agricultural equipment' is not a description that could very easily be justified.

It is also advisable that brand names or proprietary names of products are avoided as they will not be used as part of a tariff description. Likewise it is possible to describe goods on the basis of the materials of which they are made, but it is the application to which the products are put which is often more important. Describing computer hardware as 'Plastic components' would clearly be unacceptable.

So exporters should take advice from their buyers and at least consider if there is scope for a legitimate choice of product descriptions used for particular overseas markets. It should be said, however, that Customs & Excise would adopt the view that the tariff allows only one valid classification for any commodity.

Origin

Once overseas Customs have accepted the tariff classification, or
re-classified the goods themselves, then the tariff will indicate
the range of controls, such as duty, tax, licence and quota, which
apply to each particular commodity. In the case of the Community tariff the controls are actually integrated into the body of
the classification (known as the Schedule). Such controls may
be selectively applicable depending on the origin of the goods.
This is because the EC has agreed a wide range of free and
preferential trade agreements with other trading nations. These
can be broken down into:

Free Trade	EFTA COUNTRIES (Austria, Sweden, Switzerland, Finland, Norway & Iceland) Malta, Israel, Cyprus, Faroe Islands (previously Yugoslavia) Algeria, Morocco and Tunisia Egypt, Jordan, Lebanon and Syria Poland, Hungary, Czech and Slovak Republics
Preferential Trade	African, Caribbean and Pacific (ACP) (known as the Lome Convention countries) Overseas Countries and Territories (OCT) (ex-colonial countries of EC member states) Generalised System of Preferences (GSP) (other developing and under-developed countries)
EC Association	Turkey (transitional period towards full membership)

The Free Trade agreements above are all bi-lateral, that is they
give EC goods free entry into the overseas market as well as
vice-versa. The Preferential agreements, which allow for free or
reduced duty , are sometimes applicable to EC imports only and
not necessarily EC exports to those countries.

Figure 10.6: European Community C of O

1 Consignor	No. **FG** 616035	ORIGINAL
	EUROPEAN COMMUNITY	

2 Consignee

CERTIFICATE OF ORIGIN

3 Country of Origin

4 Transport details (Optional)

5 Remarks

6 Item number; marks; numbers, number and kind of packages; description of goods

7 Quantity

8 THE UNDERSIGNED AUTHORITY CERTIFIES THAT THE GOODS DESCRIBED ABOVE ORIGINATE IN THE COUNTRY SHOWN IN BOX 3

MANCHESTER CHAMBER OF COMMERCE & INDUSTRY

Place and date of issue; name, signature and stamp of competent authority

Manchester

..............19

Manchester Chamber of Commerce & Industry

DTI/XP 13026

The John Oldham Printing Group Huddersfield

Thus it may well be that the duty, and perhaps other controls, that commodities attract can be avoided by their originating in particular countries of supply. All such trade agreements are based on very precise rules of origin.

If goods are genuinely wholly produced in a particular country then proof of origin is not normally a problem, however where goods are processed in some way it can become more difficult. The principle used by most Customs authorities is that of **sufficient transformation**. In simple terms, the Customs will require a breakdown of the component elements of a product and require a sufficient proportion of the value of the finished product to be originating, that is wholly produced, in that country. At the very least the processing of the goods should change the whole of the tariff classification. In practice Customs will insist on varying proportions of value to be originating.

Rules of origin are invariably very complex because the Customs are attempting to control what is known as **Deflection of Trade**. This describes the shipping of goods via a third country to establish an erroneous origin. Foe example Japanese Video Cassette Recorders, shipped into Malta, where they are re-labelled and repacked and shipped into the EC as of Maltese origin and therefore duty free. Clearly repacking is never 'sufficient transformation' and such a process would be a serious offence.

Certificates of Origin (C of O)

We have already established that the export invoice is sometimes accompanied by other supporting documents. In the cases where a declaration of origin on the invoice is insufficient then a variety of other documents may be appropriate dependant on the country of destination, and, in some cases the goods. These are:

1 **European Community C of O** (Figure 10.6.)
   Issued by Chambers of Commerce they can be certified by the Chamber, along with the invoices, or may be self-certified by the exporter.

Figure 10.7: Arab British C of O

CERTIFICATE OF ORIGIN

Consignor : المرسل 1	K 201958	ORIGINAL
	Consignor's ref	4
Consignee : المرسل اليه 2	شهادة منشأ	
	CERTIFICATE OF ORIGIN	
	Originated in : منشأها 5	
Method of Transport : مرسلة بواسطة 3	Remarks : ملاحظات 11	

Marks and Numbers : الأرقام والعلامات	Quantity and Kind of Packages : كمية ونوع الطرود	Description of Goods : مواصفات البضاعة	Weight (gross & net) : الوزن (الصافي والاجمالي) 6

THE UNDERSIGNED AUTHORITY CERTIFIES THAT THE GOODS DESCRIBED ABOVE ORIGINATE IN THE COUNTRY SHOWN IN BOX 5

تشهد السلطة الموقعة أدناه أن البضائع المذكورة أعلاه منشأها البلاد المذكورة في الحقل رقم ٥

غرفة التجارة العربية البريطانية
ARAB-BRITISH CHAMBER OF COMMERCE

مكان وتاريخ الاصدار Place and Date of Issue   Issuing Authority سلطة الاصدار

861   Arab-British Chamber of Commerce

2 **Arab British Chamber of Commerce C of O**

As above, but specific to Arab League trade and certified and legalised along with the invoices. (Figure 10.7.)

3 **Certificates of Value & Origin**

Described earlier in this chapter as a form of export invoice. The origin declaration is incorporated in the invoice. May apply to ACP, OCT or GSP countries.

4 **Status and Movement Certificates**

In the previous chapter we identified the function of the Transit element of the SAD in terms of moving through Customs posts of transit. You may recall that since the 1st of January 1993 this has applied only to goods destined for EFTA countries. In such cases the T2 status of goods is also certified by the transit document.

In addition, for all those free trade countries mentioned above, a specialized, so-called, Movement Certificate is appropriate. This is the EUR 1 which is a four page document requiring authentication by UK Customs. Such authentication may require the provision of proof of origin to the Customs authorities. For consignments below £3,585 in value (previously covered by the EUR 2), or where the exporter was previously allowed to issue EUR 1s which had been pre-authenticated by Customs, then the Movement Certificate is replaced by the following invoice declaration:

'I the undersigned, exporter of the goods covered by this document declare that, except where otherwise indicated, the goods meet the conditions to obtain originating status in preferential trade with ... (state EFTA country) and that the country of origin of the goods is ... (state EC member state).'

The above declaration is not appropriate to Poland, Hungary or the Czech and Slovak Republics where the full EUR 1 and EUR 2 are required. Also the EUR 2 is still applicable to low value postal consignments to Cyprus, Malta and Israel. It should be noted that value limits are subject to change.

Trade with Turkey is quite a specialized area as they are Associate members of the Community. Exports to Turkey are covered by a particular form of Movement Certificate, the **ATR 1.**

Figure 10.8: EUR 1 Movement Certificate

MOVEMENT CERTIFICATE

1. Exporter (Name, full address, country)	**EUR1 No.** P 017601
	See notes overleaf before completing this form.
	2. Certificate used in preferential trade between
3. Consignee (Name, full address, country) (Optional)	**THE EUROPEAN ECONOMIC COMMUNITY** and
	(Insert appropriate countries or groups of countries or territories)

4. Country, group of countries or territory in which the products are considered as originating EEC	5. Country, group of countries or territory of destination

6. Transport details (Optional)	7. Remarks

If goods are not packed indicate number of articles or state "in bulk" as appropriate.

8. Item number: marks & numbers	Number and kind of packages (1): description of goods	9. Gross weight (kg) or other measure (litres, cu. m, etc.)	10. Invoices (Optional)

(2) Complete only where the regulations of the exporting country or territory require.

11. CUSTOMS ENDORSEMENT	12. DECLARATION BY THE EXPORTER
Declaration certified Stamp	I, the undersigned, declare that the goods described above meet the conditions required for the issue of this certificate.
Export document (2):	
Form————————No.————	
Customs office	
Issuing country or territory:	
UNITED KINGDOM	(Place and date)
Date	
(Signature)	(Signature)

C 1299   1   F 4990 (August, 1984)

Printed in the UK for HMSO
Dd 8857711 3/85 600M FCS/0107

Whilst the major consequence of origin is the potential avoidance of Customs duties it should also be noted that origin will also be relevant to the application of other controls such as quotas and to the collection of accurate trade statistics. It may even be the case that financial aid has been linked with purchases from particular countries.

Value

Once Customs have decided on the **description** and the correct **origin** of the goods then it may be the case that ad valorem charges are applicable. In such a case the invoice value, often referred to as the Transaction Value, serves as the base for the calculation of charges, invariably a CIF or CIP value. In the cases where the charge is specific to a particular quantity it is still the invoice which supplies the relevant information. In the UK, as in a number of other countries, a statement of value is required, in addition to the invoice, for anything but low value consignments. These statements are the C105 and C109 (General Valuation Statement) in the UK and are often lodged by the clearing agent on the basis of information provided by the trader.

Just as with description and origin the Customs procedures are designed to avoid any manipulation of the value of consignments which could cause anything but an 'equitable market value' to be quoted. The potential manipulation is, of course, an under-valuation of the goods in order to minimise the duties and taxes payable on such value. The importer may, for example have already paid in advance or be arranging transfers of funds for elements of value not invoiced. Invoice valuations may be rejected by Customs in which case they have other methods of arriving at an acceptable value, (to them that is). Within the EC there are in fact five other methods of valuation if the invoice value is not acceptable.

It may seem rather silly but there can also be cases where values on invoices are actually over-estimated. The offence here is usually an infringement of that country's exchange control regulations, that is, the buyer is moving hard currency out of the country. This may be held illegally in bank accounts outside the country.

The information given throughout this chapter leads us to the inevitable conclusion that sensible exporters should take a direct interest in the controls which their goods attract at destination, and how the document set prepared here affects the application of such controls. The three vital pieces of information, description, origin and value are probably the pieces of information most manipulated in international trade. The reputable exporter should be wary of the consequences of co-operation in obvious mis-declarations as, whilst direct action may only be taken against the importer, the long term consequences to their trade in that market may be unacceptable. It may also be the case that this leads to export mis-declarations to UK Customs for which the chance of more direct action is obviously greater.

Customs Management

This, and the previous two chapters, have examined the whole range of Customs controls from export, through transit to import. The first point to bear in mind is that compliance with Customs requirements is mandatory and, for no other reason than non-compliance can be expensive, it is important that exporters are aware of those procedures which affect their exports. Remember the point made at the beginning of chapter 8 – ignorance is never an excuse. However if we start from the premise that compliance is essential this does not preclude opportunities for good management to reduce the impact of Customs controls on a company's international trade.

An analogy, which may not appear at first to be directly relevant, is that of a case which was heard at the European Court of Justice some years ago. The company concerned had been fined a very large amount of money for unlawful claims of agricultural subsidies and its appeal was being heard. The peculiarities of the Court's procedure require that all the legal arguments are prepared in writing prior to the brief verbal hearings. In this case their argument was in three parts:

1 We committed no offence and should not be fined at all.
2 We did commit the offences but the fine should be reduced.
3 Can we have time to pay (please)?

The fact that all three arguments were presented at once seemed totally logical to the advocates concerned.

So how is this relevant to the way exporters approach Customs procedures? It is simply that the same logic applies. You should:

1 Avoid controls and charges completely.
2 Minimize the costs, and consequences, of those that cannot be avoided.
3 Take as long as possible to comply or pay.

Avoidance

First, a very important point. Evasion of Customs controls is illegal, avoidance is good management. There is a growing number of 'Tax Avoidance' consultants, but no 'Tax Evasion' consultants. Of the procedures we have examined in the last three chapters several do provide opportunities.

Description
A selective and informed choice of product description could reduce charges and avoid quota restrictions.

Origin
Correct statements of origin, properly documented, can again avoid all charges.

Inward Processing Relief
If imported goods are re-exported relief or drawback of duty can be arranged.

Returned Goods
Goods exported and subsequently returned within three years, in basically the same state, can avoid duty and tax.

Temporary exports

Certain types of goods which are temporarily exported can avoid all Customs controls and charges by the use of an ATA Carnet. We have seen that a Carnet is simply a book of vouchers. In the case of the ATA Carnet ('Temporary Admission ... Admission Temporaire), which is issued by Chambers of Commerce, three categories of goods are covered: exhibition goods; samples; and professional equipment.

All of these will enter one or more countries only to leave at a later date. As long as all the goods which enter actually leave, then the vouchers of the ATA Carnet replace all other Customs procedures.

It should be emphasized that this does preclude the sale of exhibition goods or samples in the overseas market. Also if samples are genuinely of no commercial value then they are not subject to Customs controls anyway and the ATA would be irrelevant. Remember, it is Customs who decide what is of commercial value and what is not. Professional equipment can be a very wide definition including tools, measuring equipment, props, costumes, sound and lighting systems, instruments, and display and demonstration equipment.

Up to the end of 1992 the EC used an equivalent document called the Community Carnet, but since the removal of internal frontiers on the 1st of January 1993, this document has become obsolete. By definition the ATA is also of no relevance to EC movements.

Freezones

A number of ports and depots throughout the world have been designated, by their government authorities, as Freezones. They are areas in which goods are exempt from Customs controls. In the UK they are:

Belfast Airport
Birmingham
Cardiff
Southampton
Prestwick Airport
Liverpool

and there are many more throughout the world. They typically receive goods as imports and allow a wide range of handling, and selective processing, without any Customs interference until the goods leave the Freezone area. If goods are re-exported they actually attract no Customs controls whatsoever.

Minimize

If we cannot actually avoid controls and charges then we should look to at least reduce them to a minimum.

Valuation
It is important that the genuine transaction value is evidenced by the invoice but it may also be the case that certain monetary amounts can legitimately be excluded. This does differ from one country to another but it may be that items such as on-carriage (the transport costs from port of entry to final destination), turn-over taxes, commissions, royalties and documentation fees can, and should be, excluded from the valuation.

Outward Processing Relief
Where goods are exported and re-imported following processing, the re-imports attract relief of part of the duty. The procedure must be agreed prior to the original export.

Period Entry
The cost of Customs entries can be reduced by the use of computer systems to make periodic entries on tape or disc. The opportunities for regular exporters to do this are continually increasing and sufficient export consignments can lead to:

Local Export Control
This allows export clearance of full loads out of approved exporter's premises.

Take time

Whatever charges and controls are unavoidable it makes sense to take as much time as is allowed before compliance or payment.

Warehousing

Many countries, including the whole of the EC, allow imported goods to remain in a Customs warehouse, in which case they do not become subject to Customs controls. In the EC, goods can be left for up to six years in the warehouse, but the handling allowed is severely limited in that the goods can be checked and re-packed but no real processing will be allowed. The goods do not have to comply with controls or pay duties and tax until they leave the warehouse.

Deferment

Both duty and tax can be deferred in many countries so that it is paid some time after the time of import. In the UK approved traders and agents can supply guarantees which defer the payment of duty until the 15th of the following month. Tax, such as VAT, can be deferred in the same way, or, for EC imports, can be accounted for on the VAT returns.

Conclusion

The last three chapters have covered what might appear to be a bewildering array of customs procedures and controls. There is, however, a logic to the current situation facing UK exporters and there is little doubt that an appreciation of the developments, particularly since our membership of the Community in 1973, will lead to easier compliance with mandatory procedures and a greater awareness of the possibilities for cost saving which can be provided by a broader knowledge and better understanding of Customs requirements.

Questions for Discussion

1 The UK exporter is required to produce export invoices in a variety of forms. Describe the different types of invoices in common use, and how the exporter would arrange for their production.

2 An understanding of the role and importance of Customs and the available procedures is essential to all those engaged in international trade.

   (a) Outline the changes that were made to the Customs tariff used by UK exporters and freight forwarders in January 1988.

   (b) Why is it so important that exporters know the correct tariff code for both UK and overseas customs authorities?

3 Write brief notes on the following:

   (a) EUR 1;

   (b) ATR 1.

11

Risk Management

The exporter faces a great many risks in conducting business internationally quite apart from the fact that the buyers may not be particularly keen to buy their goods. It is not the purpose of this book to look in any detail at the pure marketing risks which all organisations face in attempting to identify and satisfy, profitably, demand overseas. Even assuming that we have an established market for our products and services there still exist many potential practical problems in ensuring that such business actually leads to the receipt of sufficient revenues. We can identify three major risks which must be addressed by the typical exporter.

Physical Risk

Goods moving internationally face a very real risk of physical loss or damage. This may simply be damage caused to the goods in handling and transit, possibly due to inadequate packing or bad handling, or loss due to accidental diversion or deliberate pilferage or theft. Because of the length of international journeys, the range of transport modes involved, the increased handling and the great variety of conditions encountered by the goods then it is clear that the risks are generally far greater for export consignments than those for domestic movements. A statistical breakdown of the causes of loss or damage on a international journey would look something like:

Poor handling and stowage	44%
Physical damage on/in conveyance	33%
Theft and pilferage	22%
General Average	1% (see later)

It is possible for the exporter to arrange for insurance cover for all of these risks.

Credit Risk

Even if the goods arrive complete and undamaged the problems do not stop there because there is the risk that the buyer will not actually pay for the goods. This may be perfectly legitimate in that there is a contractual dispute between buyer and seller; after all the exporter may have shipped total rubbish to the importer. However we must accept that non-payment may be the result of the dishonour of the buyer. This takes many forms from simply not accepting the goods, through taking over the goods and merely delaying payment, to simply not paying for the goods. It is possible for the exporter to arrange insurance cover for such risks.

Exchange Risk

Even if we are able to deliver goods in good condition to the buyer and the satisfied buyer pays us on time it is still possible for the unwary exporter to lose money. In the event that the exporter is invoicing in a foreign currency it is possible that the Pounds Sterling funds eventually received, following exchange of the foreign currency revenues, are less than was anticipated because of fluctuations in the relevant exchange rates. It is **not** possible for the exporter to arrange insurance cover for such risks. It is however possible to manage for the possibility of such risks.

Cargo (Marine) Insurance

Many form of insurance cover exist throughout the world but there is little doubt that one of the oldest forms of insurance is that of marine insurance. In the UK the first rationalization of the marine insurance market was devised by an Elizabethan Act of Parliament in 1601, to be followed by the development of the Corporation of Lloyd's which allowed, and still allows, underwriters to offer insurance cover. Until quite recently the language of marine insurance continued to use the flowery phrases of Elizabethan English, but modernization in the 1980s has supplied us with more efficient, but some might say, a lot less interesting policies.

The principle of 'averaging' is at the heart of marine insurance and is perfectly described by a phrase taken from the original Elizabethan Act, 'so that ... it cometh to pass that ... the loss lighteth rather easily upon many than heavily upon few, and rather upon them that adventure not than those that do adventure ...'. Wonderful stuff, and a very precise description of the fact that if only one or two people carried all the risks of, for example, a sea voyage, then they might be less inclined to adventure. It was in fact an encouragement to trade internationally because the risks were shared by a large number of people; in fact the Act goes on to say, '... whereby all merchants, especially the younger sort, are allured to venture more willingly and more freely'. The underwriters of such risks were actually so called because they signed their name under the risk, stated on 'the slip', along with other underwriters who also took part of the risk. To this day Lloyd's underwriters accepts risks on behalf of their 'syndicates' and company underwriters accept risks on behalf of their companies.

It should be noted that modern international trade now involves modes of transport other than sea freight and it is probably more appropriate to use the expression '**cargo insurance**' which covers road, rail and air freight movements, as well as the common combinations of transport modes now used.

General Average

This is one of the oldest principles of cargo insurance and still has relevance today. It covers the situation where

> there is extraordinary sacrifice or expenditure, intentionally and reasonably incurred, for the purpose of preserving the imperilled property involved in the common maritime adventure.

This will include situations where goods are jettisoned to save the ship, or are damaged by water used to extinguish a fire, or the vessel is diverted to a port of refuge, and many other situations where loss of certain goods preserves the rest of the cargo and the ship. The basic principle is that all the parties involved, including the vessel owners, contribute to the loss. General Average is declared and an Average Adjuster will, eventually, calculate the amount of the claim. It is often necessary for the cargo owners to sign a General Average Bond and for the insurers to provide a General Average Guarantee, in order to obtain possession of the goods from the carrier. As all standard policies cover General Average claims then the cost of the claim will be met by the insurers.

Insurance?

An exporter can choose not to insure the goods against loss or damage in transit and simply carry this risk. This does, however pose a number of problems:

1 The terms of sale agreed between seller and buyer may impose a requirement on the seller to arrange for cargo insurance. This would apply to terms such as CIF, CIP, and may apply to DDU and DDP. In such cases the seller would have to arrange adequate insurance and prove it with documentation.
2 In the event of loss or damage it may be that action is possible against the carriers in charge of the goods at the time. The carriers have limitations on their liability (see chapter 7)

and it requires some expertise to sustain successful claims. One of the advantages of a Cargo Insurance Policy is that the exporter does not have to carry out actions against liable carriers.

The situation in practice is that the vast majority of exporters arrange for insurance cover against the physical risk of loss or damage to the goods in transit. So how do they arrange this?

Specific (Voyage) Policy

It is perfectly feasible for an exporter with an international consignment to ship to approach an insurance company, invariably through an insurance broker, and request that an insurance policy be drawn up for that particular consignment. This is often referred to as a Voyage Policy as it covers only that specific shipment. A typical company Voyage Policy form is illustrated in figure 11.1 and the traditional Lloyd's Voyage Policy in figure 11.2. It should be noted that the Lloyd's policy, the SG (Ship or Goods) form in use from 1779, became obsolete in 1983 with the introduction of the modern language Marine All Risks Policy (MAR).

Figure 11.1: A typical company Voyage Policy

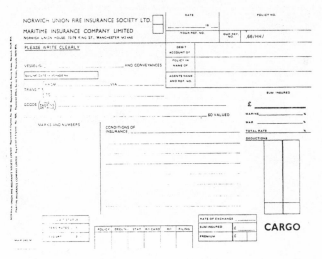

Figure 11.2: A traditional Lloyd's Voyage Policy

(No.)

Any person not an Underwriting Member of Lloyd's subscribing this Policy, or any person uttering the same if an authorised, will be liable to be proceeded against under Lloyd's Acts.

S.G.

£ 559.00

Printed at Lloyd's, London, England.

INSTITUTE DANGEROUS DRUGS CLAUSE.

"It is understood and agreed that no claim under this Policy will be paid in respect of drugs to which the various International Conventions relating to Opium and other dangerous drugs apply unless

(1) the drugs shall be expressly declared as such in the Policy and the name of the country from which, and the name of the country to which they are consigned shall be specifically stated in the Policy

(2) the proof of loss is accompanied either by a licence, certificate or authorisation issued by the Government of the country to which the drugs are consigned showing that the importation of the consignment into that country has been approved by that Government, or, alternatively, by a licence, certificate or authorisation issued by the Government of the country from which the drugs are consigned showing that the export of the consignment to the destination named has been approved by that Government; and

(3) the route by which the drugs were conveyed was usual and customary."

No Policy or other Contract dated on or after 1st Jan., 1924, will be recognised by the Committee of Lloyd's as entitling the holder to the benefit of the Funds and/or Guarantees lodged by the Underwriters of the Policy or Contract as security for their liabilities unless it bears at foot the Seal of Lloyd's Policy Signing Office.

Be it known that Reckitt and Watson Ltd.

as well in *their* own name as for and in the name and names of all and every other person or persons to whom the same doth, may, or shall appertain, in part or in all, doth make assurance and cause *themselves* and them, and every of them, to be insured, lost or not lost, at and from

Warehouse Hackney via London to Warehouse Belo Horizonte via Rio de Janeiro

Upon any kind of goods and merchandises, and also upon the body, tackle, apparel, ordnance, munition, artillery, boat, and other furniture, of and in the good ship or vessel called the Rail and/or Conveyance and S.S. Ionian sailing 1st May, 19xx.

whereof is master under God, for this present voyage, or whosoever else shall go for master in the said ship, or by whatsoever other name or names the same ship, or the master thereof, is or shall be named or called ; beginning the adventure upon the said goods and merchandises from the loading thereof aboard the said ship, *as above* upon the said ship, &c., *as above* and so shall continue and endure, during her abode there, upon the said ship, &c. And further, until the said ship, with all her ordnance, tackle, apparel, &c., and goods and merchandises whatsoever shall be arrived at *as above* upon the said ship, &c., until she hath moored at anchor twenty-four hours in good safety ; and upon the goods and merchandises, until the same be there discharged and safely landed. And it shall be lawful for the said ship, &c., in this voyage, to proceed and sail to and touch and stay at any ports or places whatsoever *and wheresoever for all purposes* without prejudice to this insurance. The said ship, &c., goods and merchandises, &c., for so much as concerns the assured by agreement between the assured and assurers in this policy, are and shall be valued at

£559.00 on 5 cases electric drills.
With average in accordance with the terms and conditions of the Institute Cargo Clauses (W.A.) including Warehouse to Warehouse.

Touching the adventures and perils which we the assurers are contented to bear and do take upon us in this voyage : they are of the seas, men of war, fire, enemies, pirates, rovers, thieves, jettisons, letters of mart and countermart, surprisals, takings at sea, arrests, restraints, and detainments of all kings, princes, and people, of what nation, condition, or quality soever, barratry of the master and mariners, and of all other perils, losses, and misfortunes, that have or shall come to the hurt, detriment, or damage of the said goods and merchandises, and ship, &c., or any part thereof. And in case of any loss or misfortune it shall be lawful to the assured, their factors, servants and assigns, to sue, labour, and travel for, in and about the defence, safeguard, and recovery of the said goods and merchandises, and ship, &c., or any part thereof, without prejudice to this insurance ; to the charges whereof we, the assurers, will contribute each one according to the rate and quantity of his sum herein assured. And it is especially declared and agreed that no acts of the insurer or insured in recovering, saving, or preserving the property insured shall be considered as a waiver, or acceptance of abandonment. And it is agreed by us, the insurers, that this writing or policy of assurance shall be of as much force and effect as the surest writing or policy of assurance heretofore made in Lombard Street, or in the Royal Exchange, or elsewhere in London.

1. Warranted free of capture, seizure, arrest, restraint or detainment, and the consequences thereof or any attempt thereat ; also from the consequences of hostilities or warlike operations, whether there be a declaration of war or not ; but this warranty shall not exclude collision, contact with any fixed or floating object (other than a mine or torpedo), stranding, heavy weather or fire unless caused directly and independently of the nature of the voyage or service which the vessel concerned or, in the case of a collision, any other vessel involved therein, is performing) by a hostile act by or against a belligerent power ; and for the purpose of this warranty "power " includes any authority maintaining naval, military or air forces in association with a power.

Further warranted free from the consequences of civil war, revolution, rebellion, insurrection, or civil strife arising therefrom, or piracy.

2. Warranted free of loss or damage

   (a) caused by strikers, locked-out workmen, or persons taking part in labour disturbances, riots or civil commotions ;

   (b) resulting from strikes, lock-outs, labour disturbances, riots or civil commotions.

   (c) Should the risks excluded by Clause 1 (F.C. & S. Clause) be reinstated in this Policy by deletion of the said clause, or should the risks or any of them mentioned in that clause or the risks of mines, torpedoes, bombs or other causes of war be insured under this Policy, Clause (b) below shall become operative and anything contained in this contract which is inconsistent with Clause (b) or which affords more extensive protection against the aforesaid risks than that afforded by the Institute War Clauses relevant to the particular form of transit covered by this Insurance is null and void.

   (b) This Policy is warranted free of any claim based upon loss of, or frustration of, the insured voyage or adventure caused by arrests restraints or detainments of Kings Princes Peoples Usurpers or persons attempting to usurp power.

And so we, the assurers, are contented, and do hereby promise and bind ourselves, each one for his own part, our heirs, executors, and goods to the assured, their executors, administrators, and assigns, for the true performance of the premises, confessing ourselves paid the consideration due unto us for this assurance by the assured, at and after the rate of

25p %

IN WITNESS whereof we, the assurers, have subscribed our names and sums assured in *LONDON, as hereinafter appears.*
N.B.—Corn, fish, salt, fruit, flour, and seed are warranted free from average, unless general, or the ship be stranded ; sugar, tobacco, hemp, flax, hides and skins are warranted free from average under five pounds per cent., and all other goods, also the ship and freight, are warranted free from average under three pounds per cent. unless general, or the ship be stranded.

Now know Ye that We, the Assurers, members of the Syndicate(s) whose definitive Number(s) in the attached list are set out in the Table overleaf, or attached overleaf, hereby bind Ourselves, each for his own part and not one for another, and in respect of his due proportion only, to pay or make good to the Assured all such Loss and/or Damage which he or they may sustain by any one or more of the aforesaid perils, and so that the due proportion for which each of Us the Assurer is liable shall be ascertained by reference to his proportion as ascertained according to the said list of the Amount, Percentage or Proportion of the total Sum assured which is in the said Table set opposite the definitive Number of the Syndicate of which such Assurer is a member.

IN WITNESS whereof the Manager of Lloyd's Policy Signing Office has subscribed his Name on behalf of each of Us.

LLOYD'S POLICY SIGNING OFFICE.

M.E. Wallington

Dated in London, the 2nd April, 19xx. MANAGER.

(13-11-80)
(15-1-43)
(16-6-50)
(90-11-61)
(75-2-64)

L.P.O. 60

(In the event of loss or damage which may result in a claim under this Insurance, immediate notice should be given to the Lloyd's Agent at the port or place where the loss or damage is discovered in order that he may examine the goods and issue a survey report.)

It may be difficult to make out the fine print of the SG form but an examination would reveal that the cover offered is somewhat antiquated as in, 'men of war, fire, enemies, pirates, rovers, thieves, jettisons, letters of mart and countermart, surprisals, takings at sea, arrests, restraints, and detainments of all kings, princes, and people ...'. Whilst pirates do still attack cargo vessels it will be clear that modern trade requires cover which is a little more sophisticated. Incidentally a letter of mart permits piracy on certain foreign vessels, and was granted, for example, to Francis Drake by Elizabeth I, the letter of counter-mart saying you have to stop now. For many years this basic Lloyd's policy was extended by the addition of clauses produced by the Institute of London Underwriters, known as the Institute Cargo Clauses, which were basically 'All Risks', 'With Average' (WA) covering specified partial loss, and 'Free from Particular Average' (FPA) excluding part losses, War Clauses and Strikes, Riots and Civil Commotions Clauses (SRCC) were often added as well as a number of quite specialized clauses covering particular situations or types of goods. The update in 1983 saw the SG form replaced by a very simple MAR policy, the cover being expressed in the new clauses which are now (A), (B) or (C), plus War Clauses and Strikes Clauses. In simple terms, Cargo Clauses (A) are the equivalent of 'All Risks' and (B) covers less than (A) and (C) covers less than (B), with a corresponding decrease in the insurance premiums. There is also an Institute Cargo Clauses (Air) which are the equivalent of the (A) clauses but obviously for air movements. A detailed examination of the clauses provided by the insurance underwriters or brokers would clearly be of use to the exporter, but a brief comparison of the clauses is shown below.

	(A)	(B)	(C)
Loss or damage reasonably attributable to:			
Accidental damage, theft, malicious damage	✓	–	–
Fire or explosion	✓	✓	✓
Vessel stranded, grounded, sunk or capsized	✓	✓	✓
Collision with any external object except water	✓	✓	✓
Discharge of cargo at a port of distress	✓	✓	✓
Earthquake, volcanic eruption or lightning	✓	✓	–

Theft	✓	–	–

Loss or damage caused by:

General Average sacrifice	✓	✓	✓
Jettison	✓	✓	✓
Washing overboard	✓	✓	–
Entry of sea water	✓	✓	–
Total loss of any package overboard or dropped whilst loading or unloading	✓	✓	–

Later in this chapter we will look at what might be seen as more important, that is, what risks are excluded from these policies.

Therefore an exporter approaching an insurer for a Voyage Policy would now receive a MAR policy (figure 11.3) with attached clauses and pay the appropriate premiums.

Figure 11.3: Marine All Risks (MAR) Policy

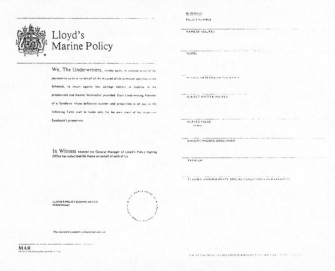

This is a perfectly feasible operation for the exporter making, perhaps, one or two consignments a month but it would clearly be very time consuming to approach an insurer for potentially hundreds, or even thousands, of shipments which the average exporter will be making. There has to be a better way, and, of course, there is.

Open policy

The most common situation is that exporters approach insurance companies and agree the raising of a policy which is drawn up to cover many shipments and not just one. This may be a **floating policy** which is raised for a particular value which is gradually reduced by the value of each shipment until it is used up and requires renewal. This type of policy is less common than it used to be, particularly because they often require the pay-ment of an averaged premium in advance. By far the most common form of policy is properly referred to as the **permanently open policy**, so called because it will be drawn up for a period of time, subject to renewal, and will allow any number of shipments over that period. The expression often used is that the policy is 'always open irrespective of declarations'. The wording of such a policy, designed to cover every shipment by that particular exporter, might be:

Per: Any Conveyances and/or Power Vessel or held covered at a premium to be arranged and/or Air and/or Parcel Post.

Voyage: World/World via any route and including transshipment.

On: Electrical Materials and/or other materials.

Such a policy could hardly be more open, covering the shipment of any materials, from anywhere and to anywhere, by any route, and by any means of transport. It will usually contain a schedule of premium rates which will depend on the country of destination and the level of cover, and the Institute Cargo Clauses detailing the actual cover.

These open policies are sometimes referred to as **declaration policies** because the exporter is making shipments which the insurers know nothing about until they are declared to them, which they must be periodically. But first the exporter has a problem with the document set.

Under the contracts we mentioned earlier in which the exporter is responsible for arranging, and paying for, cargo insurance then there is a clear need to include, in the set of documents,

Figure 11.4: Example of an insurance certificate

ORIGINAL   CERTIFICATE OF INSURANCE   No. MCR/ 130079

Exporter

Exporter's Reference

EAGLE STAR

MARINE DEPARTMENT
EAGLE STAR HOUSE 58 MOSLEY STREET MANCHESTER M60 1QS

This is to Certify that

have Insured the undermentioned Risk with this Company.

Marine Insurance Policy No.

Vessel/Aircraft Etc.	Port of Loading	Insured Value (state currency)
Port of Discharge	Place of Delivery	

Marks, Nos. and Container No.; No. and Kind of Packages; Description of Goods (specify Nature of Hazard if any)

CONDITIONS OF INSURANCE

Subject to the following Clauses:

Institute Cargo Clauses (A)/(Air)
Institute War Clauses (Cargo)/(Air Cargo)
Institute Strikes Clauses (Cargo)/(Air Cargo)
Institute Classification Clause
Institute Radioactive Contamination
Exclusion Clause
Institute Replacement Clause as applicable.

The Institute Clauses stated herein are
those current at the time of
commencement of the risk hereunder.

NOTE:– It is necessary for the Assured to give prompt notice to Underwriters when they become aware of an event for which they are 'held covered' under this insurance and the right to such cover is dependent on compliance with this obligation.

IMPORTANT.– IN ORDER TO FACILITATE THE SETTLEMENT OF CLAIMS THE ASSURED ARE ADVISED AS FOLLOWS:

SURVEY AND PAYMENT OF CLAIMS: In the event of loss or damage for which the Company may be liable, immediate application for survey should be made to

or to the nearest Institute of London Underwriters' agent (see local directories) or to the nearest Lloyd's agent.

CLAIMS PAYABLE IN

EAGLE STAR INSURANCE COMPANY LIMITED	For
J. H. Bishop *Chairman* This Certificate is not valid until countersigned by a duly authorised person.	Dated Signature

HEAD OFFICE: 60 ST MARY AXE LONDON EC3A 8JQ

some documentary proof that the contractual obligation to arrange insurance cover has been performed. The problem is that the exporter only has one open policy and it is not practical to send that to buyers as part of the document set. It is probably buried in the Company Secretary's safe anyway. The solution is that the exporter will produce an **insurance certificate** for each individual shipment.

Such certificates will be completed by the exporter on blank forms supplied by the insurers, which have been pre-signed by the underwriter. An example is reproduced in figure 11.4 and it will be clear that they contain only very basic information regarding the shipment. Thus the production of documentary evidence of the cargo insurance is accomplished by the relatively simple completion of an insurance certificate, and this is invariably acceptable. The only situation in which an insurance certificate would not be acceptable is where a Letter of Credit insists on an insurance policy. In such a case the bank would reject a certificate as being inferior to a policy and the exporter would have to obtain a Voyage Policy from the insurers, or, of course, have the Letter of Credit changed.

Figure 11.5: Example of a declaration form

EAGLE STAR

MONTH 19

MARINE DEPARTMENT FROM: DECLN NO.

DATE	METHOD OF TRANSIT/VESSEL	VOYAGE/TRANSIT	INTEREST AND PACKING	INSURED VALUE	RATE	PREMIUM
				£		

Finally the exporter has to declare all the shipments made, to the insurance company, in order for them to calculate, and invoice for, the insurance premiums. This is done periodically, usually monthly, either on paper declaration forms supplied by the insurers (figure 11.5), or by providing copies of the certificates produced over that period. It is possible for such information to be supplied on computer tape or disk or even transmitted direct into the insurance companies' computers as electronic messages. (EDI is discussed in chapter 13.)

Principles of Insurance

It is important that exporters have a basic understanding of some of the underpinning principles of insurance generally, and particularly their practical implications to cargo insurance.

Insurable interest

This expression was actually used in chapter 3 with reference to one of the functions of trade terms such as FOB, FCA, CIP and so on, in that they identified a point in the journey where the risk of loss or damage to the goods transferred from the seller to the buyer. Technically there is actually a transfer of the 'insurable interest' in the goods.

The principle of insurable interest is a vital one to all forms of insurance. In order to take out a policy the policy holder must have an insurable interest in the insured matter. In the case of cargo insurance this means that they must 'benefit from the safe arrival of the goods or be prejudiced by their loss'. Without such a principle it would be possible for any individual to take out an insurance policy on any eventuality they could think of. For example, a policy could be raised which paid if an English football player broke a leg during a game. If this policy were taken out by the Football Association then they would clearly have an insurable interest, but if it were possible for any individual to take out such a policy then it would simply be another form of gambling, that is a bet of premiums which pays out if a player actually does break a leg. Insurance is not there as a form of gambling and therefore the policy holder has to prove this 'vested interest'.

It is also necessary to prove insurable interest in order to make a claim against a policy and this can pose a problem if the claim is actually made by a non-policy holder. This situation can arise in contracts subject to CIP or CIF conditions. As explained in chapter 3, these terms mean that the seller is responsible for arranging the insurance and, as we have seen above, this will invariably be done under an open policy in the seller's name. However the 'insurable interest' transfers either at ship's rail port of **shipment** for CIF contracts or when the **first** carrier takes over the goods under CIP. Thus the responsibility for loss or damage to the goods transfers to the buyer at the port or depot in the UK even though the seller has insured right through to the final destination.

It is possible for the buyer to make a claim on the seller's open policy because of two clauses:

1 Claims Payable Abroad (CPA). The insurers will accept a claim either at the overseas destination, usually through the nearest Lloyd's or Company's agent, or here where the policy was issued. All they require is that the claim is properly documented, and as the documents can only be in one place then there is no possibility of dual claims. Thus it is perfectly possible for the buyer to pay the seller the full CIF or CIP value and use the documents to make the insurance claim for the insured value.

   Just what claims documents are required we will examine later but we still have the problem of the buyer establishing an insurable interest in order to make the claim. This is solved by:

2 Policy Proof of Interest (PPI). In simple terms this means that possession of the policy is sufficient to prove insurable interest. In reality it is the insurance certificate, and supporting claims documents, which provides such proof. Such certificates would be endorsed on the reverse side to make such a transfer possible, in the same way that a bill of lading may be endorsed to transfer title in the goods.

Indemnity

Most insurance is based on the fact that the insurers promise to indemnify the insured. That is, they promise to put them back into the situation they were in before the loss. It is obviously not a principle of life insurance. In practice the indemnity on cargo insurance policies is expressed as an amount of money, the insured value of the goods. Whilst it is possible that the insurers could replace lost or damaged goods with exact equivalents it is clearly impractical, and therefore cargo insurance is invariably based on Valued Policies.

The Marine Insurance Act 1906 specifies that the insured value of the goods must be the 'prime cost plus all expenses incidental to shipping plus charges of insurance'; in practice the typical insured value is CIF plus ten per cent. The additional ten per cent is there to represent the buyer's potential profit. After all, the seller's profit is in the ex-works price and if the goods had arrived then the buyer would presumably have made a profit on top of the CIF price they have agreed to pay. The insurance company are in fact indemnifying both parties. This seems even more logical when you consider the situation in which the buyer is making the claim. They claim the full CIF they have paid the seller plus a percentage to cover their lost profits. In this respect it is perfectly acceptable to the insurers to insure goods for CIF plus 20 per cent or CIF plus 30 per cent because the premiums are also calculated on the insured values.

It is possible to agree an 'excess' on the value in which case the exporter will always bear a percentage of the loss, and have no claim if the loss is below the excess amount. Alternatively a 'franchise' amount might be agreed in which case a loss below the amount would preclude a claim, as with the excess, but losses above the amount specified would be met in full, that is, the exporter would not carry any part of the loss as long as it exceeded the franchise percentage.

Uberrimae Fidei (utmost good faith)

Once again this is a principle which applies to all forms of insurance. The insurers are almost totally dependent on the insured to disclose any relevant information regarding the insured risks. Thus a person taking out a life insurance policy who failed to disclose a serious medical problem would find that the policy could be 'voided' by the insurers. There is an important application of Uberrimae Fidei to the type of open (declaration) policies commonly used for cargo insurance.

Imagine the situation in which an exporter makes a shipment by road to Germany at the beginning of June, and it arrives intact during the second week of June. At the end of June the seller must declare all the months shipments to the insurance company in order for them to calculate the premiums. However the safe arrival of the German consignment could persuade the seller to not declare the shipment because, after all, the insurance is not actually required for that consignment. This would be a clear and serious breach of good faith and, if deliberate, would almost certainly lead to the policy being voided, that is, cancelled by the insurers. It is obviously inequitable for the insured to avoid paying premiums on goods which they already know have arrived safely. Goods are declared 'safe or not safe, lost or not lost'. Good faith does work both ways. Imagine the situation in which the goods are actually written off due to a collision on their way to Germany. The insurance company's good faith is that they accept the claim, at the end of June, even though the loss occurred before declaration, that is, before they knew of the consignment.

Subrogation

In the event that loss or damage occurs due to an insured risk then a claim will be made on the insurance company. If we assume that the claim is successful then the insured will regard the matter as closed. However, if nothing else happens we have a carrier, who may well be liable for the loss or damage, who has apparently avoided any liability. It is the principle of subrogation which avoids this, in that it allows the insurance company to take action against liable carriers in the name of the insured. The exporter, or importer, must maintain any rights of action against carriers, by avoiding giving clean receipts and advising loss or damage as soon as possible, ideally within three days, but these rights are subrogated to the insurance company once the claim has been paid. It is very fair to the insured in that the claim must be paid first. The insurance company cannot make a claim on the carrier and only pay the insured if the action against the carrier is successful. The insured will have a valid claim irrespective of the carrier's liability. Also, in the unlikely event that the insurers actually receive more in their claim on the carrier than they have paid to the insured, then the insured receives the difference. The whole thing becomes somewhat more complicated because the carriers will often have taken out insurance to cover their liability to the owners of the goods. This is known as a Goods in Transit (GIT) policy and valid claims will be met by the carrier's insurance company. What this means is that claims against carriers are often made by insurance companies and that disputes may well be settled between the two insurance companies involved. See figure 11.6.

Figure 11.6: The process of subrogation

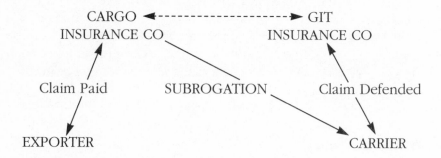

Contingency (seller's interest) insurance

Many exporters find that there are situations where they are making export shipments for which the buyer is responsible for cargo insurance. The most obvious would be CFR (C & F) shipments, although the same situation applies to FOB sales. In some markets CFR shipments are very common as the importer's country have a requirement that cargo insurance is taken out with one of their national insurance companies, rather than a foreign company in the seller's country. This is particularly common in African markets. The risk here is that loss or damage can occur and the buyer refuses to take up the goods or documents; it may even be that the buyer has not actually insured the goods. If the buyer attempts to avoid liability, and legal action is often pointless, it can lead to a substantial loss to the exporter. Seller's interest insurance covers the contingency that the buyer is responsible for insurance, loss or damage occurs, and the buyer has failed to insure. In such a case, and for a relatively small premium, the seller would be able to make a claim. It is often important that the existence of such cover is not revealed to the buyer.

Proximate Cause

It is perfectly reasonable for insurance companies to prefer that claims are made for loss or damage due to risks which are actually covered by the policy. In fact many claims fail simply because the cause of the loss is not an insured risk. Just what the insured is not covered for is covered below but first the principle of Proximate Cause needs to be explained. When a loss occurs it is often the result of not one clear event but of a series of events which, cumulatively, lead to a loss. What the insurers must do is establish the actual cause of the loss, what they describe as the 'active, efficient cause', that is the Proximate Cause. As an example of this in action consider a situation in which a road vehicle is in collision during transit. If goods are damaged in the collision then there is a valid claim as collision is an obvious insured risk. However if the goods are not damaged but the vehicle is, and this results in a delay of the journey for repairs, and your Christmas cards arrive at the wholesalers on Boxing Day then there is no claim because delay is not an insured risk. It is therefore important to investigate the process of events leading to a loss, and thus establish the Proximate Cause, and then ensure that this is an insured risk. Rather than list what risks are insured it is actually easier to identify those which are specifically excluded from the (A), (B) and (C) policies.

You are not insured for ...

1 Delay. As we have seen above, if any loss occurs because of the late arrival of the goods then there is no claim. It may be in this case that action is possible against the carrier, the transport conventions defining what would be considered unreasonable delay in delivery, but not against the insurers.

2 Wear and tear. The exporter has to plan for predictable factors which could lead to loss (perhaps of value) to the goods. Normal wear and tear is never covered by the policy and the exporter has to prepare for the possibility of, for example, a rough sea voyage. In fact the consequences of 'the ordinary action of the wind and waves', is not covered. It is, after all, no surprise that it gets a bit windy in the North Atlantic.

3 Inherent vice. This describes things which goods are apt to do and is therefore predictable. For example it is obvious that metal has a tendency to rust, particularly in damp conditions such as are found at sea, and the exporter must take steps to avoid such damage, by priming or the use of silicone gels or shrink-wrap, rather than rely on the insurance policy. Similarly cotton can rust, fishmeal ferment, concrete set and perishables go off, all of which must be managed by the exporter.

4 Ullage. This is almost a form of inherent vice but is specifically applied to liquids. In the context of cargo insurance it describes loss due to evaporation. It is a particular form of 'ordinary leakage or loss in weight or volume' which is excluded from policies.

5 Wilful misconduct of the assured. This may be obvious but it is extremely important in that the documentation supporting claims must prove that the claimant has acted prudently and that the loss is not the consequences of their direct actions or their negligence. A clear example of this would be to attempt to make a claim for damaged goods which included bills of lading which were claused 'inadequate packing'. Any claims where there is evidence of insufficient or unsuitable packing are likely to fail.

Claims documents

Assuming the claim is actually being made for the consequences of an insured risk the second reason that claims may fail is that they are not correctly documented. The insurance companies do not require excessive documentation and ask for nothing that is not relevant to the claim. The documents typically requested would include:

1 Original policy or certificate. Bearing in mind that the policy is proof of interest (that is, insurable interest) this is essential. It also describes the subject matter, insured value and appropriate clauses.
2 Invoices and packing specifications. Needed to assess the percentage of a part loss and specifically where lost or damaged goods were packed within the consignment.
3 Original bill of lading or other transport document. Proves the goods were in apparent good order and condition when shipped and evidences the contract of carriage, should action later be taken against the carrier.
4 Survey report or other evidence of loss or damage. An independent report of the nature and extent of the loss should ideally be produced by an approved agency, for example a Lloyd's Agent.
5 Landing account/weight notes at destination. The carrier's or stowage broker's record of the out-turn of the goods at destination. Useful for identifying where damage took place in the container or on the vessel or haulage unit.
6 Any correspondence with the carrier or other parties. Obviously the insurers wish to maintain any legal rights against other parties and insist that the insured do not give them away.

Not an unreasonable set of documents to require and every one there for a specific, and understandable, purpose.

Credit Insurance

Assuming the exporter is able to actually get the right goods, in perfect condition, to the right place at the right time the problems are not yet over because it may be that the buyer, for a variety of good and bad reasons, does not pay for them. The management of this credit risk is a task which occupies an increasing amount of the time and resources of the typical exporter as the credit risk in world markets increases.

There is little doubt that the credit risk faced by international traders is greater than it has ever been. In many markets, particularly third world countries, there is a probability of delay in payment and a distinct possibility of non-payment. In fact something like one third of the countries in the world would be bankrupt if they were companies, in that their liabilities far exceed their assets. This is the result of recurring world recessions in the last twenty years, which affect developed and developing countries alike, and, in particular, the increasing problem of third world debt. It is a statistic which is debated at some length but there is a lot of evidence to suggest that if one were to measure the capital flows from the first world (developed and industrialized countries) to the third world (underdeveloped and developing countries) then the surplus is on the developed countries' side. That is, more money moves from the third to the first world than vice-versa. Add to this the increasing economic problems of the emerging second world of the ex-Communist countries and world trade has enormous financial problems.

It may be useful to briefly examine the origins of such widespread credit risk, particularly in developing countries. There is much which is taken for granted by traders in developed countries like the UK. A UK company wishing to buy goods from an overseas supplier can invariably trade in Pounds Sterling. Even if the supplier does not wish to accept Pounds Sterling then they can easily be converted into US Dollars, or French Francs or Deutschmarks, or almost any other hard currency the supplier prefers.

It is not the same situation for, for example, a Ghanaian trader. It is highly unlikely that any supplier would be prepared to accept Ghanaian currency, which is Cedis incidentally, as payment for goods, and the buyer's Cedis cannot be converted into other, so called, hard currencies, being a non-convertible 'soft' currency. So how does a Ghanaian buy, and pay for, your goods? If they are lucky they are able to earn hard currencies from their own exports. Some countries would be under-developed if it were not for the good fortune they have in owning resources, invariably natural resources, which earn them hard currency. The Middle East is a perfect example of a group of countries which are rich because of natural resources. Some other developing countries, which at one time were able to export commodities at good market prices, have found that a down-turn in world commodity prices has severely reduced their earnings. This group would include a number of Latin American, African and Australasian countries.

Finally there are many countries which have no valuable resources, and in fact have trouble feeding themselves. In the latter two cases the only way that funds can be made available to pay for imports is to borrow, and this is the core of the problem of credit risk – third world debt. We are now in a situation in which many overseas countries cannot even service their debts, by making interest payments, and where millions of Dollars worth of loans are being written off by western banks. In such a situation the exporter has to be extremely careful in managing the risk of non-payment.

In the next chapter we will examine the range of methods of payment available to the exporter which can provide varying degrees of security, from the most secure, cash in advance, to the least secure, open account. The security which the exporter enjoys is also, obviously, improved by a sensible approach to credit control, involving the proper use of credit information, credit limits for individual buyers and operative blacklists. All of this can be made much easier by the operation of a credit insurance policy.

The basic risks can be broken down into two categories:

1 Buyer risk: Default, dishonour, insolvency, failure to take up goods.
2 Country risk: (sovereign risk): Government action, for example failure to transfer currency.

The exporter's assessment of risk must take into account both aspects.

Credit risk insurance is provided by a number of specialist organizations, the most important of which are:

NCM Credit Insurance Ltd

Formerly a government department known as Export Credits Guarantee Department (ECGD) and now a Dutch owned limited company, covering over 20 per cent of UK exports. Since its privatization in 1991 the basic policy has not changed and is typically a comprehensive short term policy covering credit periods of up to two years.

Cover is available for both buyer and sovereign risk subject to the seller operating within either written credit limits from the insurers or discretionary limits which can be calculated from the company's trading experience. The limits are obviously affected by the method of payment in use. Generally NCM would require a fair spread of an exporter's business but are prepared to negotiate premiums for selective contracts, which could include pre-shipment, as well as post-shipment cover. They insist that the seller bear a percentage of the loss, paying 90 per cent of the loss due to buyer default or insolvency, and 95 per cent of loss due to sovereign risks, the purpose of this being to maintain some interest from the seller in recovery of the debt. As with contingency cargo insurance the existence of a credit insurance policy should not be revealed to the buyer.

Export Credits Guarantee Department

This remains a government department but is concerned only with contracts with credit periods over two years and generally with project finance. This includes a range of pre-shipment and supplier credit arrangements which relate to the sometimes complex payment schemes associated with overseas projects.

Private underwriters

There an increasing number of companies offering international credit insurance who can supply almost any form of cover subject to the agreement of appropriate premiums. They include:

1 Lloyd's Underwriters (of course);
2 Trade Indemnity;
3 Pan Financial; and
4 Black Sea & Baltic.

all of whom have offices in London. There are also a number of overseas-based companies operating in an increasingly competitive market, including:

1 HERMES (Germany);
2 COFACE (France);
3 COBAC (Belgium);
4 SIAC (Italy);
5 CIGNA Worldwide (USA); and
6 Swett & Crawford (USA).

Generally, credit insurance policies operate in a similar way to the open cargo insurance policies examined earlier, although each insurer will come to their own particular administrative arrangements. Typically premiums will be negotiated in advance, in some cases being averaged over all customers and markets, and it may be that a fixed fee or advance payment of a percentage of premiums is required.

Insurance and the exporter

The typical exporter will operate both cargo and credit insurance policies and therefore conducts business in the knowledge that such security exists in the event that things go wrong which are, of course, outside of their control. However it is very important to understand that:

1 The security operates only in the situation where the exporter is not at fault. We established earlier that, pretty obviously, there is no cover where the loss is due to the misconduct of the exporter, but the situation may not always be clear cut. For example there may be a situation in which the sellers consider that they have fulfilled all contractual obligations, but the buyer disagrees. A typical example would be dispute regarding the quality of goods supplied. In such a case there is not necessarily clear misconduct on the seller's part but nevertheless the insurance companies will not entertain a claim until the contractual dispute is settled. If, however, the sellers can prove, to the satisfaction of the insurers, that the buyer's complaint is simply an excuse for delay or dishonour, which is not uncommon, and that they have fulfilled the contract, then a claim will be accepted. The moral is that exporters do need to maintain a high quality of administration, and the documentation evidencing it, to ensure that they can prove performance of all their contractual obligations.

2 The insurers expect the insured to minimize not only the possibilities of loss but also the consequences of losses when they happen. An example of this, which was mentioned earlier, is the fact that claims on carriers for loss or damage should be made as soon as possible, and certainly within three working days. The basic, and very important, principle is that the insured must act as 'a prudent man uninsured'. With apologies for the male gender (this is a quote from Lloyd's underwriters in the 1600s) the phrase does concisely describe the expectations of the insurers. The policy is not a safety net for a lack of concern on the sellers behalf, and all insured parties must conduct their business as if an insurance policy does not exist.

Exchange Risk

It is becoming more and more common for UK exporters to do business with overseas buyers in currencies other than Pounds Sterling. The currencies used would invariably be the 'hard' convertible currencies of developed countries and often the currency of the buyer's country. It may also be the case that business, say, from the UK to Saudi Arabia is actually conducted in a third currency, commonly US Dollars. The main reason for exporters to do this is an attempt to offer buyers, particularly those in developed markets, a package deal based on Delivered prices in their own currency. A quotation Ex Works in Pounds Sterling to a French buyer has severe disadvantages when compared with others Delivered Duty Paid in French Francs.

The other reason is that, in the cases where the UK exporter chooses to deal in Pounds Sterling with overseas customers, then there is a clear possibility of risk for the buyer in that the cost of the Pounds Sterling they need to pay, in terms of the amount of their own currency needed to buy it, may well increase due to fluctuations in the relative values of the two currencies. It is a fact of modern commerce that the exchange rates of currencies are subject to, sometimes, large movements. The apparent failure of the Exchange Rate Mechanism (ERM), and the certain devaluation of the Pound Sterling, in Autumn 1992, is an illustration of the extreme fluctuations in rates which can be generated by market activities which cannot be controlled by governments.

Because of the importance of the Balance of Payments to the value of a country's currency relative to others, there is a perfect logic to the economic theory which describes the corrective mechanism which controls such fluctuations. To use the UK as an example, if the Pound weakens against other currencies, that is, becomes worth less in that it takes more Pounds to buy the same amount of foreign currency, then UK exports become cheaper to foreign buyers and therefore UK exports increase, the Balance of Payments deficit reduces, and the Pound strengthens. The reverse situation is that a strengthening Pound makes exports more expensive to the buyers and the reduction in exports leads to a weakening Pound. Wonderful in theory until one considers the fact that many UK exporters, especially the bigger ones, choose to invoice in foreign currencies and the situation above operates in reverse. For example the exporter receiving US Dollars, with a weakening Pound, actually benefits from the change.

Movements in exchange rates are broadly subject to supply

and demand within the market for currencies. This is affected by the demand for trading currency, that is, an increase in German exports can lead to an increased demand for Deutschmarks, but also by the differences in interest rates from one country, and one currency, to another. The higher the interest rate available the more that currency will be demanded.

It is the long term expectation that the Pound will weaken against other hard currencies, plus the risk free package deal to the buyer, which has led to a marked increase in foreign currency invoicing by UK exporters over the last twenty years.

The simple risk faced by the UK exporter is that the calculated export price, based on predominantly Pounds Sterling costs, which is then converted to a foreign currency price at the current exchange rate, has to be calculated some time in advance of the eventual receipt of those funds and the pounds Sterling revenues may well be less than was planned.

Assuming that the decision is taken to invoice some overseas buyers in their own currencies then the exporter has a number of options in relation to the management of the risk.

Do nothing

Not a very dynamic approach but nevertheless one which could be justified. It is simply the case that the exporter may well be prepared to accept whatever the exchange rate happens to be when the foreign currency payment is actually received. The rate on that day, which is known as the spot rate, may actually favour the seller, if the Pound has weakened against that currency. It also has the advantage of simplicity, which makes it very attractive to many traders.

However, we must accept that the opposite situation could apply and there is a clear risk that the seller could lose substantial revenues, possibly even sustain losses, should the exchange rate movement have gone against them. This is a particular problem where the amounts involved are large and if the profit margins are small. Therefore the average exporter looks for ways in which to minimize or remove the risk.

Currency accounts

The most obvious way to remove the exchange risk is not to exchange at all. That is, the seller simply keeps the foreign currency in foreign currency accounts. The absence of exchange control regulations within the UK means that the UK exporter can maintain accounts, in any currencies, in the UK. In many cases it will also be possible to hold foreign currencies in accounts overseas, that is, French Franc revenues could be kept in a French Franc account with Credit Lyonnaise in Paris, but this does depend on whether the overseas market allows such external accounts.

Apart from the fact that any exchange risk is eliminated it may also be the case that the interest earned on such accounts, which would depend on the type of account, could be superior to interest rates paid on Sterling accounts. It may even be possible to borrow foreign currencies at beneficial rates.

However the main benefit of currency accounts applies to the situation in which a company is selling and buying in foreign currency. The ideal situation would be where the receipts and payments actually balanced each other out, but there are still great benefits even when there is no balance, any shortfall being made up by borrowing currency and any surplus being held in interest bearing accounts. Also there is often the option to take advantage of movements in spot rates by exchanging currency where there is a revenue benefit.

Forward exchange contract

It is possible to approach a bank and be given a rate for selling (receipts) or buying (payments) foreign currency at a future time. What this does is to guarantee an exchange rate to the trader, at the time when prices are being calculated, and allows them to rely on that rate irrespective of the actual spot rate at the time of the exchange. The banks will quote 'forward rates' for anything from one month to five years, but the standard periods are three, six and 12 months.

The rates they offer differ depending on whether the bank is buying or selling the currency and will be expressed as a 'premium', for currencies strengthening, which is deducted from the spot rate or 'discount', for weakening currencies, which is added to the spot rate. Figure 11.7 shows a typical range of rates against the Pound for US Dollars, at a premium, and Belgian Francs, at a discount.

Figure 11.7: A typical range of forward rates

	Close	One Month	Three Months
US	1.4785 - 1.4795	0.37 - 0.35 cpm	0.86 - 0.83 pm
Belgium	53.85 - 53.95	15.00 - 19.00 cdis	41.00 - 48.00 dis

In the case of the US Dollar the rate of 1.4785 is the current spot selling rate (importer buys) and the rate of 1.4795 is the buying rate (exporter sells). The expression cpm defines a premium in terms of 100th of a cent and cdis a discount in terms of 100th of a Franc. As the Dollar is at a premium then the one month forward buying rate would be

1.4795 less 0.35 = 1.4760.

The equivalent rate for the Belgian Franc would be

53.95 plus 19.00 = 54.14.

The exporter can arrange a contract with the bank to sell the foreign currency receipts expected from a particular consignment at a fixed (forward) rate at the end of a particular time period. In our example of the US Dollars then the exporter would sell a specified amount of Dollars at 1.4760 in one month's time.

The great advantage of forward exchange contracts is the fact that the exporter knows exactly what rate will be used when the currency is eventually received and converted. However there are potential problems in that the contract must be met even if the payment has not been received from the overseas buyer. This would entail the exporter having to purchase the correct amount of US Dollars, at the spot rate, in order to meet the forward contract, and then have to convert the eventual Dollar payment, again at spot. It also means that the exporter cannot take advantage if the actual spot rate is better than the forward rate.

In the cases where the exporter has some doubt about the exact time payment would be received then it is possible to negotiate an **option forward**.

This would fix a rate which could be taken up over a period of time that is, one to three months, and therefore give an element of flexibility to the timing of the exchange. However, this does not give the exporter the option to take up the forward rate or not; the forward exchange contract **must** be honoured at some time during the period allowed. Also the bank will attempt to quote a rate which will be the best for them over that time period.

Currency option

In this case the exporter does have the option to take up the forward rate or to ignore it and convert at spot if that is more favourable. There will still be a fixed forward rate, known as the 'strike rate', and either a stated date or a time period for that forward rate to be taken up. In return for the option to take the forward rate or ignore it the exporter (or importer, of course) will pay an 'up front' premium, the amount of which is dependent on the 'strike' rate agreed and the time period.

Contrary to popular belief, the forward rates used in the above contracts are not the bank's guess at what the rates will be in the future, but are simply a spot rate adjusted to take into account the differences in the interest rates for the two currencies, and effectively compensates the party who has held the currency with the lower interest rate for the period of the contract.

Summary

We started this chapter be examining the range of risks faced by an exporter and have attempted to identify the ways in which the typical exporter deals with such risks. In brief they are:

1 Physical loss or damage – Cargo Insurance Policy.
2 Non-payment – Credit Insurance Policy.
3 Loss on exchange – Currency Accounts or Forward Exchange Contracts.

However none of the solutions mentioned above are compulsory. Traders have a perfect right to choose not to insure against these risks and may have goods reasons not to. If, for example, the costs of the premiums on an insurance policy actually exceed the claims then it could actually be more cost-effective not to insure. This should also be coupled with the fact that the better the level of professionalism displayed by the trader, notably in terms of shipping the goods, credit control and payment collection, then the less important becomes the 'safety net', of the insurance policy.

Questions for Discussion

1 Briefly describe the meaning of the following terms:
   (a) Average Bond;
   (b) subrogation;
   (c) open cover;
   (d) insurable interest.
2 A marine insurance contract is said to be one of the 'utmost good faith'. Explain what is meant by this and state in what circumstances an insurer might not settle an exporter's claim for loss of, or damage to, goods?

12

Methods of Payment

As the majority of companies trading internationally are profit making, or are at least attempting to be profit making, then it is fairly obvious that the receipt of payment is essential to that purpose. As we have seen in the previous chapter, there are a number of factors which can directly affect the proper receipt of payment, including lost or damaged goods, default of the buyer, exchange fluctuations and, of course, the broad area of a genuine contractual dispute, and it may be the case that the exporter can arrange forms of insurance cover for some of these risks. However, whether insurance exists or not, it is clearly the responsibility of the exporter to operate in a way which maximizes, and ideally guarantees, the possibility of payment being received in full and on time. This primarily relates to the choices made regarding the terms and methods of payment used for particular countries and customers. Also, as will be obvious as we examine these methods, the whole export order process needs to be carried out correctly in order to ensure collection of payment. In particular the documentary procedures, and the quality of documents they produce, very often are the deciding factor as to whether the money is paid or not.

To clarify the distinction made above, the **terms** of payment are the time allowed for payment to be made, that is, the credit period allowed. This is usually expressed as sight payment, where no credit period is allowed and payment is required on sight of the documents, or in blocks of 30 days, for example 30,

60, 90, 180 days, following a date specified in the contract which could be from sight of documents, or from receipt of the goods, or from date of shipment or even from the invoice date. The **method** of payment is the means by which the money will be paid and the exporter has a range of choices which offer varying degrees of security. Ranking the methods from the least secure to the most secure they are:

Least secure	Open Account
	Bills of Exchange
↓	Documentary Letters of Credit
Most secure	Cash in advance

Choosing Terms and Method of Payment

The trader obviously has to make a choice as to the appropriate terms and method of payment right at the beginning of the process when the quotation is first made and this choice will be affected by a variety of factors.

The Market

Certain methods of payment are clearly more common in particular markets than are others, so the exporter invariably has a 'rule of thumb' as to the usual method for a particular market. In this context it is no surprise that for the high risk markets, for example West Africa, then cash in advance is not uncommon and Letters of Credit are very common. On the other hand a developed market like Germany exhibits a preponderance of Open Account contracts. There are occasional apparent anomalies where methods have become traditional for certain markets or market groups which seem inappropriate. In this context it is very common to deal with some very rich, and very safe, Middle Eastern markets on Letter of Credit terms even though the risk may seem to be minimal.

The Buyer

Irrespective of the traditional and accepted method of payment in a particular country, the seller's perception of the buyer risk, or lack of it, can override any 'rule of thumb'. The seller's perception may simply be based on a trading history with a buyer over a period of time which has established an element of trust which allows for methods of payment such as Open Account in what are regarded as Letter of Credit markets. Alternatively, the opposite might apply and Letters of Credit might be demanded in Open Account markets if the seller has reason to doubt the reliability of a specific buyer. In this context the exporter would need to have good reason to demand, for example, a Letter of Credit from a reputable German buyer as there is a distinct possibility that the prospective buyer might take such a request as a personal insult.

Such decisions should be the result of the operation of a credit management system which takes a pragmatic approach to the calculation of buyer risk and establishes operative credit limits based on the methods of payment in use. It may be that the seller is operating a credit insurance policy which will generate approved methods of payment and related credit limits provided by the insurance company. One of the advantages of a credit insurance policy is the quality of information available to the insurers which enables them to make decisions regarding the level of risk they are prepared to cover. The sensible exporter will also, and may be required to, use other sources of information regarding the credit worthiness of individual buyers such as Bank Reports or Status Reports from the DTI or private business information companies such as Dun & Bradstreet International.

The Competition

This does overlap with the two factors mentioned above in that the typical method of payment adopted in a market is clearly the one most likely to be offered by the competition in that market. It could be the case that the competition faced by a particular exporter is prepared to use terms and methods of payment as a marketing tool. That is, they are prepared to agree longer credit periods or less secure, and often cheaper, methods of payment in order to secure business. In such a case the exporter must seriously consider the risks inherent in matching competitive offers. It is a fact of commercial life that price and quality are not the only factors affecting the competitiveness of a particular product or service.

Any decision regarding the terms and method used must be based on the application of all the above factors and under-pinned by a very clear understanding of the operation of the various methods, the risks involved and the ways in which good management can minimize those risks.

Open Account

The least secure method of payment and therefore only used regularly in low risk markets. It is thus quite common in Western Europe and the USA. It literally means 'pay me when you like', but is obviously clarified by an agreement as to when payment will be made. This may be on receipt of documents or goods, which would invariably be sent direct to the importer, or after a credit period of typically 30, 60, or 90 days. In either case the seller is totally dependent on the buyer paying at the agreed time. What is of relevance at this point are the ways in which such payments might be transferred.

Buyer's cheque

Subject to the risk of the cheque 'bouncing' this is not a bad way to receive payment. However it is very much better to have a cheque drawn on an account in the UK, which will be cleared within three days and in hours if expedited, rather than one drawn on an account overseas. The problem is that the cheque will have to be returned to the buyer's country to be cleared and this can often take up to four weeks. We must appreciate that not every country benefits from a central clearing system and many have a large number of banks, and it could be that problems arise which extend this time period or even mean, on occasions, that the cheque will not be cleared.

Banker's draft

An importer can purchase from his bank a draft in favour of the exporter drawn on a bank in the exporter's country. It is, in effect, a cheque drawn by one bank on another and is therefore more secure than the buyer's cheque. There is still the time delay in the draft being raised and posted to the exporter and it should not be forgotten that the draft is as secure as the bank drawing it up, and even banks go out of business (pretty regularly in some countries).

International transfer

These represent the fastest way, and probably the most expensive, of making payment and result in the exporter receiving cleared funds direct into the bank account. There are actually three ways in which the transfers can be made:

1 Mail transfer;
2 Cable or Telex transfer; or
3 SWIFT.

The latter method is the fastest and stands for Society for Worldwide Interbank Financial Telecommunications. It is an automated inter-bank system and offers a secure and rapid method of financial transfers between compatible computer terminals. In some areas, like Western Europe, SWIFT may be used automatically.

Finally, however the transfer is to be made, it is important that the exporter makes it absolutely clear where the money should go. An obvious point but one which some exporters fail to consider. The seller's documents, in particular the invoice, should include:

1 Bank name;
2 branch address;
3 account name and number; and
4 sort code (6 digit number at the top right hand corner of your cheques).

It is very much in the seller's interest to minimize the delay between the buyer paying and those funds being cleared and available. The delay is sometimes referred to as 'Float Time' and a survey in the late 1980s estimated that it cost UK exporters at least £60 million per annum in extra charges and lost interest.

Bills of Exchange (Drafts)

Referred to as Documentary Collections by the banks, the use of Bills of Exchange, sometimes called Drafts, introduces a new documentary requirement for the exporter in that the Bill of Exchange will be drawn up by them in addition to the other shipping documents. The security which Bills of Exchange offer is based on the fact that the procedures involve the banks in arranging for collection of payment from the buyer on behalf of the seller.

The exporter, having agreed such a method of payment with the buyer, will draw up a Bill of Exchange which will form part of the document set which will be sent to their bank in the UK. The layouts of Bills of Exchange do vary but a typical blank Bill is shown in figure 12.1

Figure 12.1: A Typical Bill of Exchange

№ Exchange for Manchester 19

At pay this of Exchange to the Order

the Sum of

Value which place to Account

To

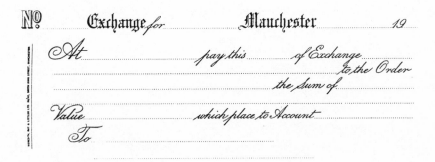

However it is not necessary to use a particular printed form and in fact a much simpler layout, as shown in figure 12.2, would be just as acceptable.

Figure 12.2: Simple layout of a Bill of Exchange

Birkenhead Paper Mills
Merseyside

No. *1234* . . . .

Date *24th June 1993*
For . . . *£35,000* . . .

AT . . . *Sight* . . .**PAY THIS FIRST OF EXCHANGE (SECOND UNPAID)**

TO . . . *Ourselves* ....

THE SUM OF . . .*Thirty five thousand pounds* . . .**VALUE RECEIVED**

TO . . . *Sweeping Sing Fat Ltd*
. . . *High Street, Singapore* . . .

FOR BIRKENHEAD PAPER MILLS

....

SIGNED..............................
DIRECTOR

The point is that a Bill of Exchange is defined in terms of the information it contains rather than the way it is laid out. The following definition, from the English Bill of Exchange Act 1882, is supposedly the finest legal definition in the English language.

> . . . an unconditional order in writing, addressed by one person (the drawer) to another (the drawee), signed by the person giving it, requiring the person to whom it is addressed to pay on demand, or at a fixed or determinable future time a sum certain in money to, or to the order of, a specified person or to bearer (the payee).

The expressions in brackets are the titles the banks would use to identify the parties. The exporter is the **Drawer** in that they actually draw up the Bill of Exchange and the importer is invariably the person to whom it is addressed and therefore the **Drawee**. The Drawee is the **Payer** or **Acceptor** of the Bill and the money will be paid, at the specified time, to the **Payee**, which is usually the exporter but could be another party or even the Bearer, that is, the person holding the Bill.

The difference between a Bill of Exchange and a Promissory Note, which though rare is still seen in Europe, is that the Bill is a demand for payment from the seller, whereas a Promissory Note is a promise to pay from the buyer.

As we shall see, the Bills are either drawn up at sight (figure 12.2) or at a number of days after sight. A typical 60 day Bill is shown in figure 12.3.

Figure 12.3: A typical 60 day Bill of Exchange

Payable together with all bank charges.

At ....60 days........... sight of this FIRST of Exchange (second ....21st June...19.xx.... of the same tenor and date unpaid)

Pay to the Order of   No. ....250..............

...................LUSTRE   FIBRES   LTD.,.......................................

the sum of.....Two hundred and ninety six pounds ——————————————

—————————————————————————————————————

———————————————————————————————————

....55p.Value received

To....SUNFLAG   KNITTING   MILLS   (NIGERIA) LTD.......

PLATEAU   ROAD,   APAPA - LAGOS,   NIGERIA...................

£ 296.55

For   LUSTRE   FIBRES   LTD.,

A. J. Hadleigh

DIRECTOR

268

The parties involved in this Bill are:

1 Drawer – Lustre Fibres Ltd.
2 Drawee – Sunflag Knitting Mills (Nigeria) Ltd.
3 Acceptor – Sunflag Knitting Mills (Nigeria) Ltd.
4 Payee – Lustre Fibres Ltd (sometimes expressed as 'ourselves').

The sum of £296.55, always expressed in words and numbers, will be paid 60 days after the Drawee has had sight of the Bill and documents. The reason why a Bill should contain the words 'first of exchange second unpaid' is that it is common for two, or even three, Bills to be drawn up. This is based on the same, rather antiquated logic, of having two or three Bills of Lading (see chapter 7) designed to ensure that at least one arrives successfully at destination. The second Bill will contain the words 'second of exchange first unpaid'.

Once the exporter has drawn up the Bill/s of Exchange and assembled the full set of shipping documents, they are then sent to their bank along with the appropriate completed Letter of Instruction. The major banks use their own versions of instruction forms but figure 12.4 shows a typical one. Many of the instructions are in the form of tick boxes and they will include clear reference to the procedures followed not only by the UK bank but also the overseas bank. The documents will be dispatched either to the UK bank's branch or correspondent, or one specified by the exporter, in the buyer's country, who will make the collection.

Sight Draft

In the case where the amount is payable at sight, that is, no credit period will be allowed, the overseas bank will require the buyer to pay the due amount at sight of the documents. The reason this provides security for the seller is that the bank will not release the documents to the buyer unless payment is made. This is referred to as **Documents Against Payment (D/P)** and, particularly if a Bill of Lading is part of the document set, the buyer will not be able to take possession of the goods without first paying for the documents.

Figure 12.4: A typical Letter of Instruction

National Westminster Bank PLC

Drawer/Exporter	Date
	When corresponding please quote our full reference: **BCE/OBCC/**

Drawee	From: **National Westminster Bank** Outward Bills PO Box No 75 · 38 Colmore Circus · Birmingham B4 6DJ · United Kingdom · Telephone 021-234 2000 · Telex 339271 NWBBHM G · Swift Code NWBKGB 2LB · Facsimile 021-234 2411

To:

Please deal with the enclosed remittance in accordance with the instructions marked X below

Deliver Documents on		Acceptance	Payment

If documents are not taken up on arrival of goods please advise us immediately, stating reason, and - (All charges accrued on the goods are for the drawers account).	Warehouse Goods	Do Not Warehouse
	Insure Against Fire	Do Not Insure

Documents: If enclosures are not as specified the balance will follow by next mail.

Bill of Exchange	Comm'l Invoice	Cert/Cons Inv	Cert of Origin	Collect **all** charges including ours of:		
Ins Pol/Cert	Bill of Lading	Parcel Post Rec't	Air Waybill	Collect all of your Bank charges, stamps etc	Charges may be waived	Yes	No
Comb Trans Doc				Insurance covered by Drawee	Carrying Vessel	

Whereabouts of any missing Original Bill of Lading	If necessary accept a deposit in local currency together with Drawee's written undertaking to take all possible action to ensure prompt remittance of Sterling/Dollars and to make good any exchange loss. Advise date paid in local currency.

If unaccepted ➤	Protest	Do Not Protest	and advise reason, by ➤ and confirm case of need, where given, has been advised	Telex/Swift	Airmail
If unpaid ➤	Protest	Do Not Protest	and advise reason, by ➤ and confirm case of need, where given, has been advised	Telex/Swift	Airmail
Acceptance/Payment may be deferred until goods arrive	Yes	No	After final payment remit proceeds by	Telex/Swift	Airmail

In case of need refer to:	For guidance	Accept their instructions

Special proceeds instructions:

Special Instructions: Please acknowledge receipt, quoting both your and our reference numbers.

Date of Bill of Exchange	Tenor of Bill of Exchange	Amount of Collection

General Instructions (Applicable in so far as they may be modified or contradicted by the instructions above or on the Bill).

Acknowledge receipt, quoting both your and our reference numbers.
Advise acceptance and due date promptly
Advise non-acceptance and/or non-payment giving definite reason for refusal, and confirming that the case of need, when given, has been advised.
Send all advices by Swift or airmail unless instructed otherwise.
Term bills not already accepted should be presented immediately on receipt, and after acceptance, should be held for payment at maturity.
When collections cover consignments addressed to yourselves by parcel and/or airfreight, the relative packages should be released in accordance with the instructions given for the release of documents.
If documents of title are attached and are not taken up on arrival of the consignment or any difficulty arises, please advise us immediately, stating the reason.
Meanwhile, please ensure that the goods are properly protected but do not insure them.
All charges accrued on the goods are for the drawee's account.
Failure on your part to comply with all instructions given will be at your sole responsibility.
Subject to Uniform rules for Collections (latest revision) International Chamber of Commerce.

Bill is already accepted	Yes	No
Charges to be taken in	Currency	Sterling

Credit Sterling Account Number

Apply to Forward Contract Number

Credit Foreign Currency A/c No.

Signature

Termed Draft

Where the exporter has agreed to allow a credit period, for example 60 days, then the Bill is referred to as a Termed Bill or Usance Bill. The latter description describing the fact that the buyer has a period of use of the goods before having to pay. The credit term allowed in the Bill is usually from Sight of the Bill but they can also be drawn up with terms which run from the date of shipment (as evidenced by the transport document), the date of the Bill or even the date of invoice. It would not escape the buyer's attention that a 'credit' period which included the transit time for the goods is not exactly a full usance period.

In the case of a Termed Bill the overseas bank will not collect payment in return for the documents but will instead release the documents against **Acceptance** of the Bill. This usually requires only a signature, of the Drawee, and often a company stamp. The credit term of the Bill is known as the **tenor** and when this expires, that is, 60 days later, the Bill is said to have **matured** and will be represented for payment. This procedure is described as **Documents Against Acceptance (D/A)**.

The exporter should appreciate that in the case where documents have been released against Acceptance there will be no automatic payment transfer when the Bill matures. The buyer must still make the payment and it is perfectly possible for dishonour to take place. It may, of course, be due to the fact that the buyer has a genuine complaint and has withheld payment for good reason.

In the cases where there is non-payment of a Sight Bill, or non-acceptance of a Termed Bill, or non-payment of an accepted Bill on maturity, it is important in many markets that a **protest** is made. Whilst this procedure does not apply in every country overseas there are many in which the lack of a protest will lead to a loss of all legal rights against the buyer. As any protest must be made the next working day (in practice three days' grace are allowed) then it is important that the banks are instructed in advance. As can be seen from the sample Instruction Form in figure 12.4, there is a clear requirement for such an instruction. Even in the cases where the exporter has little desire to take

Figure 12.5: Example of a protest

By This Public Instrument

Be it known and made manifest that on the ....22nd....... day of ......JUNE......
in the year......ONE THOUSAND NINE HUNDRED & SEVENTY NINE......I Frank Odunayo
Akinrele, Notary Public, duly authorised, admitted and sworn, practising in Lagos, Nigeria,
West Africa do hereby certify that on this the......22nd......day of......JUNE......
IN THE YEAR OF OUR LORD ONE THOUSAND NINE HUNDRED &
at the request of......ARAB BANK NIGERIA LIMITED (BALOGUN SQUARE)......
of the Colony of Lagos, Nigeria, Bankers and holders of the original Bill of Exchange a
true copy of which is on the other side written, I, Frank Odunayo Akinrele of the said
Colony, Notary Public, duly authorised, admitted and sworn, did cuase the said Bill of
Exchange to be taken to No.....26 Kingomdy STREET, LAGOS NIGERIA......... and to
be produced and exhibited to....XYZ ELECTRICAL STORES LIMITED......
on whom it was drawn, at No....26 Kongodmy Street, LAGOS NIGERIA
......................and cause to be demanded
payment thereof,....When J.Smith (Jr.) Brother for and on behalf of
XYZ Electrical Stores Limited, Said:- "My Director is not in office
but he will be informed to make necessary arrangement for payment."

and so, I am unable to obtain payment of the said Bill of Exchange.

Whereupon, I, the said Notary, at the request aforesaid, did cause protest to be
made and by these presents do solemnly protest against the drawers of the said Bill of
Exchange and all other parties thereto, and all others concerned for Exchange, re-exchange,
and all costs, damages, charges and interest present and future for want of payment of the
said Bill of Exchange.

Thus done and protested at Lagos in the presence of:-

....
......(A.O. ADEYEYE)
......130, Broad Street,
......Lagos Nigeria

Dated the......22nd......day of......JUNE IN THE YEAR OF OUR LORD
ONE THOUSAND NINE HUNDRED

Which I Attest,

......F. O. AKINRELE
Public, Nigeria.

2k
NIGERIA

legal action then the protest can be sufficient to prompt payment from a buyer who is simply 'playing for time'. Also, lists of protested Bills are published in the financial press or bank gazettes of some countries and buyers will usually wish to avoid this. Finally some credit insurance companies, including NCM Ltd, will require protest to be made as part of the policy requirements. Figure 12.5 reproduces an example of a protest which was actually made in Nigeria, but the names have been changed to protect the guilty.

The above procedures describe what are known as Documentary Collections in that the bank handle the set of shipping documents as well as the Bill of Exchange. It is possible to arrange for what are known as Clean Collections in which the documents are sent direct to the buyer, rather than to the bank, the Bill of Exchange being handled by the banks in the normal way. This is only used where there is a large element of trust between seller and buyer and the Bill is simply a convenient way to collect and transfer the payment.

It is even possible to simply instruct an overseas bank to release the documents against payment without including a Bill of Exchange. This is known as **Cash Against Documents** but does not provide the security that a Sight Draft can and operates according to local practice rather than a set of rules.

In this respect the advantage of both Clean and Documentary Collections is that the banks handling such collections invariably operate under the same set of procedural rules. These are known as the **Uniform Rules for Collections** and are a publication of the International Chamber of Commerce (*ICC Publication No. 322*), available from your local Chamber of Commerce.

Avalised Bills of Exchange

As we have seen a Termed Bill accepted by the Drawee is not a guarantee of payment on maturity, but it is possible to arrange for the accepted Bill to be avalised by the buyer's bank. This must be arranged in advance and involves the bank adding their '**Pour Aval**' endorsement, or guarantee, to the accepted Bill. In such a case the exporter has a bank's promise to pay rather than the buyer's. This is not as secure as a Letter of Credit in that the buyer must accept the Bill of Exchange first, but it does have the great advantage of producing an accepted Bill which can be discounted. This describes the process whereby it is possible to receive a discounted amount of the Bill value at the time of acceptance rather than wait for it to mature. The 'Pour Aval' on the Bill means that a number of agencies will be prepared to advance funds; in particular there are financial institutions who specialize in what is known as '**forfaiting**' who will advance funds at good rates. Such forfaiters will also become involved in long term forfaits of high value Bills, such arrangements perhaps extending over four Bills maturing over a period of two years or more.

Documentary Letter of Credit (L/C)

Most exporters will feel that a promise from a bank to pay is an improvement on a promise from the buyer and we have seen that the addition of a bank's Pour Aval on an accepted Bill of Exchange gives distinct advantages. The ultimate form of bank guarantee used in international trade is that of the Letter of Credit which, in simple terms, is a letter from a bank promising to pay an amount of money. However the typical operation involves the use of Documentary Letters of Credit which promise to pay only if the documents stated on the Credit are provided by the exporter. In this respect they are very much conditional guarantees of payment.

The procedure, which begins with the seller and buyer agreeing payment by Letter of Credit, requires the buyer to arrange for the credit to be opened by their bank at the time the order is placed. From the exporter's point of view, the Letter of Credit would need to be received before the order was accepted and checks on its acceptability would take place right at the beginning of the order process.

The buyer will instruct their bank, known as the **Opening** or **Issuing** bank, to raise the L/C and agree with them the specific documentary requirements. The credit will then be passed to the exporter, known as the **Beneficiary**, through the Issuing bank's correspondent bank in the exporter's country. If this bank happens to be the exporter's bank then it is pure coincidence and it may be the case that a transcribed, retyped, version of the original Credit is what the exporter will eventually see.

The UK bank may simply pass the Credit to the exporter, in which case they are the **Advising** bank and the exporter has the Issuing bank's promise to pay subject to the provision of the required documents. It may be that the UK bank adds its confirmation to the Credit, that is, its own promise to pay, and will be referred to as the **Confirming** bank. As we will see later the UK exporter may feel that the Confirmation of a UK bank is an improvement on the Issuing bank's promise.

Once the Credit is received by the exporter it is important that it is checked immediately to ensure that the documentary requirements, and the time periods allowed, are acceptable. If amendments are required it is advisable to request them immediately from the Issuing bank, through the Advising or Confirming bank.

Assuming that the Credit is acceptable to the exporter then they will proceed with the manufacture, packing and shipping of the goods in order to produce a set of shipping documents in compliance with the Credit. These documents will be presented to the UK bank who will check that they comply with the Credit requirements and, assuming they find no discrepancies, they will pay the exporter. Figure 12 .6 shows the basic procedure. Unfortunately the reality is not always quite so simple and in fact the statistics show that almost 60 per cent of document sets presented to UK banks against Credits are rejected because of documentary discrepancies. They actually go wrong more often than they go right. To see why such problems are experienced it is necessary to look in more detail at the Letter of Credit process.

Figure 12.6: Documentary Letter of Credit procedure

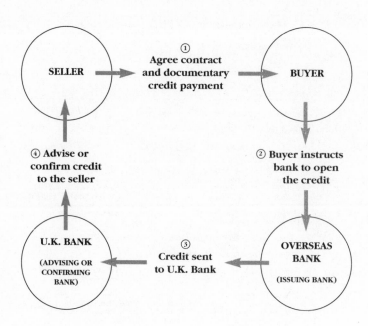

Documentary Requirements

Figure 12.7 is an example of a typical Letter of Credit and it can be seen that the documentary requirements are very specific. The average Credit will require:

Drafts (Bills of Exchange)

These are often drawn on the Issuing or the Confirming bank. That is to say that the Drawee on such Bills will be a bank rather than the buyer. The Bills will reflect whether the Credit is payable at Sight or contains a credit term as can be seen from figure 12.8 which is a 90 day Bill drawn on Barclays, and 12.9 which is a Sight Draft drawn on Barclays. In both cases the Bill will contain a clause referring to the relevant letter of Credit. Assuming that no documentary discrepancies are found, the

Figure 12.7: A typical Letter of Credit

3 National Westminster Bank PLC

International Banking Division
Documentary Credits Department – Overseas Branch

---

4 United Kingdom Seller Limited
Baltic House
27 Leadenhall Street
London EC3

Dear Sirs

We have been requested by **2** Traders Bank of Japan, Tokyo, Japan to advise the
issue of their irrevocable Credit Number 01/765 in your favour for account
4 of JAPAN BUYER CORPORATION c/o NYK Line 3-2 Marunouchi 2-Chome, Chiyoda-ku,
Tokyo 100, Japan for £100,000 (SAY ONE HUNDRED THOUSAND POUNDS STERLING).

5 available by your drafts on us at .... sight accompanied by the
following documents namely:

5 1. Signed Invoices in triplicate certifying goods are in accordance with
Contract No. 1234 dated 23 October 19   between Japan Buyer Corporation and
United Kingdom Seller Limited.

5 2. Marine and War Risk Insurance Certificate covering "all risks" warehouse to
warehouse, for 10% above the CIF value, evidencing that claims are payable in Japan.

5 3. Complete set 3/3 Shipping Company's clean "on board" ocean Bills of Lading
made out to order of the shippers and endorsed to order of "Traders Bank
of Japan", marked "Freight Paid" and "Notify Japan Buyer Corporation c/o
NYK Line 3-2 Marunouchi 2-Chome, Chiyoda-ku, Tokyo 100, Japan".

Covering: Mechanical Spare Parts CIF Tokyo, Japan.

Shipped from UK Port to Tokyo, Japan.

Partshipment prohibited   Transhipment prohibited

Documents must be presented for payment within 15 days from the date of shipment.

We are requested to add our confirmation to this Credit and we hereby undertake
to pay you the face amount of your drafts drawn within its terms provided such
drafts bear the number and date of the Credit and that the Letter of Credit and
all amendments thereto are attached.

The Credit is subject to Uniform Customs and Practice for Documentary Credits
(1983 Revision), International Chamber of Commerce Publication No. 400.

Drafts drawn under this   [X] Payment
Credit must be presented to us for   [ ] Negotiation } not later than 14 December 19
                                       [ ] Acceptance

and marked "Drawn under Credit Number 01/765/NWB/2A of Traders Bank of Japan.
2 Tokyo, Japan   Dated 1 November 19

Note: On the grounds of security the above Credit, whilst accurate in content, is used for illustrative purposes only.

1 Buyer/Applicant   **4** Seller/Beneficiary

2 Issuing/Opening Bank   **5** Documents Required

3 Advising/Paying/Confirming Bank

bank will pay against the Sight Draft or will accept the Termed Draft. These Bills are known as **Bank Bills** and such a Bill, drawn on and accepted by a UK Clearing bank would be 'Good Paper' in that a discount of the Bill would be very easy. The acceptance by, for example Barclays bank, of a Bill due to mature in 90 days would be seen as an absolute guarantee of payment on maturity. In fact Barclays would be happy to discount their own Accepted Bills.

Figure 12.8: A 90 day Bill of Exchange

£4,108

London
11th August 19..

AT 90 DAYS AFTER DATE OF THIS FIRST OF EXCHANGE (SECOND OF THE SAME TENOR AND DATE BEING UNPAID) **PLEASE PAY TO OUR ORDER THE SUM OF** STERLING POUNDS FOUR THOUSAND ONE HUNDRED AND EIGHT ONLY FOR VALUE RECEIVED

Drawn under Irrevocable Credit of Barclays Bank International Ltd.,

168 Fenchurch Street, London No. FDC/2/6789 dated 20th July 19..

To: Barclays Bank International Ltd
168 Fenchurch Street
London EC3

For and on behalf of
SPEIRS AND WADLEY LTD

W. H. Speirs

Director

Figure 12.9: A Sight Draft

£4,108

London
11th August 19..

AT SIGHT OF THIS SOLA OF EXCHANGE PAY TO OUR ORDER THE SUM OF STERLING POUNDS FOUR THOUSAND ONE HUNDRED AND EIGHT ONLY FOR VALUE RECEIVED

Drawn under Irrevocable Credit of Barclays Bank International Ltd.,

168 Fenchurch Street, London No. FDC/2/6789 dated 20th July 19..

To: Barclays Bank International Ltd
168 Fenchurch Street
London EC3

For and on behalf of
SPEIRS AND WADLEY LTD

W. H. Speirs

Director

Export Invoices

These will be required in a prescribed format (see chapter 10) and in sufficient numbers. Any required certifications and legalisations must be arranged and it may be that Certificates of Origin or other status documents are requested.

Insurance Policy or Certificate

This will be necessary if the contract is one which requires the exporter to arrange for the cargo insurance, that is, CIF, CIP, DDU or DDP. Such cover must be for the risks and the amount specified.

Transport Documents

These could be Bills of Lading, Air Waybills, Road or Rail Consignment notes (see chapter 7) or even Freight Forwarder's receipts.

The above represent the typical documentary requirements on a Credit but there could obviously be a number of additional documents depending on the specific consignment involved. These may include Packing Specifications, Consular Invoices, Inspection Certificates, Clean Reports of Findings, Standards Certificates, Black List Certificates, Psychosanitary Certificates, Veterinary Certificates and Halal Certificates.

The Letter of Credit will also impose other conditions on the exporter, most notably the strict time limits imposed on shipment and document presentations, and will allow, or not allow, transhipment and partshipment. Obviously there will be a fixed value which cannot be exceeded.

Doctrine of Strict Compliance

The problems arise when the exporter presents the documents, against the Credit, to the UK bank who will examine them to assess whether they comply with the Credit requirements. The banks operate on what is known as the **Doctrine of Strict Compliance** which means that they insist that the documents comply **exactly** with the Credit requirements.

As illustrations of how far the banks will take the Doctrine of Strict Compliance the following are examples of typical bank rejections:

1 ABC Engineering Ltd are described as AVC Engineering Ltd on the Credit. Despite the fact that they are obviously the beneficiaries of the credit they would have to have the Credit amended or produce a letterhead with their name spelt wrongly.

2 20,000 **rells** of Insulating Tape are described on the Credit and the exporter uses the correct description of **rolls** on the invoice, which the bank, of course, reject. In their defence they would say that there may be a technical trade expression which distinguishes **rells** from **rolls**.

3 A quantity of 5.000 Kg Industrial Laminate is described as 5,000 Kg on the invoice and the bank reject for an incorrect description. You will have noticed that there is a (,) instead of a (.) .

The above examples, which mostly relate to word descriptions, are the result of the detailed examination which the exporter's documents receive when presented, and there are many other reasons for rejection which are mentioned below.

The justification of such a level of compliance is that, if payment were made by the UK bank, they having found no discrepancies, then it is probable that the Issuing bank would find such discrepancies and therefore refuse to pay the Advising bank. The situation is even worse for the UK Confirming bank who will pay the exporter **without recourse** and will not be able to recover any funds should the Issuing bank not pay.

The banks do not operate wilfully or independently in rejecting documents presented to them but apply a very strict set of rules which are known as the *Uniform Customs & Practice for Documentary Credits*. These rules are again a publication of the International Chamber of Commerce and the version which has operated from 1st January 1994 is *ICC*

Publication No. 500. These were an update of ICC No. 400 (produced in 1983) and have taken into consideration technological innovations, judicial decisions and the developments of day-to-day practice. Copies are available from Chambers of Commerce or the banks.

Avoiding Rejection

The first solution for the exporter is to attempt to ensure that the Letter of Credit is acceptable when it is received. A number of organizations, including the banks, will provide Letter of Credit checklists which can be useful for this purpose, and an abbreviated version would look like this:

1 Is it irrevocable?
2 Is it confirmed or advised (by a UK bank)?
3 Is your name complete and spelt correctly?
4 Are the shipping and expiry dates acceptable?
5 Is the value sufficient?
6 Is the description of the goods correct?
7 Is the quantity correct?
8 Is shipment allowed from (and to) the correct ports or depots?
9 Are part and transhipments allowed?
10 Are the documents required obtainable?
11 Are specific agents or carriers required?
12 Is an insurance policy or certificate required?
13 What risks must the insurance cover?
14 Is the Credit subject to the UCP No. 400 or 500?

An understanding of the most common discrepancies which UK banks find in examining Documentary Credit presentations can be instructive in terms of the UK exporter avoiding common rejections. A current 'top ten' would include:

1 Late shipment.
2 Documents not presented in time (within time allowed or 21 days).
3 Credit expired.

4   Absence of documents requested in the Credit.
5   Claused Bills of Lading.
6   No evidence of goods 'shipped on board'.
7   Description of goods on invoice differs from that on the Credit.
8   Documents inconsistent with each other.
9   Insurance not effective from the date of shipment.
10 Bill of Exchange not drawn up in accordance with the Credit.

It can be seen from the above that the bank not only check the documents against the Credit, but also against each other. This means that rejections can happen even when there is no specific breach of a Letter of Credit requirement. An example of this would be a case where the shipping marks shown on the invoice differ from those on the Bill of Lading. The bank would reject the documents even though a specific shipping mark is not mentioned on the Credit at all.

In the event that documents are rejected by the bank then the exporter has a number of possible strategies:

1   The discrepancies can be corrected and the documents re-presented to the bank. (The 60 per cent statistical rejection rate is on **first** presentation and it is often possible to re-present and obtain payment on second presentation.) Another example of bank practice is illustrated by the fact that, if the original error/s are corrected and the documents re-presented to the bank, they may well accept that the original causes of rejection are now acceptable but could reject because the time limit for presentation of documents (time specified in the Credit or 21 days) has by then expired. The fact that the documents were originally presented some days before is irrelevant, the time periods applying to the receipt of an acceptable set of documents.
2   In the event that the errors cannot be corrected then the exporter must except that the security of the Letter of Credit has been lost. The bank may simply contact the buyers, via the Issuing bank, and inform them of the nature of the discrepancies. The buyers then have the right to accept or

reject the documents as they see fit. After all, it is the exporter who has breached a contractual obligation. It may be that the documents themselves are dispatched to the Issuing bank 'for collection', which means that we have reverted to a Bill of Exchange to collect payment, or even that the documents are sent to the buyer 'in trust'. In either case the buyer has the right to reject the documents and therefore reject the goods. It is possible for the UK bank to pay 'with recourse' and usually against a form of indemnity from the exporter, although this may only be available for certain discrepancies, such as late (stale) documents.

When the goods are actually on the way to, or have even arrived at, the destination, this merely adds to the problems of the exporter. To take this just a stage further, the situation in which goods have arrived at the destination and the buyer has legitimately rejected the documents, is a very difficult one for the exporter. The worst consequence is that, if the goods are not cleared (into the importing country) or re-exported (returned to the exporting country) then they will eventually be auctioned off. The more congested the overseas port or depot is then the sooner this will happen. It could easily be only a matter of weeks rather than months.

In such a case there is a clear hierarchy in terms of the distribution of the auction revenues. Top of the list?

1 Customs & Excise (you guessed it); followed by
2 demurrage charges (fines for delay);
3 other warehousing & storage charges;
4 auctioneer's fees;
5 any other receiving authority charges;
6 any outstanding carrier's charges; and last and very definitely least
7 the owners of the goods, that is, the exporter.

A situation to be avoided at all costs ... particularly when the person who picks up the goods at auction just happens to be the original buyer who rejected the documents in the first place.

So the security of the Letter of Credit brings with it a clear responsibility for the exporter to produce a set of documents which comply exactly with the Credit and with each other. Should discrepancies occur it is almost guaranteed that the bank's checking system, which may involve two or three separate examinations, will find them and the security of the Credit is lost. The Documentary Letter of Credit is very much a **conditional** guarantee of payment.

Types of Letters of Credit

Irrevocable

An irrevocable Credit cannot be cancelled before expiry without the consent of both parties, that is, opener and beneficiary. It is irrelevant if the buyers change their mind or even go out of business. The only thing that can invalidate the Credit is if the issuing bank go out of business, or a government moratorium means that trading must cease with a particular country.

Revocable

It is possible, but unusual, to trade with revocable Credits which, as the name suggests, can be cancelled by either party. The obvious problem for the exporter is the possibility of the buyer simply cancelling the guarantee. The Credit will not be labelled **revocable** in large letters but will contain, in small print at the bottom, a phrase such as:

> This credit is therefore subject to cancellation without notice and the above particulars are for your guidance only.

They are only used where the parties are closely related and as a means of efficient funds transfer, not as security of payment.

Confirmed

As mentioned above it may be in the exporter's interests to obtain the promise of the UK bank to pay, by adding their confirmation to the Credit, in addition to the Issuing bank's promise. Whether this is insisted upon or not should depend on an informed assessment of the reliability of the Issuing bank and not simply be a blanket request. After all the UK is not the only country in the world with safe banks. There may also be situations where the openers do not allow confirmation of their Credits, for example it is common to trade with Iran on Unconfirmed 360 day credits.

Transferable

In the cases where a 'middleman' operates between a manufacturer and an end-user it is possible for a Credit to be raised showing the agent as the beneficiary but also allowing the transfer of a percentage of the credit to the manufacturer. The difference is the agent's profit and the manufacturer must meet the conditions of the Credit to obtain their payment, just as the agent must. In similar situations it may be that the first Credit, paying the agent, is used to raise a second Credit for a lesser amount, paying the manufacturer, with identical documentary requirements. These are known as **back to back** Credits.

Revolving

Where a series of identical shipments are to be made it is possible to raise one Credit to cover all of them, rather than a separate Credit for each shipment. They are known as revolving because after payment against a shipment the amount payable is reinstated for the next shipment.

Deferred payment

These are becoming increasingly popular where a credit term has been agreed but the parties wish to avoid raising a Bill of Exchange under the Credit. This will usually be because the Bills attract stamp duty in the issuing country. When correct documents are presented the bank do not 'accept' a Bill of Exchange but instead give a 'letter of undertaking' advising when the money will be paid. Such Credits are very common in Spain and Italy.

Standby Credits

This type of Credit is unusual in that both parties hope it will never be used. They are used where the seller is trading on open account but requires some security of payment. They require the Issuing bank to make payment to the seller on presentation of documents evidencing non-payment by the importer. They have the advantage of being regulated by the Uniform Customs & Practice rules and are becoming more common in markets like the USA.

Summary

The Documentary Letter of Credit is an important and very common method of payment in international trade, primarily because of the security it offers to the exporter. However we must accept that the security of the bank guarantee inherent in the Credit is tempered by the documentary conditions imposed. It is an unfortunate fact that more than half the presentations to UK banks are rejected on first presentation because of documentary discrepancies. It is vital that exporters not only establish systems which eliminate documentary errors but that they also understand the 'rules of the game'. The banks do not invent reasons for rejection, they genuinely play by the rules, and the rules are the *Uniform Customs & Practice for Documentary Credits (ICC Brochure No. 500)*. Copies are available from

Chambers of Commerce along with a *Guide to Documentary Credit Operations (ICC No. 415)*. Forewarned is forearmed.

Cash in Advance or With Order

Finally the most secure method of payment for the exporter, if you can get it. In chapter 11 we examined the problem of the increasing credit risk in world markets and briefly looked at its origins. It is because of exporter's perceptions of this risk, and the fact that they do not regard Letters of Credit as an absolute guarantee, that there has been a clear increase in the incidence of advance payments. It is increasingly the case that overseas buyers in certain high risk countries also accept it as the normal method of payment subject, of course, to their exchange controls. In this context many African buyers are regularly paying in advance. In the case of a large project it is not unusual for a percentage of the payment to be made in advance, the balance often being paid in instalments. The money can be transferred just as for an open account payment, the only difference being that the transfer takes place before shipment (or even before manufacture) against a pro-forma invoice (see chapter 3) rather than a final invoice. The ultimate Cash in Advance is the 'suitcase full of dirty bank notes' which has become familiar to some exporters.

Factors

It is possible for exporters to actually avoid the problems of collecting overseas debts by 'factoring' them to specialist financial institutions. The factors will take over the invoices of the exporter and pay a percentage of their value. This is calculated on the trader's average credit period and extent of bad debts, and is often paid at the end of an agreed period from the invoice dates. The exporter is therefore able to accurately predict receipts with all the cash flow advantages that entails. The larger factors operating internationally are obviously very adept at credit control and debt collection. This will invariably cost more than if the exporter were to successfully collect their own debts and it does smack of 'passing the buck'.

Countertrade

Over the last twenty years there has been an enormous increase in countertrade throughout the world and the recent break up of the state-planned economies of Eastern Europe has only served to accelerate this development. Some estimates suggest that in anything up to 33 per cent of world trade, countertrade at least forms part of the negotiations, although final payment might actually be made in currency. It is obvious that the severe hard currency shortages which have been mentioned earlier in this chapter lead to countertrade being seen as the only way in which international trade can occur in some situations.

The expression countertrade actually covers a variety of possible procedures.

Barter

The direct exchange of goods for goods. Overseas markets with excess (sometimes) commodities trade them for negotiated quantities of imported goods with no cash changing hands. It is not uncommon in Africa and Latin America, and is preferred by some oil-dependant economies. There are specialist consultants who will handle the disposal of the bartered products on behalf of the exporter.

Counterpurchase

As a condition of securing the export order the seller undertakes to purchase goods or services from that country. Two contracts are agreed, one sale and one purchase, and payments are made on negotiated cash or credit terms. The counterpurchase contract can be anything from ten per cent to 100 per cent (or even more) of the value of the export sale.

Buy-back

A form of barter in which the suppliers of capital equipment, such as manufacturing plant, agree to accept payment in the form of the output of the manufacturing unit. An important variation of this is practised by Ikea who establish or upgrade factories, mostly in Eastern Europe based on Western European equipment, and buy-back the production. This has the distinct added advantage that the small to medium sized European manufacturers supply plant and equipment direct to, say, Poland but receive payment from Ikea.

Offset

A condition of the export would be that materials and components which originate in the importing country are incorporated in the finished product which they eventually receive. This is particularly relevant to high technology products such as aircraft and defence systems and may even involve the exporter participating in the establishment of production units in the overseas market.

Evidence Accounts

Traders with significant levels of business in certain markets may be required to arrange an equivalent amount of counterpurchased exports from that country. For example, a multinational company with a local manufacturing subsidiary may be required to balance the import of materials and equipment with equivalent exports. The 'evidence account' attempts to record the balance of imports and exports over a period of time.

Questions for Discussion

1 Recent surveys have shown that over 50 per cent of documents presented to banks under a Letter of Credit are rejected

because of discrepancies. Why is it important that the documents are correct and give examples of errors that may be found with transport documents which would be rejected by a bank.

2 Explain the following terms used in connection with Bills of Exchange:

(a) D/A;

(b) D/P;

(c) protest;

(d) clean;

(e) discounted.

13

The Future

The world is a constantly changing place and international trade operates at the cutting edge of that change. This not only relates to the problems of marketing products and services in the incredible variety of commercial environments encountered in the dynamic and often volatile arena of international trade, but also the constant development of physical distribution techniques and procedures.

This book has addressed the subject of international physical distribution as it exists towards the end of 1993 but it is obvious that the situation can, and will, change. Even during the writing of this book some major changes have taken place, particularly in the area of Customs controls, and many exporters must feel that it is something of a full time job just keeping up with the changes. However, it should be said that virtually every development in transport and documentation has served to make the job of exporting actually easier. This is not always obvious, and change is not often welcomed even when it does improve things, but an understanding of the purpose and functions of the documents and the procedures does help, not only in keeping up with the changes, but in understanding the reason for them and the advantages they often offer.

This chapter will examine a number of developments which are continuing initiatives which began some time ago, and will also attempt to identify, or even predict, improvements yet to come. In the former case there is a constant and continuous development of the use of computers in the export office, invariably encouraged by outside agencies such as the Customs & Excise, and the Single European market goes from strength to strength. In the latter case the effects of the Channel Tunnel on the movement of UK exports to the Community is still a matter of supposition rather than fact.

Placing the procedural changes, with which we are particularly concerned, in the context of the Single European Market, the breakup of eastern Europe and the development of the Pacific Rim countries, to name just a few global developments, highlights the problems traders have in just keeping up with the pace of change.

First let us look at the practical aspects of document production in the modern export office.

One-Run Systems

The number of documents associated with an export transaction has always been a problem for exporters. As we have seen, each consignment requires a set of export documents, often in multiple copies, and, quite apart from selecting the correct documents for a particular consignment, there is a clear logistical problem in actually producing them. The traditional method has been to simply type the documents, using carbon for multiple copies, but the obvious problem here is the inefficiency of multiple typing. It is not unusual for the same basic set of information to be typed, laboriously into the correct boxes, up to ten times. The limitations of carbon paper not only mean that 18 copies of an invoice, which could be insisted on, require something like three typings, but also that the quality of copies can leave a lot to be desired. In addition it is not only a very time consuming activity but also a very boring one. This leads not only to problems with the morale of staff but inevitably raises the error rate, and we have seen in the previous chapter that very minor typographical errors on documents will have major consequences in terms of getting paid, or rather not getting paid, against a Letter of Credit.

Solutions to these problems have been developing since

the 1950s, originally in Scandinavian countries, and in 1962 the Joint Liaison Committee on Documents used in the International Carriage of Goods (JLCD) was formed in the UK. This was in response to the United Nation's Economic Commission for Europe working party which investigated the possibilities for standardizing and simplifying international trade documentation. The JLCD was to become, in 1970, the very influential arm of the DTI known as SITPRO (Simpler Trade Procedures Board) which still plays a major part in documentary and systems developments worldwide.

SITPRO has played an important role in the simplification of documentation in three different ways:

Reducing the number of documents

Since their inception SITPRO have attempted to persuade all the parties involved in international trade to co-operate in the use of standard documents rather than dozens of separate ones performing the same function. A very successful example of this, which is described in chapter 4, is the introduction of the National Standard Shipping Note which replaced the large number of Port and Dock notes previously used to deliver goods into the receiving authority's premises. Some 40 documents were replaced by one, fulfilling exactly the same purpose. The introduction of a Common Short Form Bill of Lading is another, although less successful, example, and they played an important role in the development of the Single Administrative Document (SAD). In this context SITPRO operate within a global network of similar organizations and are concerned with standardization internationally and not just in the UK.

Alignment

The problems associated with documents were not just to do with number but also layout, that is to say, the differences in layout. Until the 1960s there was not even a standard size for documents let alone layout. We now take for granted that the vast majority of export documents are A4 size and that they have very similar layouts, in that information will occur in the same place on many documents. This standard format, originally known as the 'UN Layout Key', means that the majority of international trade documents are 'aligned' with each other. The UK aligned series of export documents produced by SITPRO are known as Top Form 2 and many documentary examples reproduced in this book form part of that set.

Document production systems

Alignment of documentation does not just provide the advantage of easier completion but, more importantly, allows the use of automatic methods for producing documents. These 'one-run' systems solve the problems of multiple typing and have led to the current and growing use of computers in the export office. The majority of SITPRO's work now centres around the expansion of computerized systems and the very important developments of the electronic means of communicating information. More of that later, but first a look at how one-run systems actually work.

Overlays

The simplest method, and one which is still valuable to many companies, is based on the production of one master document from which all other documents can be produced. Figure 13.1 shows a typical master which would be completed by the exporter, ensuring that the information is correct, and all the other required documents are produced by the use of overlays. An overlay is available for almost every export document and consists of a transparent film which allows through the information needed on a particular document, masks out information not required and (sometimes) substitutes specialist sections not on the original master. The overlay, on top of a master document, can then be photocopied to produce the completed document in as many copies as are necessary. Not only is this much faster than repetitive typing but also if the master is correct then every

Figure 13.1: A typical master document

© SITPRO 1992

MASTER DOCUMENT

Exporter VAT no.	Invoice no.	Customs reference/status
	Invoice date	Carrier's bkg. no.	Exporter's reference
	Buyer's reference	Forwarder's reference
Consignee VAT no.	Buyer VAT no.	
Freight forwarder VAT no.	Country of despatch Carrier	Country of destination code
	Country of origin	Country of final destination
Other UK transport details	Terms of delivery and payment	
Vessel/flight no. and date	Port/airport of loading	
Port/airport of discharge	Place of delivery	Insured value	EUR 1 or C. of O. remarks

Shipping marks; container number | Number and kind of packages; description of goods * | Item no. | Commodity code

Quantity 2 | Gross weight (kg) | Cube (m³)
Procedure | Net weight (kg) | Value (£)
Summary declaration/previous document

▶ LIMIT OF SAD BOX 31

Commodity code
Quantity 2 | Gross weight (kg) | Cube (m³)
Procedure | Net weight (kg) | Value (£)
Summary declaration/previous document

Commodity code
Quantity 2 | Gross weight (kg) | Cube (m³)
Procedure | Net weight (kg) | Value (£)
Summary declaration/previous document

Identification of warehouse | FREE DISPOSAL | Trade term | Invoice total (state currency)
| | | Total gross wt (kg) | Total cube (m³)

Ocean freight payable at | Signatory's company and telephone number
Number of bills of lading | Name of signatory
Original   Copy
| Place and date
| Signature

Vertical left margin text: * DANGEROUS GOODS : Refer to IMDG, ADR, IATA, CIM, and UK regulations as appropriate and specify : proper shipping name; hazard class; UN no.; flashpoint °C

SM01

Export Trade Connections : 0908-221172 SITPRO Approved Licensee No. 10

Figure 13.2: A typical overlay

© SITPRO 1987

COLLECTION/DELIVERY ORDER

Exporter   Ⓐ

Exporter's reference

Forwarder's reference

Collection address if different from Ⓐ   Ⓑ

Other UK transport details e.g. delivery address   Ⓒ

Haulier   Ⓓ

Vessel/flight no. and date | Port/airport of loading

Port/airport of discharge

Shipping marks; container no. | Number and kind of packages; description of goods | Gross weight (kg) | Cube (m³)

DANGEROUS GOODS
Specify: proper shipping name; hazard class; UN No.; flashpoint °C
Shipper must provide the appropriate Dangerous Goods Declaration

IMPORTANT — DOCUMENTS TO BE COLLECTED
Collect documents from Ⓐ Ⓑ

Deliver documents to Ⓒ Ⓓ or:-

Total gross weight of goods | Total cube of goods

Prefix and container/trailer number(s) | Seal number(s) | Container/trailer size(s) and type(s) | Tare wt (kg) as marked on CSC plate | Weight of container and goods (kg)

Received the above number of packages/containers/trailers in apparent good order unless stated hereon | For and on behalf of

Haulier's name

Vehicle reg. no. | Date

Driver's signature | Signature and date

SITPRO Approved Licensee No. 10

document produced from it will also be correct. The overlay system, used correctly, eliminates errors in documentation. It is even possible to use this system with spirit duplicating machines, although such equipment is not found in many modern offices, and copiers with in-built overlays, which can be programmed to produce a set of documents, are available on the market. Overlays can even be created for internal company documents as well as those required for third parties. Figure 13.2 shows a typical overlay.

Computer Systems

The fact that many companies are now using computers for many of their administrative procedures does allow even more efficient document production systems than the use of overlays. Whether the organization is using small PC type computers or huge mainframes, the software is available to produce all export documents, including the new requirements for EC Sales Lists and Supplementary Statistical declarations (chapter 8). Many software houses now offer systems but the industry standard, as an 'off the peg' program, is SITPRO'S SPEX. The typical system will operate on the basis of a database containing information on buyers, forwarders, carriers, products and terms of delivery and document information such as declarations and signatories. The 'master document' is actually produced on screen, using the database, and the appropriate documents are produced on anything from a dot matrix to a plain paper laser printer. It is also possible to produce a master for photocopy overlays.

Whether exporters use simple overlays or more complex computerized procedures, the use of 'one-run systems' provides a number of clear advantages:

1 Reduction in the cost of document preparation. (SITPRO claim that the cost is halved.)
2 Avoidance of errors and documentary discrepancies.
3 Greater speed.
4 Better quality documents.

The subject of computerization of export procedures is one which does not stop with just the production of documentation, efficient as that may be, because computers offer many other advantages, particularly in the field of communication.

The UK Customs & Excise are world leaders in the development of computerized Customs procedures. Over 80 per cent of imports are now cleared with Direct Trader Input (DTI) involving, usually, a clearing agent keying information direct into the Customs' computers. Under the Customs Handling of Import & Export Freight (CHIEF) initiatives, and the Customs Freight Business Review in 1991, the intention is to increase the computerization of export information. Along with the movement of Customs controls from the ports to the Inland Clearance Depots and then into the trader's premises, the UK Customs are encouraging traders to supply information on magnetic tape or 3.5 inch diskette or by even more sophisticated electronic data transmission. As more and more organizations develop computer systems, especially for invoicing, stock control and document production, it is logical for Customs to promote the use of those systems to provide information and their 'Systems Audit Techniques' are increasingly moving their controls into trader's premises, avoiding the need to actually delay the movement of goods. The development of Electronic Data Interchange (EDI) is perhaps most important in terms of the future of export procedures.

Electronic Data Interchange (EDI)

The simple principle of EDI is based on the fact that if, for example, an exporter, is using computers to print documents containing information, then that information can be more efficiently transferred as an electronic message to another computer, than by posting paper. As an example of EDI in operation take the situation in which an exporter is keying information into computers to set up a master document on screen; instead of printing out a Cargo Instruction Form for their shipping agent, they would transmit the screen information direct to the agent's computer. The same situation applies in terms of communicating with carriers, banks, insurance companies and even the buyer. Rather than use 'bits of paper' and the postal services to send information, electronic messages from one computer to another are transmitted, instantaneously, via telephone lines (or even satellite).

The requirements for the development of EDI, and 'paperless exporting', are that the computers themselves are part of a compatible system and that they share the same language. Major development in both of these areas in terms of the growth of compatible networks and the agreement on a common format of messages (27 in all) in the form of EDIFACT, have made EDI a reality, and a growing one, in world trade, companies like IBM and ICI having already established operative systems.

In looking at developments which occur outside the export office, but directly affect the physical distribution of something like 65 per cent of UK exports, it is impossible to underestimate the effect of the emergence of a Single European Market. In chapters 8 to 10 we have examined the specific procedural changes faced by exporters from the 1st of January 1993, in particular the development of Intrastat procedures, but there are many other aspects of the Single Market which affect the UK trader.

The Single European Market

> After 1992 Europe will turn in on itself and become a sprawling, sluggish entity about as relevant to the outside world as the Austro-Hungarian Empire . . . a decadent pleasure resort.

Irrespective of the accuracy of the above statement, it is instructive to consider the source of the quote, which was, in fact, an American economist. It says more about the attitude of people outside the European Community (EC), than it does about the Community itself, to the development of a true Single European Market.

In chapter 8 we took a close look at the nature of the European Community as a Customs Union and emphasized the fact that this was far more than just a free trade area. The development of the Single Market can be seen as moving the EC further ahead into something which is even more than a Customs Union. To understand the current situation within the EC it is useful to look at the route taken to get here, that is the historical developments which have led us to a single market.

At the end of the Second World War in Europe there were many people who were concerned to establish a situation which would ensure that such a conflict could not happen again. After all there had been two major European wars this century and a third had to be avoided at all costs. Two Frenchmen were particularly important in these developments: Robert Schuman, the French Foreign Secretary at the end of the war, and Jean Monnet, a very influential civil servant. They proposed many ideas such as a European Political Community and a European Defence Community which did not find enough support but they were able to realize one proposal which saw the birth of the European Community and that was a **European Coal & Steel Community (ECSC)**. This was set up by the Treaty of Paris 1952 and included the 'original six' of France, West Germany, Italy, and the Benelux countries of Belgium, the Netherlands and Luxembourg. The UK declined to join, considering that its coal and steel was its own business.

It may seem strange that the ECSC was designed to avoid a third world war but the logic was that co-operation on the major source of power (coal) and the major material for the manufacture of armaments (steel) would preclude any single country from diverting its economic resources into a war effort. Also some of the major coal and steel resources in Europe lie in the Ruhr and this area had been a thorn in the side of the French and Germans for centuries. Strasbourg is at its centre, a major French city which has changed hands on a number of occasions and is now seen, particularly by the French, as the centre of the Community.

The ECSC worked so well that the members decided to expand their co-operation in to other areas. This gave rise to two more communities which were set up by the Treaties of Rome 1957.

EURATOM

The European Atomic Energy Community is, in effect, an update of the ECSC and has the huge added benefit of co-operative research.

European Economic Community

Clearly the most important development and one which expanded the co-operation of members into a wide range of other areas, particularly towards the development of a Custom Union.

When the UK eventually joined in 1973, along with the Irish Republic and Denmark, it actually joined all three communities, the ECSC, EURATOM and the EEC. Since then they have combined their secretariats and it is now possible to refer to the European Community, which was enlarged by Greece in 1981 and by Spain and Portugal in 1986. We now have a Community of 12 member states, with Turkey as an associate member, and a European Economic Area which includes the EFTA countries of Austria, Sweden, Finland, Norway and Iceland (and Switzerland eventually), many of which will be full members in the near future.

By the will of (most) of the members, the influence of the Community, and the level of co-operation between member states, another giant step forward was taken with the Single European Act 1987. This was the result of the Ceccini Report in 1985 which suggested the barriers to trade which still existed within the EC cost anything up to £130 billion per annum. It is the measures which were proposed, most of which have now been implemented, by the Single European Act which this chapter will examine.

The concept of a Single European Market (SEM) centres around the '**four freedoms**' expressed in the intention of the Act to establish:

> an area without internal frontiers in which the free movement of goods, persons, services and capital is ensured in accordance with the provisions of the treaty

This was to be achieved by an increase in the power of the European Parliament and a corresponding reduction in the subjects which required a unanimous vote on the Council of Ministers.

It is those factors which specifically affect the movement of goods which we will now address.

Barriers to Trade

The original Ceccini Report identified three main types of barrier to trade:

1 Physical
   (a) Customs
   (b) Transport
2 Fiscal
   (a) VAT
   (b) Excise
3 Technical
   (a) Standards
   (b) Certification

and the almost 300 proposals made in the Single European Act, to be enacted by the end of 1992, sought to remove these barriers to the benefit of the member states and citizens of the EC. Whilst, at the time, this seemed a ridiculously ambitious prospect, the reality is that by the end of 1992, of the 282 final proposals, 255 were agreed by the Council of Ministers. The Single Market, to all intents and purposes, was created on the 1st of January 1993. The following is a brief look at the measures which addressed, and substantially removed, these barriers to trade.

Customs

From the 1st of January 1993 the transit systems controlling the movements of intra-Community trade ceased to exist, as did the use of 'T' forms within the EC. In addition the need for export and import declarations on the Single Administrative Document (SAD) were replaced by the Intrastat procedures. These are examined in detail in chapters 8 and 9 but perhaps the most important development is the fact that the Customs assume that goods 'are Community goods in the absence of anything to the contrary'. What this means is that the vast majority of goods (and people) moving in the Community do not encounter any Customs interference whatsoever. Customs controls are directed at trader's premises, where the goods attract specific controls, and are based on information and intelligence to enable more efficient targeting. The fact that in the first six months of 1993 the Dover Customs were able to stop four times the quantity of drugs which were confiscated during the same period in 1992 does illustrate the advantages of the removal of mandatory controls on all goods.

Transport

Road
The restrictions imposed on the operation of road hauliers by the need for permits, which were restricted by quota in many countries, were almost completely removed. Also we are moving towards a liberalization of Cabotage within EC markets. Cabotage describes the movement of goods domestically by a foreign carrier, for example a French registered haulier carrying goods from London to Manchester. Whilst Cabotage is not actually legalized, then an increasing number of Cabotage permits is leading to what will be a free market for road transport throughout the Community by July 1998. Future developments also include the establishment of a common Road Fund (Tax) Disc, known as a Vignette, by the 1st of January 1995.

Sea
There are moves towards the legalization of Coastal Cabotage throughout the EC (it is actually already permitted in the UK) and the establishment of a EC register of ships (EUROS) which it is hoped would reduce the problems of flags of convenience and subsidized competition.

Air and rail

Less progress has been made in these areas due to the powerful and entrenched interests (including governments) involved. The principle intention is still to establish a free market and the introduction of elements of Cabotage on air routes and the break up of British Rail, allowing some elements of competition, are steps in the right direction.

Fiscal

The situation at the moment is that, whilst the EC has a Common Customs Tariff and therefore the duty rates are the same for each member, there are major differences in the levels of VAT and Excise charged in each member state. The VAT rates range from exemptions (that is zero) to 38 per cent and the excise differences on alcohol, tobacco and hydrocarbon fuels are even greater.

Chapters 8 and 9 examined the technicalities of VAT and Excise payments but the removal of internal frontiers is intended to have the general effect of levelling out the differences in rates from one country to another. The logic being that the high tax and excise countries, like the UK, will loss revenues to cross-border shopping and will have to lower them in the long term. The abolition of the limits on duty paid purchases for private consumption on the 1st of January 1993 and the proposed abolition of duty free sales within the EC on the 30th June 1999 are all part of this development.

A development which affects both transport and fiscal arrangements is the change in the arrangements for VAT on freight. Between 1992 and 1996 two situations apply:

1 If the carrier and the customer operate in the same member state the carrier will charge VAT on their invoice and this will be claimed as input tax in the normal way.
2 If the carrier and the customer are in different states the carrier will zero-rate their invoice (bearing the customer's VAT Number in another member state) and the customer shows the input and output tax, in the same way as imports

would be subject to the Postponed Accounting System.

This duplicates the situation applicable to goods, described in chapter 8, and will revert to the 'home' sales system of charging VAT in 1996 in the same way. That is, Community suppliers of goods or freight will charge VAT on the sales invoice.

Technical

The problems addressed here concern the fact that many manufacturers were involved in costly product modifications in order to meet the differing technical requirements from one member state to another. This was exacerbated by the fact that the inspection procedures could be onerous, often requiring the use of the importing country's inspection authorities, and the absence of standard test certificates. The 'New Approach to Technical Harmonisation' involves:

1 No new barriers to be created without the approval of the Technical Committees of the Commission.
2 The establishment of minimum European standards, based on protecting the health and safety of people and animals, and the environment generally. Each member state's standards to be approved against these minimums.
3 Agreement on approved testing bodies and a mutual recognition of test certificates issued by approved bodies. In some trades this involves the use of a standard test certificate in every member state.

Thus the three problem areas of Physical, Fiscal and Technical barriers to trade have seen great advances since the passing of the Single European Act in 1987, and progress will continue in the 1990s.

Other areas of change which possibly have a less direct affect on the typical exporter include:

Financial services

It has been estimated that the fragmentation of the range of financial services within the EC, due to restrictions on the location of banks, regulations governing personal accounts and exchange controls, costs some £14.3 billion per annum. The solutions to this are:

1 The freedom of establishment of services ... subject to home country licensing but host country regulations.
2 Liberalization of capital movements.
3 Common standards of disclosure to investors and shareholders.

Public purchasing

This represents almost 15 per cent of the Gross Domestic Product of the EC and a range of restrictions have been removed. There is now a need for **transparency** which requires that tenders above a certain value are advertised in the *European Journal* and precludes complex tender procedures. Discriminatory specifications are no longer allowed and a general refusal to consider foreign bids will be controlled by an established compliance procedure.

Intellectual property

This expression describes the range of basic know-how, much of which can be protected by legislation. Important elements are:

1 Patents which protect original designs or processes. There is now a Community Patents Convention which allows mutual recognition of patents granted within member state's individual legislation. The intention is to go further and establish a Community Patents Office which will regulate genuine pan-Community patents.
2 Trade Names and Marks. There are at the moment ten separate systems for registration of marks. The intention is to establish a Community trade mark.

Competition law

Articles 85 and 86 of the Treaty of Rome 1957 already provide legislation designed to prevent 'agreements which prevent, restrict or distort competition' and the 'abuse of a dominant position'. There will be no change in these areas but the Commission does intend to concentrate on their enforcement as, in their own words, 'an increased freedom to operate in the Community by 1992 will be jeopardised by unofficial and illegal arrangements'.

In brief, other topics addressed include **state subsidies** based on the principle that 'aid is incompatible with a Single Market'; the approximation of **Company Law** to protect shareholders, the environment and the consumer; and mutual recognition of **Professional Qualifications**.

The above is obviously a very shallow investigation of the elements of the Single European Act and its role in creating the Single European Market, and is designed to give a broad overview and identify those areas that individual exporters may need to address with regard to their particular business.

There is little doubt that the Community will expand over the next few decades, a Community of 25 countries being perfectly feasible, as the EFTA countries come in, along with Cyprus, Malta and the newly democratized Eastern European countries of Poland, Hungary and the Czech and Slovak Republics, and there is little doubt that further steps will be attempted in the establishment of a genuine Common market. In this respect the Treaty of Maastricht came into force on the 1st of November 1993 and all nationals of the 12 member states became citizens of the European Union. The union plans to have a common foreign and security policy which may lead, in time, to a common defence policy. The other 'pillar' of Maastricht, that of Economic and Monetary Union, leading to a single currency, is still on the agenda for most member states although the possibility of this occurring by 1996 are not good, to say the least. The only immediate change is the replacement of the words 'European Community' with the words 'European Union'.

It may be that the American economist quoted at the beginning of this section is correct, but it is far more likely that such comments reveal a genuine fear that the development of a trading block, the size of an expanded Community, towards a real Single Market, does pose direct threats to the economic dominance of countries like the United States of America.

The development of computerized trade procedures and the growth of the Single Market are two of the major areas of development facing exporters in the future, but at least they can be assessed in terms of what has gone before and as part of processes which have been evident for some time.

It is, however, far more difficult to predict the effects of other changes facing international traders in the years to come. These include:

The Channel Tunnel

Opening for business in the summer of 1994, it is planned that 35 freight trains will run, each way, every day, leading to a trebling of rail freight from and to the continent with a total of 6.5 million tonnes anticipated in the first year. This will partly come from a growth in the size of the market but how much will be generated by taking business from the RO/RO ferries is not clear. The ferry companies themselves, particularly in the north of Britain, seem to feel that their new generation vessels will remain profitable.

It is to be hoped that an increase in rail freight across the Channel will lead to a reduction in the amount of heavy goods moved by road in the UK, which is a much higher proportion than all of our Western European partners, and an increase in the number of rail movements. In this context it is likely that there will be a significant increase in the movement of goods and passengers by air in the next twenty years. It is already clear that much larger widebody aircraft will be operating and a 300 per cent increase in the air freight fleet is anticipated.

The world in which the international trader attempts to do business represents a complex, and constantly changing, environment. To succeed, a company must have a clear strategy, in terms of market selection and market plans, and must appreciate the importance of the physical distribution aspects of that plan to the matter of collecting payment. Any exporter that underestimates the importance of quality order processing procedures and the relevance of correct documentation to trouble free movements and the collection of payment will invariably have to 'pay to learn'.

It is hoped that the information in this book will go some way towards improving the understanding, and the efficiency, of exporters competing in overseas markets. The single most important economic activity, that of exporting, is too important to be left to amateurs.

Questions for Discussion

1 Describe the functions of SITPRO and give examples of how they have simplified the procedures affecting UK exporters.
2 The increasing use of computers in export offices offers great advantages to the exporting company. Describe how they can be used for the production of export documents.

14

Further Questions for Discussion

1 State briefly when and why you would need to use the following documents:
   (a) Export Cargo Shipping Instruction (ECSI);
   (b) House Bill of Lading;
   (c) EUR 1;
   (d) SAD;
   (e) Combined Transport Bill of Lading;
   (f) Clean Report of Findings.

2 The following are initials of organizations closely involved with the international transport of goods. What are their full names and give brief details of their respective functions:
   (a) IMO;
   (b) ICC;
   (c) IATA;
   (d) SITPRO.

3 Write brief notes on when and why the following carnets would be used:
   (a) TIR;
   (b) ATA;
   (c) Carnets de Passage.

4 The following terms are used when goods are shipped by sea. Write a brief summary of your understanding of each of them:

(a) break-bulk;
(b) notify party;
(c) consolidation;
(d) NVOCC;
(e) unitization.

5 Describe the important features of the following 'pairs' of documents and distinguish between them:
(a) a Certificate of Origin – an Inspection Certificate;
(b) a Bill of Lading – a Charter Party;
(c) a FIATA Bill of Lading – a House Bill of Lading;
(d) a Letter of Credit – a Letter of Indemnity.

6 Write notes to show your understanding of the following:
(a) Electronic Data Interchange (EDI);
(b) vertical and horizontal organization of an export office;
(c) Export Merchants and Confirming Houses;
(d) bonded goods.

Appendix

Sample Freight Calculation

(reproduced with the kind permission of Tony Symes, examiner for The Institute of Export)

Your company has received an enquiry from a customer in Uruguay for assorted machinery to be shipped to their warehouse. The following information is necessary to calculate a Delivered Duty Paid (DDP) Canelones price.

Packing Specification

2 cases each 800 Kg	Dims. 100 x 125 x 75 cm
4 cases each 775 Kg	Dims. 100 x 135 x 100 cm
3 cases each 850 Kg	Dims. 100 x 100 x 125 cm
Ex Works (EXW) price	£60,000
Freight Rate	Tilbury/Montevideo US $285.00 per 1,000 Kg/ 1 CBM (cubic metre) (Exchange rate: US $1.80 = £1.00)
Pre-carriage to Tilbury	£235.00
FOB charges	£125.00
On-carriage from Montevideo	£430.00
Custom Clearance	£75.00

Cargo Insurance premium   0.60% (of CFR Montevideo
PLUS 10%)

Customs Duty   25% (on CIF Montevideo)

Taxes & Stamp Duty   5% (on CIF Montevideo
PLUS duty)

2 cases x 800 Kg = 1,600 Kg   100 x 125 x 75 cm = 1.875 CBM
4 cases x 775 Kg = 3,100 Kg   100 x 135 x 100 cm = 5.400 CBM
3 cases x 850 Kg = 2,550 Kg   100 x 100 x 125 cm = 3.750 CBM
Total Gross Weight 7,250 Kg (7.25 metric tonnes)
Total Cube 11.025 CBM

Therefore freight will be charged on measurement and not weight.

Freight Quotation

	£
Ex Works (EXW) price	60,000.00
Pre-carriage to Tilbury	235.00
FOB charges	125.00
FOB Tilbury	**£ 60,360.00**

Freight Tilbury/Montevideo:
US$ 285.00 per 1,000 Kg/1 CBM on 11.025 CBM
11.025 x US$ 285.00 = US$ 3142.12 x 1.80   1,745.62

CFR Montevideo   £ 62,105.62

Insurance premium £0.60%
(based on CFR Montevideo + 10%)   (a)   409.90

CIF Montevideo   £ 62,515.52

Customs duty
(25% of the CIF price)   (b)   15,628.88

Taxes and stamp duty
(5% of the CIF price plus duty) (c) 3,907.22
On-carriage charges from Montevideo 480.00

Customs clearance charges in Montevideo 75.00

DDP Canelones £ 82,606.62

(a) Insurance premium is calculated by adding 10% to the CFR price (£62,105.62 + £6,210.56 = £68,316.18) then multiply by £0.60% (**not** 60%).
(b) CIF price £62,515.52 x 25%.
(c) CIF price £62,515.52 + duty to be paid (£15,628.88 = £78,144.40 x 5%).

Index